D1766119

*The Illustrated Guide to
Mason's Patent Ironstone China*

The Illustrated Guides to Pottery and Porcelain
General Editor
GEOFFREY A. GODDEN

Subjects include

LOWESTOFT PORCELAIN by Geoffrey A. Godden
MASON'S PATENT IRONSTONE CHINA by Geoffrey A. Godden
ROCKINGHAM CHINA by Dennis Rice
WORCESTER PORCELAIN 1751–1793 by Henry Sandon
VICTORIAN PARIAN WARE by C. and D. Shinn
STAFFORDSHIRE SALT-GLAZED STONEWARE
by Arnold R. Mountford

Others in preparation

Also by Geoffrey A. Godden
VICTORIAN PORCELAIN
BRITISH POTTERY AND PORCELAIN, 1780–1850
ENCYCLOPAEDIA OF BRITISH POTTERY AND
PORCELAIN MARKS
ANTIQUE CHINA AND GLASS UNDER £5
AN ILLUSTRATED ENCYCLOPAEDIA OF
BRITISH POTTERY AND PORCELAIN
THE HANDBOOK OF BRITISH POTTERY AND
PORCELAIN MARKS
MINTON POTTERY AND PORCELAIN OF THE
FIRST PERIOD, 1793–1850
CAUGHLEY AND WORCESTER PORCELAINS, 1775–1800
STEVENGRAPHS, AND OTHER VICTORIAN SILK PICTURES
COALPORT AND COALBROOKDALE PORCELAINS

Frontispiece. A rare biscuit (unglazed) china bust; this unmarked but
another example bears the mark 'Published by C. J. Mason & Co.'
c. 1826–30. *Dr. D. Rice.*

The Illustrated Guide to

MASON'S PATENT IRONSTONE CHINA

The Related Ware—'Stone China',
'New Stone', 'Granite China'—
and their Manufacturers

GEOFFREY A. GODDEN
F.R.S.A.

BARRIE & JENKINS
LONDON

23 AUG 1973

© 1971 by Geoffrey A. Godden
First published 1971 by
Barrie & Jenkins Ltd,
2 Clement's Inn, London WC2
Printed and bound in Great Britain by
Butler and Tanner Ltd,
Frome and London
Colour printing by
Colour Workshop Ltd,
Hertford
Set in Monotype Imprint
SBN 257.65117.9

Contents

List of Plates

All between pages 114 and 115

COLOUR PLATES

MONOCHROME PLATES

Preface

Some years ago I purchased a mass of typescript notes from the now destroyed Staffordshire rate records. This material included an unpublished manuscript entitled *The Mason Potters of Lane Delph*, with the preface dated 1929. The notes had been compiled by the late Alfred Meigh and were purchased from his executors.

Having acquired this manuscript and the copyright of all Alfred Meigh's material, I had it in mind to enlarge upon the basic research and eventually publish a new book on the Masons. This plan was brought forward by many years when I discovered, whilst looking for entirely different material, the catalogues of two important sales of Mason's Ironstone china held in 1818 and 1822. These documents are of vital importance as they prove how wide was the range of Mason's Ironstone ware produced at these dates—five and nine years respectively after the patent was granted. The publication of this contemporary information, together with Alfred Meigh's original research and with additional material gleaned from many sources, now permits the story of Mason's Ironstone to be fully told. The timing of the completion of this work happily coincides with the successful launching of the new series of *Illustrated Guides* published by Messrs. Barrie & Jenkins Ltd.

My main wish is to show, by means of a large selection of illustrations, the range and qualities of Mason's Ironstone china and to help collectors to differentiate between the early pieces and those produced by firms that took over the original moulds and designs after the company's bankruptcy in 1848.

The various related durable Ironstone-*type* bodies, ranging from the 'Stone China' of the opening years of the nineteenth century to the 'Granite Ware' of the second half of the century, make up a most important part of English ceramic history. Probably, more of such wares were exported to America and other overseas markets in the nineteenth century than any other type of ceramic; and their manufacture was by no means limited to the Staffordshire potters. Chapter V contains basic details of one hundred and thirty-five manufacturers and their marks, so that the whole range of Ironstone-type wares is featured in this book.

Mason's Ironstone china is decorative and relatively plentiful. Its acquisition affords much pleasure, and I hope that owners or would-be owners will derive helpful and stimulating information from the following pages.

GEOFFREY A. GODDEN,
14 SOMPTING AVENUE,
WORTHING, SUSSEX, ENGLAND.

Acknowledgments

I wish to record my gratitude to the late Alfred Meigh for his research into the history of the Masons and their various premises, and to Reginald G. Haggar for his generous help over many years.

I am also indebted to Mr. J. S. Goddard of Messrs. Mason's Ironstone China Ltd. for his interest in the present work and for his kindness in allowing me to examine the early Mason copper plates, etc., which have been passed down to the present firm: 'Sole reproducers of Mason's patterns and shapes'.

My appreciation to Messrs. Christie, Manson & Woods Ltd. and to Messrs. Phillips, Son & Neale Ltd., the well-known fine art auctioneers, is twofold —to past directors for preserving the early nineteenth century catalogues of Mason's Ironstone wares sold by them in 1818 and 1822, and to the present directors for permitting me to make full use of the material in this work.

Other new material has been obtained from contemporary records housed at the Guildhall Library, the National Newspaper Library and the Public Record Office, with the assistance of their courteous staff. Acknowledgment must also be made to Mr. Francis Baxendale, Mr. Christopher Gilbert, Mr. Derek Harper, Mr. Bevis Hillier, Mr. C. Shingler and Mr. Alan Smith for their valuable help.

The illustrations have been taken from specimens in the possession of the following individuals or firms (in the case of dealers and auctioneers, it must be understood that the items will now have passed to other hands) to whom I am indebted for their assistance and interest. Other examples are from museum collections, and I am also most grateful for the splendid co-operation which I have enjoyed from the various museum directors, curators and their staff: L. J. Allen Esq.; Beaverbrook Art Gallery, Fredericton, Canada; Messrs. Chichester Antiques; Messrs. Christie, Manson & Woods; Messrs. Delomosne & Son Ltd.; Messrs. Godden of Worthing; Mr. & Mrs. B. Halls; D. Harper Esq.; City of Liverpool Museums; Messrs. Marshall Field & Co. (Chicago); Miss M. Martin; Messrs. Mason's Ironstone China Ltd; P. Nelson Esq., Stow-on-the-Wold; Northampton Museum; Dr. D. Rice; Messrs. Sotheby & Co.; City Museum & Art Gallery, Stoke-on-Trent; the late Mrs.

M. Symes; Dr. M. Tanner; the Victoria & Albert Museum; and Mrs. F. R. Webster.

These sources are acknowledged in the caption to each illustration. Other uncredited photographs are of objects in the author's collection. These, and the numerous illustrations from the stock of Messrs. Godden of Worthing, were posed and photographed by Derek Gardiner, A.I.B.P., of Messrs. Walter Gardiner of Worthing.

Chapter I

Miles Mason, 'Chinaman' and Porcelain Manufacturer

MASON'S CHINA

Miles Mason . . . has established a manufactory at Lane Delph, near Newcastle-under-Lime . . . his article is warranted from the manufactory to possess superior qualities to Indian Nankin China, being more beautiful as well as more durable, and not so liable to snip at edges . . .

This is part of the first recorded advertisement relating to Miles Mason's newly introduced porcelain—an advertisement which appeared in the *Morning Herald* of 15th October 1804. It is interesting to see that at this date, nine years before the patent for Ironstone china, Miles Mason was fully aware of the desirability to make strong durable china, not liable to 'snip' or chip, and that he was fully aware that the public wanted gay goods in the tradition of the 'Nankin' ware that was being imported from China. This important knowledge of the market had been gained from his earlier experience as a London 'Chinaman', or retailer of pottery and porcelain— experience that was to be of the utmost value in later years, for the Masons were primarily concerned to give the public what it wanted: inexpensive, strong, durable, useful wares painted in gay, cheerful patterns.

Miles Mason was born in December 1752, the son of William Mason of Dent in Yorkshire. He is said to have worked in the Bank of England and to have struck up a friendship with Miss Ruth Farrar, whose father had been an important Chinaman (latterly in partnership with Richard Garrett) dealing mainly in imported Chinese porcelains at 131 Fenchurch Street, London. Richard Farrar had died in May 1775, leaving over £30,000 to his daughter, who was then only nine years old. Miles Mason subsequently married her in 1782, and took over the business at a period between 1780 and 1784— probably in about September 1783, when he joined the Glass Sellers Company.

Owing to the rising duty on imported Chinese porcelain and to the growing competition from English manufacturers, the London retail business in Oriental wares became less remunerative as the eighteenth century drew to a close. Consequently, Miles Mason turned his attention to the manufacture of his own porcelain. He first obtained a partnership in the Islington Pottery, Liverpool. This factory (formerly worked by John Pennington) was under the management of Thomas Wolfe and John Davenport from c. 1792 to 1796; but on Davenport's retirement, John Lucock and Miles Mason were taken into partnership under the title 'Thomas Wolfe & Co.'.

However, the *London Gazette* of 5th July 1800 records the dissolution of the partnership of Thomas Wolfe & Co. (Thomas Wolfe, Miles Mason and John Lucock or Luckcock) of the Islington Pottery, Liverpool:

> Notice is hereby given that the partnership heretofore subsisting between Thomas Wolfe, Miles Mason and John Luckcock and established at Islington, Liverpool, in the county palatine of Lancaster, in the china-manufactory, under the firm of Thomas Wolfe & Co. is this day dissolved by mutual consent. Witness the parties hands this 7th Day of June 1800. Thomas Wolfe, Miles Mason, John Luckcock.

The *London Gazette* also records the dissolution of a further Mason & Wolfe partnership between George Wolfe of Lane Delph, Staffordshire, and Miles Mason of London:

> Whereas the partnership lately subsisting between us Miles Mason, of Fenchurch Street in the City of London, china merchant, and George Wolfe of Fenton Culvert, otherwise Lane Delph, in the Parish of Stoke-upon-Trent, in the County of Stafford, trading under the firm of Mason & Wolfe of Lane-Delph, as Manufacturers of Earthenware in the Staffordshire potteries, is this day dissolved by mutual consent: and all debts to the concern are to be paid into the hands of the said Miles Mason, who will discharge every just demand against the said partnership: as witness our hands this 5th Day of July 1800. Miles Mason. George Wolfe.

It will be observed that Miles Mason was described as 'china merchant', not as a potter. This, together with the fact that the London directories include Miles Mason or Miles Mason & Co. at 131 Fenchurch Street until 1802 (Holden's directory of 1802 lists Mason & Elliot at the Fenchurch Street address) with a further address at 41 Finsbury Square, which was probably Mason's private address, makes it seem likely that Miles Mason's role in the early partnerships at Liverpool and Lane Delph, Staffordshire, was largely confined to managing the London retail and wholesale establishments.

The Liverpool partnership which traded as Thomas Wolfe & Co. produced a class of rather hard-looking porcelain which is unmarked. Mr. Alan Smith (Keeper of Ceramics and Applied Art, Liverpool Museum) has excavated interesting factory wasters from the Wolfe site, of which some representative pieces are shown in Plates 1 and 2. As this porcelain is Liverpool rather than true Mason, it is not discussed here at length; but it is relevant to note that most of the discovered 'wasters' bear blue-printed Chinese-style landscape designs similar to the imported Chinese porcelain in which Mason dealt in London, and that these styles of pattern were continued by Miles Mason when he commenced to make his own porcelain in Staffordshire.

Turning our attention to the Staffordshire Potteries, we know that the pre-1800 partnership between Miles Mason and George Wolfe had operated on the site of the Victoria Pottery (later worked by James Reeves) because a map incorporated in J. Allbut & Son's *Staffordshire Directory* of 1802 records 'Mason & Co.' on this site. These works were advertised in the *Staffordshire Advertiser* of 9th November 1805:

CAPITAL POTWORKS

TO BE LET

and entered upon at Martin-mas next.

All these compleat set of Potworks situate at Lane Delph in the Staffordshire Potteries, now and for several years past occupied by Mr. Miles Mason, as a china manufactory, together with an excellent modern sashed House and necessary out buildings, adjoining thereto . . .

The use of the word 'china' rather than earthenware is interesting. As I do not know of any marked Miles Mason (or 'M. MASON') earthenware, it may perhaps be presumed that the early Miles Mason productions were confined to porcelain.

Be that as it may, the works were apparently not let, for in April 1807 they were advertised for sale by auction, the description stating that the works were then 'in the tenure and holding of Mr. Miles Mason'. The full description reads: 'Lot 1. All that eligible, complete, and new erected set of Pot-works, and dwelling-house thereto belonging, situate at Lane Delph aforesaid, now in the tenure and holding of Mr. Miles Mason; and also a piece or parcel of Land, marked and staked . . . The above potworks are advantageously situated not only for coal, but also for water, there being a constant run of water through the land above mentioned commanding a ten feet fall capable of working a small mill, which will be very useful for grinding Potters' materials . . .'

After vacating the Victoria Pottery at Lane Delph, Staffordshire, Miles Mason moved to a factory, later known as the Minerva Works, at Fenton. The first available rate records in which Miles Mason is listed at these Fenton premises, which were owned by Thomas Broade, cover the period August 1807 until November 1812. The next available Fenton rate record relates to April 1815 and shows the same works under the name of George Mason

—Miles Mason's son. In the rates records of April 1817, the premises are listed as 'void'. In subsequent rate records, Felix Pratt & Co. are shown in occupation.

There were, however, two separate factories worked by the Masons from July 1811 to 1817—the Minerva Works mentioned above and the Bagnall factory. The rate record of July 1811 shows 'Miles Mason & Son' as the occupiers of Sampson Bagnall's pottery at Fenton, but from 1812 to 1816 William Mason's name is given. From 1817 to 1822 the works reverted to Miles Mason in name; but it is likely that, in practice, Miles' sons Charles and George were managing the works. They certainly continued there after their father's death; and in the 1816 and 1818 directories Miles Mason is recorded as living in Liverpool, not at Fenton.

The earliest recorded reference to Mason's china or porcelain, is an advertisement contained in the *Morning Herald* of 15th October 1804:

MASONS' CHINA

It has hitherto been the opinion, not only of the public, but also of the manufacturers of this country, that the earths of these kingdoms are unequal to those of foreign nations for the fabrication of china. Miles Mason, late of Fenchurch Street, London, having been a principal purchaser of Indian [Chinese] porcelain, till the prohibition of that article by heavy duties, has established a manufactory at Lane Delph, near Newcastle-under-Lime, upon the principle of the Indian [Chinese] and Sève [sic] china. The former is now sold only at the principal shops in the City of London and in the Country as British Nankin. His article is warranted from the manufactory to possess superior qualities to Indian Nankin china, being more beautiful as well as more durable, and not so liable to snip [chip] at the edges, more difficult to break, and refusable or unitable by heat, if broken. Being aware that, to combat strong prejudices with success something superior must be produced; he, therefore, through the medium of his wholesale friends, proposes to renew or match the impaired or broken services of the nobility and gentry, when, by a fair trial or conjunction with foreign china, he doubts not that these fears will be removed, and in a short period the manufactories of porcelain, by the patronage of the nobility of this country, will rival, if not excel, those of foreign nations. N. B. The articles are stamped on the bottom of the large pieces to prevent imposition.

The significant points contained in this interesting advertisement are that by 1804 Miles Mason had left London and had 'established a manufactory at Lane Delph', that his wares were apparently marketed under the name 'British Nankin' and that the larger pieces bore an impressed mark 'to prevent imposition'. The description 'British Nankin' does not, incidentally, appear to have been first introduced by Miles Mason at the time of his

October 1804 advertisement, for it was used some two and a half years earlier by Thomas Brocas in connection with Coalport ware.*

The reference to an impressed mark would seem to refer to the standard 'M. MASON' mark rather than the words 'British Nankin', for no pieces bearing this description have been recorded. The description was used, however, by Mr. Phillips, the New Bond Street auctioneer, in the same year as the above-quoted advertisement:

> A Table Service of blue and white china, British Nankin, containing 18 dishes in sizes, 2 soup tureens and stands, 4 sauce tureens and stands, 1 salad dish, 4 sauce boats, 4 vegetable dishes with covers, 4 baking dishes, 6 dozen meat plates, 2 dozen soup plates, 2 dozen pie plates and 2 dozen cheese plates.
> (Lot 378. Sale on July 6th, 1804. This seemingly complete and perhaps new dinner service was sold for £15/4/6).

A blue-printed plate which could well be similar to that described above, from the 1804 catalogue, is shown in Plate 4. It bears the impressed name mark 'to prevent imposition', to use the wording of the 1804 *Morning Herald* advertisement. This mark can be seen on the reverse of one of the Chinese-style Mason plates featured in Plate 3.

The plates shown in Plates 5 and 6 do not bear the impressed Mason name mark, although I believe that they are copies of Oriental ware or replacement pieces to Chinese services and the 1804 advertisement makes a special point of the fact that to prove his new wares Mason 'proposes to renew or match the impaired or broken services of the nobility and gentry . . .'. Plate 6 shows a copy (or replacement) of a typical Chinese export market plate as made in the second half of the eighteenth century to special order, with the owner's crest, armorial bearings and motto worked into the centre or into the border. While the original Chinese pieces were typical hard-paste porcelain turned to a thin gauge, the English replacements are quite different, both in the type and quality of the body and in their thicker gauge and heavier weight.

Many factories made replacements to Chinese services as pieces became damaged, and reorders were placed with London retailers or direct with the English manufacturerers. Examples such as that shown in Plate 5 have even been attributed to the Bow factory (c. 1747–76), but in general style and in their apparent date—about 1800—they link conveniently with Miles Mason's first essays in making, on his own account, English copies of the Chinese porcelain which he had previously sold as a London retailer.

To return again to Miles Mason's 1804 advertisement in the *Morning Herald* and the statement that 'the articles are stamped on the bottom of the large pieces', the impressed name mark was often inconspicuously placed on the footrim, where it normally takes the form 'M. MASON'. As the footrim was sometimes ground level, the mark can be very indistinct. In fact, I have

---

* *Coalport and Coalbrookdale Porcelains*, Barrie & Jenkins Ltd., 1970.

purchased several specimens as unmarked, only to find traces of the impressed mark when washing the articles. This, coupled with the point that only the larger pieces were marked at all (cups and saucers were not marked), explains why the quality and range of Miles Mason's porcelain is not generally appreciated.

Incidentally, it is likely that Miles Mason was indirectly responsible for the introduction of porcelain manufacture at the Wedgwood pottery during the 1812–22 period, for in 1810 Mason visited the Wedgwood company's London shop, the manager of which reported back to Wedgwood:

> Mr. Mason of Lane Delph is in town and he called upon me, and in the course of conversation said that we should sell immense quantities of china here, if we had it—and that he should be very happy to make it for you. His china is I believe very good, and he has great orders for it . . .

Miles Mason porcelain is not discussed in detail in this book, which deals with the later Ironstone ware, but Plates 3 to 16 illustrate some standard shapes. This interesting porcelain will be discussed at length in a subsequent book. It must be stated here, however, that the early Miles Mason Staffordshire porcelain of the probable period 1802–13 (when the new Ironstone china was introduced) is of fine quality and is tastefully designed. Most examples found today are teaware, but fine dessert services and even large dinner services were made, as were vases and other rare objects such as bulb pots. Many specimens show the Chinese influence and reflect both the Oriental wares sold by Mason in his London shop and the popular taste of the period.

Chapter II

The Development of Ironstone-Type Earthenware

Miles Mason's third son, Charles James Mason, took out his famous patent for 'Ironstone china' in 1813 (see page 80). He was, however, by no means the first to introduce a durable earthenware body able to compete in price, as well as in quality, with the imported and highly fashionable Chinese ware.

The first of these special bodies often bears the mark 'Turner's Patent'. This compact body was patented in the names of William and John Turner in January 1800. Part of the specification reads:

> A new method or methods of manufacturing porcelain and earthenware, by the introduction of a material not heretofore used in the manufacturing of those articles. The material is known in Staffordshire by the names 'Tabberner's Mine Rock'; 'Little Mine Rock'; 'Mine Rock' or 'New Rock'. It is generally used as follows—ground, washed and dried, mixed with certain proportions of growan or Cornish stone, previously calcined, levigated and dried, a small quantity of flint similarly prepared is also added, but in different proportions according to the nature of the ware . . .

Ware made under this patent bears the written mark 'Turner's Patent' and normally displays decoration in Chinese taste, although some rare and fine specimens depict English views (see Plates 135 and 136). Dessert services were a feature but all examples are comparatively rare, partly because the Turner brothers became bankrupt in July 1806. S. Shaw, writing in 1829 (*History of the Staffordshire Potteries*), suggests that the rights were sold to Josiah Spode, probably some months before the bankruptcy was announced.

Spode, of Stoke-on-Trent, certainly produced a similar heavy durable earthenware body, but the date of its introduction is in doubt. Leonard Whiter, in his excellent book on Spode ware, suggests that the Spode stone-china body was not introduced until 1813 or 1814, to compete with the newly patented Mason Ironstone china; but I believe that Spode stone china was on the market first. Spode called his ware 'Stone China' to emphasise its

7

strength; a later variation was known as 'New Stone'. The Spode ware is of the finest quality, neatly potted, thinly turned and, in general, well produced. Again, the painted or printed designs show strong Chinese influence, occasioned by the popular Chinese export porcelain they were imitating. Fine large dinner and dessert services were made, as well as a host of other articles (see Plates 126 to 131).

Messrs. Davenport, of Longport in Staffordshire, produced stone china early in the nineteenth century which often rivals the Spode examples in quality and design. Both Spode and Davenport included their names in their 'Stone China' marks. Typical marked examples are illustrated in Plates 107 to 109. But other firms produced comparable decorative Japan-style designs on 'Stone China', 'Semi Porcelain', 'Opaque China', and similarly titled bodies, without including their own names.

The identity of many of these makers will probably never be known, but one of the leading manufacturers was undoubtedly Messrs. Hicks & Meigh of Shelton, in the Staffordshire Potteries. Their working period was from 1806 to 1822, when they were succeeded by Messrs. Hicks, Meigh & Johnson (1822–35). Blue printed marks, incorporating the words 'Stone China' with the Royal Arms or a crown, were extensively used, and fine dinner and other services were produced.

The marks and basic details of many Stone China and Ironstone-type pottery manufacturers are given on pages 51 to 101.

The popularity of this durable, gaily decorated 'Stone China'-type ware cannot be denied. While the 'landed gentry' probably preferred the more expensive porcelain services, there was a vast middle-class market for the less expensive but more utilitarian stone china ware.

It was this market which Charles James Mason sought to expand and satisfy when he introduced his 'Patent Ironstone China' in 1813. The choice of name was a masterly stroke that did much to popularise his new ware and outsell his already existing rivals. Each word has meaning: 'Patent' suggesting a new, unique discovery; 'Ironstone' suggesting great strength and durability; 'China' suggesting a delicate ware capable of gracing any table or home— and although this 'Ironstone China' is normally regarded as an earthenware today, some thinly potted pieces do in fact show a slight translucency. The lasting qualities of 'Ironstone China' are attested to by the fact that it would be difficult to find an adult in the civilised world who has not heard the term first put into the ceramic vocabulary by Charles James Mason in July 1813.

The abstract of the patent reads:

A process for the improvement of the manufacture of English porcelain, this consists of using the scoria or slag of Ironstone pounded and ground in water with certain proportions, with flint, Cornwall stone and clay, and blue oxide of cobalt.

The details are given more fully in the full patent specification, after the usual written preliminaries:

. . . The Ironstone which contains a proportion of argil and silex is first roasted in a common biscuit kiln to facilitate its trituration, and to expel sulphur and other volatile ingredients which it may contain. A large earthen crucible is constructed after the exact model of an iron forge, a part of the bottom of which is filled with charcoal or coaks (sic); these, having been previously strewed with ore and about one third part of lime, are raised to an intense heat by a strong blast of air introduced under the coaks at the bottom.

By this heat ore is fused, and the fluid iron drops through the fuel to the bottom, then follows the scoria, which floats upon the top of the fluid iron. This latter scoria, or as the workmen call it slag, is the material used in the manufacture of china, and is much impregnated with iron, and of a compact and dense structure. The slag is next let off by a hole through the forge into a clean earthen vessel, where it cools. . . . The scoria is next pounded into small pieces and ground in water to the consistence of a fine paste at the flint mills of the country. This paste is next evaporated to dryness on a slip kiln well known amongst potters. Thus evaporated to dryness, it is used with the other ingredients to the following proportions, viz.:

	Cwts.	Qr.	Lbs.
Prepared Iron Stone	3	—	—
Ground Flint	4	—	—
Ground Cornwall Stone	4	—	—
Cornwall Clay	4	—	—
Blue Oxide of Cobalt	—	—	1

These, having been mixed together with water by the slip maker, are again evaporated on the slip kiln to the proper consistency for use . . .

Several authorities have stated that the materials mentioned in the patent would not, on their own, make a workable ceramic body, and that the patent specification was a misleading front. Be this as it may, from 1813 the brothers George and Charles James Mason produced a durable, heavy earthenware bearing the trade name 'Patent Ironstone China', with or without the Mason name preceding the new descriptive title.

In view of the controversy over the workable qualities of Mason's patent specification, I asked the Director of the Ceramic Testing Laboratory at the North Staffordshire College of Technology at Stoke to analyse an early impressed marked 'Mason's Patent Ironstone China' plate. The result was:

Silica (SiO_2)	76%
Alumina (Al_2O_3)	18.87%
Potash (K_2O)	1.77%
Lime (CaO)	1.31%
Soda (Na_2O)	0.75%
Ferric Oxide (Fe_2O_3)	0.41%

Titanic Oxide (Tio$_2$)	0·40%
Magnesia (Mgo)	0·25%
Loss (Calcined at 950°C)	0·44%

As a comparison, I also sent a marked example of Ridgway's 'Stone China' of about 1820. The resulting analysis read:

Silica (SiO$_2$)	72·71%
Alumina (Al$_2$O$_3$)	21·48%
Potash (K$_2$O)	2·02%
Lime (CaO)	1·15%
Soda (Na$_2$O)	1·08%
Ferric Oxide (Fe$_2$O$_3$)	*0·43%*
Titanic Oxide (Tio$_2$)	0·40%
Magnesia (Mgo)	0·20%
Loss (calcined at 950°C)	0·35%

The Director of the Ceramic Testing Laboratory (Dr. W. L. German, D.Sc., M.Sc., Ph.D., F.R.I.C., F.I.Ceram.) comments that the small amount of iron (ferric oxide (Fe$_2$O$_3$)) found in the marked sample indicated that the body was *not* prepared in accordance with the published patent specification.

The patent of 1813 was granted for an initial period of fourteen years, taking the coverage up to 1827. It was not then renewed, probably as very similar bodies were in general use. William Evans, in his *Art and History of the Pottery Business*, 1846, published several recipes for Ironstone bodies. One of these was:

350 lbs. Cornwall stone.	300 lbs. Cornwall clay.
160 lbs. Blue clay.	60 lbs. Flints, 14 oz. Blue calx.
Fritt for Ironstone body:	
90 lbs. Cornwall stone.	20 lbs. Salts of soda.
Glaze:	
33 lbs. of above fritt.	33 lbs. Cornwall stone, 35 lbs. whiting, 80 lbs. white lead.

Here there is no mention of Ironstone, but in another part of the book Evans states: 'The Ironstone china is formed by introducing ground clay from the smelting furnace in the proportion of 28 (parts) for 72 (parts) of No. 3 or 8 (other recipes listed) carefully blunging (mixing) the fluids together.'

Mason's new 'Patent Ironstone' body quickly became very popular (perhaps because of its claimed cheapness rather than for its durability), as is shown by a letter preserved in the Wedgwood archives. The note is dated 19th March 1814, and is additionally interesting because it shows that Spode 'Stone China' was also popular and was linked with the new Mason Patent Ironstone china.

Every one enquires for the Stone china, made by Spode and Mason and it has a very great run. I presume you know what it is—it is a thick coarse china body, not transparent, with china patterns . . .

The original makers of Mason's Patent Ironstone China were the brothers Charles James Mason and George Miles Mason. Charles, the youngest son of Miles and Ruth Mason (see page 1) was born in London on 14th July 1791. Little is known of his early life; but he must have assisted his father and elder brother in the potting business, for when only twenty-one he took out the all-important patent for 'Ironstone China'. It is open to some doubt whether he alone invented the body. It is more probable that it was the result of experiments carried out by Miles Mason and his sons over several years. Nevertheless, the patent was in Charles James Mason's name. A month before the patent, Miles Mason had formally transferred the business to his two sons, George Miles and Charles James, who traded under the style 'G. & C. Mason'.

George Mason, Miles' second son, was born on 9th May 1789. Besides becoming an Oxford graduate, and a man of cultivated taste, he was to be a prominent figure at Stoke, being responsible in part for establishing both a mail coach through the Potteries and a police force, and introducing several other improvements—listed by Reginald G. Haggar in his excellent book *The Masons of Lane Delph*.

From 1813 to 1826, George and Charles traded in partnership—George looking after the administrative side of the large, thriving concern. After retiring from active participation, George remained in the district and may even have retained a financial stake in the pottery, for Charles James Mason's bankruptcy in February 1848 seems to have affected George's resources— a fact that would, however, be explained if George had stood security for his brother on the factory premises or on any loans. George Miles Mason died on 31st August 1859.

Apart from Miles Mason's two sons, Charles James Mason and George Miles Mason, who succeeded their father and won fame with their newly invented 'Patent Ironstone China', there was a third son—the eldest—named William. Little is known about William, but at one period he had his own factory and a retail shop in Manchester. He was born on 27th January 1785. On coming of age, in 1806, he seems to have joined his father, which accounts for the style 'M. Mason & Son', although the impressed mark remained 'M. Mason'. As previously stated, William Mason's name is given in rate records as the tenant of Bagnall's Minerva Works at Fenton from 1812 to 1816. The following document offers proof that Miles Mason and William were in partnership by March 1811 and evidence that Miles Mason was the dominant partner, even though the wording 'the manufactory of Mr. William Mason' is used.

In consequence of an advertisement having appeared in the last *Staffordshire Advertiser* [given in that of 9th, 16th and 23rd March]

noticing that Thomas Appleton had procured a parcel of moulds in an improper manner from the manufactory of Mr. Josiah Spode of Stoke, potter, and that he had carried the same to the manufactory of Mr. William Mason of Lane Delph—'We, the undersigned, Miles Mason and William Mason, partners and manufacturers of chinaware do hereby declare that so far from our soliciting or obtaining in a clandestine manner from the said Mr. Spode, his patterns moulds or shapes, or those of any other persons, we should not deem ourselves worthy of the patronage of the public, if our chinaware and shapes were not equal or something superior to any manufactory in the British Dominions.
Witness our hands this 14th March, 1811.

Miles Mason, Wm. Mason

The use of the word 'chinaware' is interesting, for the only recorded marked pieces of William Mason's products are of earthenware. This notice could well relate to Miles Mason's china or porcelain, not directly to his son's earthenware.

The reason for the insertion of this notice is evident; but the Masons turned the affair into an opportunity to advertise their own products. The same incident reveals the name of one of Mason's workmen, for the following statement was also published, together with one from Thomas Appleton, who was the person accused of stealing the Spode moulds:

...and I the undersigned Daniel Goostry, a workman of the said Messrs. Masons, do here by certify, that when Mr. Wm. Mason observed that I was going to make use of the moulds alluded to, he requested that they might not be used in his Manufactory.

Daniel Goostry

On Miles Mason's death, in 1822, William Mason took a pottery belonging to John Smith (and formerly worked by James Hancock) at Fenton Culvert. His name is given in rate records of 1823, but the record dated 29th May 1824 is marked 'Wm. Mason to Thomas Roden & Co', indicating that William Mason had lately given up the works.

William Mason's short-lived factory at Fenton Culvert seems to have produced earthenware, but only two marked specimens are at present known to me. One of these is a fine platter, 20 inches long, from a dinner service decorated with an underglaze blue landscape within an ornate wide floral and scenic panelled border. This specimen from the late Alfred Meigh's collection is reproduced in Plate 389 of my *Illustrated Encyclopaedia of British Pottery and Porcelain*. It is to be hoped that further marked examples of William Mason's earthenware will come to light, as it is inconceivable that only two examples should have survived.

William Mason also had a retail establishment at Smithy Door, Manchester, where Messrs. Wedgwood supplied creamware to him in January 1815, the order for which is still preserved. Later in 1815, he was unable to pay

Wedgwood, and his father, Miles, came to his aid. That is all we know of William.

The duration of his father's porcelain manufacture in Staffordshire falls within the period c. 1802 to c. 1813. This period could have been extended into the 1820s, as Charles and George continued the works using the original title 'Miles Mason' (& Sons). But it is more likely that the manufacture of porcelain and earthenware (marketed under the name 'semi-china') ceased in 1813, when the patent for the newly introduced 'Ironstone China' was taken out (see page 8). The success of this durable and relatively inexpensive body, over which they had sole patent rights, would quickly have taken over the whole productive capacity of the factory and caused the manufacture of competitive porcelain to be abandoned.

Miles Mason seems to have retired from active participation in the manufacturing of ceramics in 1813, leaving the business to his sons, who henceforth concentrated on the production of the new durable Ironstone body (see page 8). Miles Mason died on 26th April 1822.

Whereas sale catalogues of household goods sold in the pre-1810 era include a good proportion of Chinese export porcelain, especially in dinner services, by the late 1820s Ironstone ware had taken its place. In a sale held in January 1827, Messrs. Christie's sold:

> A dinner service of blue and white Iron-stone china, with gilt edges, consisting of two soup tureens, covers and dishes, six sauce ditto and stands, four vegetable dishes and covers, a salad bowl, nineteen dishes in sizes, two fish plates, 60 table plates, 18 soup and 48 pie plates. (Sold for £12. 12. 0.)
> A dessert service of Iron-stone china, in imitation of Oriental burnt-in, consisting of centre piece, two cream bowls and stands, 12 dishes and 24 plates. (Sold for £2. 12. 6.)

In May 1827, the contents of Clarence Lodge, Roehampton, were sold and contained:

> A dinner service of Iron-stone china, in imitation of Japan, consisting of 2 tureens, covers and stands, 2 vegetable dishes, 7 corner dishes, 6 covers, 3 sauce tureens and stands, 21 dishes in sizes, 49 table plates, 19 soup, 18 pie and 11 cheese plates. Some pieces imperfect. (Sold for £15. 5. 0d.)
> A pair of handsome octagonal Iron-stone jars, in imitation of oriental burnt in. (Sold for £5. 5. 0.)
> A pair of smaller ditto. (Sold for £3. 0. 0.)
> A vase of Iron-stone china with rams heads and the companion, broken and 2 ditto bowls. (Sold for £3. 3. 0.)
> A pair of very handsome bottles of Iron-stone china, pencilled with gold upon mazarine blue ground, and painted with landscapes and bouquets in compartments. (Sold for £3. 10. 0.)

On George Miles Mason's retirement from the partnership of G. & C. Mason in 1826, Charles James Mason traded as 'Charles J. Mason & Co.' (the '& Co.' perhaps relating to Samuel Bayliss Faraday, who died in 1844, as some rate records and *Pigot's Directory* of 1841 refer to 'Mason & Faraday'), Charles James Mason was an enlightened master potter in days when little light was evident. He was a supporter of the new unions struggling to establish themselves against strong opposition from most pottery owners, and he saw the desirability of improving working conditions and having happy, contented workmen earning a fair wage.

Mason's Ironstone China was first produced at Miles Mason's former porcelain factory known as the Minerva Works at Lane Delph, Fenton. On 13th June 1813—that is, just before the patent for the new Ironstone China was published—the brothers William, Charles James and George Miles Mason bought the Fenton Stone Works at Lane Delph, Fenton, from Sampson Bagnall. This factory had earlier been let to Josiah Spode under a lease dated July 1805. The Fenton premises were depicted on several printed marks (see page 48) and are described in two contemporary accounts:

> The manufactory of Messrs. G. & C. Mason, for Patent Iron stone china, is commodious. Here is a steam engine of some peculiarity in its construction by Holford of Hanley . . . The front warehouse is four stories high, is fire proof, and has the most beautiful facade of any in the district.*

and

> The works of Charles James Mason & Co., standing obliquely to the turnpike road, and on the line of the canal company's Railway, present an extensive front of four stories in height, inscribed in large letters 'Patent Ironstone China Manufactory' . . . A steam engine is employed here in aid of manual labour, and for the other uses of the trade.†

These 'Fenton Stone Works' were retained until Mason's bankruptcy in 1848, when they were taken by Samuel Boyle (1849–52) and then by E. Challinor & Co., whose successors worked them until c. 1896. For many years, however, the Masons also managed Sampson Bagnall's works in Lane Delph, Fenton, just below the Minerva Works. From 1811 to 1822, these premises were in the name of William Mason but were probably worked by his brothers, as William was dealing in pottery at Manchester. From 1822 to 1825, the rate records show the tenants as the executors of Miles Mason. The works were then purchased by George and Charles Mason; but in the March 1827 rate records they are shown as void or empty. The changes in the various premises are rather difficult to follow. They are set out in table form in Appendix I.

* S. Shaw, *History of the Staffordshire Potteries*, 1829.
† John Ward, *History of the Borough of Stoke-upon-Trent*, 1844.

Mr. Haggar, in his book *The Masons of Lane Delph*, tends to praise Mason's 'commercial genius' in organising auction sales of his ware throughout the country, 'producing his famous Ironstone china in bulk for this special purpose and making the fullest use of advertisement and publicity in the press, he systematically exploited every auction mart in the country, netting in succession vast sums of money. The results of this brilliantly conceived organisation were stupendous.'

This practice, however, is bad in the long term as the temptation is to include slightly faulty ware, which flood the market, encouraging the buyers to obtain cheap examples and leave the more expensive perfect articles. The local auctions also destroy the trade of the retailers (the manufacturer's main and long-term link with the buying public), who are then less inclined to re-order from the manufacturer who has stolen their trade. In general, disposal of china by auction is a good expedient when one is closing a concern and has stock to clear. It is bad when the concern wishes to continue. The same policy was the downfall of the Derby factory under Robert Bloor in the 1840s. It was, I believe, the main reason for Charles James Mason's downfall. I have, in fact, discovered a letter from an Oxford auctioneer which confirms my opinion:

> St. Clements,
> Oxford.
> December 11th, 1826.

> . . . I have recently held a sale of china for the manufactory of Mason & Co., Lane Delph, it is of a very inferior quality and they have been attack'd by the Trade here since the sale and put to some expense in Penalties. They are about attempting another sale in Oxford, but I have declined officiating for them . . .
>
> Wm. Wise

The Oxford reference librarian was able to find the original advertisement for this sale in Jackson's *Oxford Journal* of 25th November 1826. The above letter from William Wise in which he stated that he had declined officiating for Masons again should be borne in mind when one reads these rather fanciful descriptions—in all probability supplied by the manufacturers themselves. Nevertheless, the range of articles offered is illuminating:

EXTENSIVE SALE OF CHINA

at WISE's Room, in St. Clements,

In consequence of the dissolution of the Partnership of Messrs. GEORGE and CHARLES MASON, Proprietors of the extensive Works at Lane Delph, Staffordshire, Patentees of the IRON STONE CHINA, and late of No. 11, Albemarle Street, London.

Mr. WISE begs most earnestly to assure the Nobility and Gentry of Oxford and its environs, that he has been especially appointed to dispose of the whole of this truly elegant and useful STOCK by PUBLIC AUCTION; and that his Room will be opened for the view of part of this grand assemblage of China on Monday next, Nov. 27th, and on Tuesday the 28th. On WEDNESDAY, Nov. 29th, at Eleven o'clock, the Sale will commence, and continue at the same hour each following day of business, till the whole is disposed of.

As it may be necessary to enumerate part of the Stock, W.W. begs to point out the great variety of Enamel and Gilt Table Sets, with the usual additions in fashionable Society of Yacht Club Finger Bowls; Ice Pails, Wine Coolers, Stilton Cheese Tubs, Custards and Covers, Celery Vases, Salts and Pickle Saucers; Dessert Services, Punch Bowls, Hydra Jugs, Egyptian Mugs, Broth Basins &c in corresponding patterns. Breakfast Services, with the addition of Honey Pots, Egg Pipkins, Tea and Coffee Sets &c; also a supply of Unmerapoora Tea Extracters, which have entirely superseded the Rockingham Tea Pot. Complete Chamber Services with additional pieces, such as Foot Pails, Slop Jars &c. &c.

In matters of taste and ornament a selection will be seen peculiarly meriting attention. The Neapolitan Ewer rivals the best Work of Dresden manufactory [see Plate 94]; Fish Pond Bowls, of extraordinary magnitude; Siamese Jardinier and Plateaux, adopted by the Horticultural Society, for the culture of Bulbous Roots &c; a general and extensive variety of Jars, Beakers, Ornaments for the Cabinet and Mantle Piece, from French, Italian, Spanish, Chinese, Japanese, Berlin and Saxon Originals. The Blue Printed Table Services comprise a variety of this year's pattern. All other Earthenware in use will be found in the Stock.

Catalogues may be had, and the Property viewed, at the Room.

The Sale will commence each day at Eleven o'clock.

Packers from the Manufactory will attend, for the accommodation of Country Purchasers.

Other sales were held by individuals or firms closely connected with Messrs. Mason. Samuel Faraday (later Charles Mason's partner) held many sales in his own name. The press advertisements for these sales are interesting:

Mr. Farady (sic), 190 Regent Street, has certainly collected the finest stock of china ever seen in this metropolis, and has caused the art of Potting to be carried to its highest pitch in the higher branches of that interesting manufacture. The set of fine jars of English make are the finest we ever saw, and are superior to foreign productions; we understand the models cost five hundred pounds . . .

(*John Bull*, 23rd March 1828).

Other advertisements of the period include:

> ... splendid, extensive, and unique Stock of Porcelain and Earthenware
> ... comprising richly gilt table [dinner] and dessert services ... a
> variety of earthenware table sets, gadroon and plain edges, in light and
> full patterns of the newest make, rivalling China in delicacy of colour and
> elegance of patterns ... The Stock further embraces drawing room and
> vestibule vases, pot pouries, pastile burners, fine flower and scent jars,
> capacious fish globes, Italian urns, delicate diminutive specimens,
> etc. ...
> (*The London Morning Herald,* 1st April 1828).

> Many hundred table services of modern earthenware, breakfast and
> tea ware, toilet and chamber sets, many hundred dozen of baking dishes,
> flat dishes, broth basins, soup tureens, sets of Jugs, and numerous other
> articles. The china is of the most elegant description, and embraces a
> great variety of splendid dinner services, numerous dessert services, tea,
> coffee, and breakfast sets of neat and elegant patterns, ornaments of
> every description that can be manufactured in china from the minutest
> article calculated to adorn pier table and cabinet, to the most noble,
> splendid and magnificent jars some of which are near five feet high.
> (*The London Morning Herald,* 21st April 1828).

It will be noted that these flowery advertisements mention both earthenware and porcelain (or china). The Ironstone body—an earthenware—was
always described as 'china', even in the patent and in the marks.

Many faulty specimens of Mason's Ironstone China will be found. Large
tears in the body or chips (caused in the manufacture, as they are often glazed
over) are relatively common and were, I believe, finished for the auction sales
rather than rejected, as they should have been. The jug shown in Plate 63
represents the ultimate in this practice. The handle has completely come
away from the body but the resulting scars have been glazed and painted
over, resulting in a handleless jug being placed on the market.

For thirty-five years, from 1813 to 1848, the Mason Works produced a
vast quantity of Ironstone China, for the output was almost exclusively
devoted to this ware. Some rare earthenware and stoneware moulded jugs
(see Plates 72–3) etc. were made, but these represent less than one per cent
of the total. It is perhaps not surprising, then, that the market became
saturated. The novelty had worn off. Vast amounts were on the market,
and to some extent, by the late 1840s, the traditional Chinese-style designs
were outmoded. It is also probable that the Ironstone proved too durable,
reducing the demand for replacements or new services.

In view of this, it is not surprising that Charles James Mason was declared
bankrupt in February 1848. The factories and private possessions were
offered for sale by auction, the following notices appearing in *The Staffordshire
Advertiser* in March 1848:

FENTON
PATENT IRONSTONE CHINA MANUFACTORY
—

MR HIGGINBOTTOM
WILL SELL BY AUCTION
AT THE PATENT IRONSTONE CHINA MANU-
FACTORY
FENTON
THE ENTIRE OF THE FIXTURES, UTENSILS,
MATERIALS, STOCK, & BELONGING TO THE
ESTATE OF MR. C. J. MASON, ON MONDAY
(to) FRIDAY, APRIL 3rd, 4th, 5th, 6th & 7th, 1848.

A further premises was also offered:

FENTON MANUFACTORY,
TERRACE BUILDINGS
—

MR HIGGINBOTTOM
WILL SELL BY AUCTION,
AT THE MANUFACTORY, TERRACE BUILDING,
FENTON
THE ENTIRE OF THE FIXTURES, UTENSILS,
MATERIALS, STOCK, ETC. BELONGING TO THE
ESTATE OF MR. C. J. MASON ON APRIL 10th,
11th, and 12th, 1848

Further details of the factories' contents are given in other sale notices, headed: **'The Patent Ironstone Manufactory, Fenton and the Patent Ironstone China Manufactory, Terrace Buildings, also at Fenton'** —'the entire of the Fixtures, Utensils, Moulds, Green [unfired] Biscuit [once fired but unglazed] and Glossed [glazed] Stock, Materials, etc. a complete Patent Printing Machine by Pott, with 17 Engraved Rollers, and all necessary appliances for immediate work.'

'Also, at the Ironstone China Manufactory, Terrace Buildings, Fenton, the whole of the Manufactured Stock, Fixtures, Utensils, etc. the immense stock of Copper Plate Engravings, and other effects, the whole belonging to the estate of Mr. C. J. Mason . . .'

Apart from the factories, stock, unfinished goods, and all fittings, Charles James Mason's personal effects at Heron Cottage, Fenton, were offered by the assignee to the estate:

. . . The whole of the rich and modern dining room and breakfast room furniture, in rosewood, mahogany, and other woods, gilded corn-ices, draperies, magnificent pier glasses, elegant French clock in tortoi-shell (sic) and buhl; richly carved mahogany 4 post bedsteads, in chintz, damask, and morsen; hair mattresses, prime goose feather beds, mahogany wardrobes and chests of drawers, splendidly bound books, superb collection of paintings by Michant, Hutenberg, Burney, Parnell, Robarts, Nasmyth, Hill, Richards, etc.; scarce and rare prints, oriental jars and vases, patent ironstone gilded china, table [dinner], dessert, toilette, and tea services, rich cut glass and plated goods; valuable marble tables, and dressing glasses, cellar of wines, chariot, britzha, phaeton, gig, pair and single harness, cutting and kibbling mill, patent hand corn mill, and all other effects in and out of doors . . .

Charles James Mason, however, survived the bankruptcy. Perhaps his brother George came to the rescue, for in the Great Exhibition of 1851 'Charles Mason, [of] Longton, Staffordshire—Designer, Manufacturer, and Patentee' exhibited the following 'specimens of Patent ironstone china':

Garden Seats of mixed Anglo-Indian and Japanese pattern, representing an old dragon, in raised enamel on a gold ground.
[The description 'Indian' or 'Anglo-Indian' relates to Chinese based designs, the term 'Indian' being widely used in the eighteenth and nineteenth centuries for articles of Chinese origin.]
Garden seats of an Anglo-Chinese pattern, on a sea-green ground, with raised solid flowers and gilt panels.
Fish Pond bowls of Anglo-Chinese pattern; Gog and Magog, an Anglo-Indian pattern; The Water Lily, an Anglo-Japanese pattern.
Jars with raised enamel Mandarin figures and sea-dragon handles. Large jars and covers of Anglo-Indian pattern. There are also some open jars.
Jars covered; dragon handles of Anglo-Indian and Anglo-Japanese patterns, with raised solid flowers, etc.
Specimens of plates in the oriental style of pattern, on registered shapes, and Anglo-Japanese. Three jars and covers, with Anglo-Indian grounds.
A Plate, a dish, a tureen, a covered dish, a tall coffee cup and saucer, and a sugar-basin, made of the white patent ironstone china, as used in the hotels of the United States of America.
Jugs of old Indian, Japanese and gold patterns of the original shape; also Anglo-Indian and melon pattern; with oriental figures and gold ornaments. Ewer and basin, and mouth ewer and basin, with oriental figures, and a rose border.
Jars: the old India crackle, with India red grounds. A breakfast cup and saucer.
A monumental tablet, made of Ironstone, and lettered under the glaze.
Jugs, showing various patterns in Bandanna ware. Toilet ewers and basins. Antique jugs of Japanese pattern and gold ornaments. Red and gold paint jars. Zig-zag beakers, on bronze. Table ware of a Japanese pattern in blue, red and gold.

It is not clear whether these 1851 exhibits were new productions or old ware rescued from the bankruptcy or 'bought in' at the sales. The Staffordshire rate records of 1849 list Charles Mason at Mill Street, Lane End. He

c

is not listed in 1850, but in 1851 he appears at Daisy Bank, Lane End. Longton and Lane End are to all intents and purposes one, so the latter address agrees with that given in the catalogue of the 1851 Exhibition.

The list of objects shown at the 1851 Exhibition is interesting and indicates the types of ware made by Charles Mason in the late 1840s. The reference to registered shapes—'Specimens of plates in the Oriental style of pattern on registered shapes'—relates to a form registered at the Patent Office in Mason's name on 16th April 1849, after the bankruptcy. A plate of this form, with the printed Mason trade mark as well as the official registration mark, is reproduced in Plate 33. It is also interesting to read of the inclusion of 'white patent Ironstone China, as used in the hotels of the United States of America'. On the evidence of the fine vase or jar 'with raised enamel Mandarin figures and sea-dragon handles', shown in Colour Plate VI, the Mason exhibits at the 1851 Exhibition bear the printed inscription, in script letters, 'Exhibition 1851'. The standard mark shows the angular crown, which also occurs on the plate form registered in 1849 (see Plate 33).

The Potts 'Patent Printing Machine' with '17 engraved rollers' and 'the immense stock of copper plate engravings . . .' were offered for sale in the March and April 1848 auction sales. They were of vital importance, enabling other manufacturers to match Mason's services and other ware and to reproduce his most successful patterns.

The majority of these former Mason moulds, engraved copper plate designs, etc., were apparently purchased by Francis Morley of High Street, Shelton. The name MORLEY was added below Mason's former standard crown mark on ware made to Mason's designs. Francis Morley was an experienced potter, first in partnership as Ridgway, Morley, Wear & Co.—having married William Ridgway's daughter Emma—(c. 1835–42), then as Ridgway & Morley (c. 1842–5). From 1845 to c. 1858 he traded under his own name, '& Co.' being added on most marks to cover his partner, Samuel Asbury.

The next partnership, that between Francis Morley and Taylor Ashworth, during the 1858–62 period, is most important as it explains how the firm of G. L. Ashworth & Bros. Ltd. (recently retitled 'Mason's Ironstone China Ltd.') acquired the original Mason shapes and patterns. In 1862 Francis Morley retired, passing to Ashworth (with his father George L. Ashworth) the valuable Mason copper plates and trade marks which have since been used to great advantage by the present Company.

The firms listed above employed various printed marks incorporating their initials or full names (see Chapter V and my *Encyclopaedia of British Pottery and Porcelain Marks*, 1964). Some marks were adaptations of earlier Mason's marks, retaining the words 'Patent Ironstone China' and the elevation view of the factory, with the new partnership name or initials replacing those of the earlier Mason firm.

George L. Ashworth was trading under his own name from at least May 1862. Although he used the Mason printed trade mark on Ironstone ware, he also produced a wide range of earthenware which was plainly marked with his own name or initials—'A. Bros.' or 'G.L.A. & Bros.'—or with the Ashworth name (see page 53). Some, but not all, 'Mason' printed marked Ashworth ware also bore Ashworth's name impressed.

The Ashworth reissues of Mason's original shapes and decorative patterns are often difficult to distinguish from the originals, especially now that some reissues are themselves antique. In general, the body is not quite as compact or heavy as the original, although it is whiter—a floury white rather than a creamy tint. The underglaze blue parts of the design are normally lighter in tint than the dark blue original. Impressed numerals indicate a late nineteenth or twentieth century date and, in fact, they give the month number and the last two digits of the year in which the piece was manufactured, e.g. 7·06, for July 1906; but this practice has now been discontinued.

For over a hundred years, Messrs. George L. Ashworth & Bros. Ltd. have been selling in home and export markets vast quantities of their Mason's-type ware decorated with traditional Oriental-styled patterns. Mason's number one pattern, the Grasshopper design—now called 'Regency' or 'Regency Ducks'—is still proudly displayed in most china shops and stores, and there can be few homes in the British Isles that cannot boast a specimen of 'Mason's Ironstone'. In 1968, the firm of G. L. Ashworth & Bros. Ltd. took the new title 'Mason's Ironstone China Ltd.'—so the wheel has turned full circle.

Most press notices advertising the introduction of a new product tend to overstate the virtues of the article. That inserted in *The Times* in December 1813:

Patent Ironstone-china

The great importance of this article is well worth the attention of the nobility, gentry and the Public, the durability of the composition is beyond any other yet produced, and not being so liable to chip or break, which, together with its being much lower in price than any other china, it is presumed will prove a recommendation for its general utility . . .

can be regarded as an understatement. The original advertiser could have had no idea that retailers one hundred and fifty or more years later would be enjoying regular sales of the same designs, or that the objects of 'general utility' then offered would today grace the cabinets of collectors and be the subject of illustrated books.

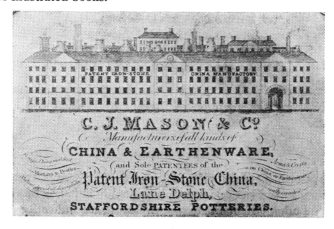

Chapter III

Mason Ironstone Ware

This chapter, which is devoted to listing objects made in Mason's Ironstone and the patterns with which they are decorated, is based not only upon many years of experience in trading in this ware but also on contemporary documents, newspaper notices and accounts.

The most important of the documents are the catalogues of two sales of Mason's stock which were held in London in 1818 and 1822. These hitherto unpublished catalogues are of the utmost importance, throwing light, as they do, on the large variety of early ware made five and nine years after the patent was granted. They are given in complete form in Appendix II.

The first sale was held on 'Tuesday, December 15th, 1818 and the two following days . . . by Mr. Christie, at his Great Room, Pall Mall.' The title page of the catalogue is given below:

A
CATALOGUE
OF
A MOST VALUABLE AND EXTENSIVE STOCK
OF
ELEGANT AND USEFUL
CHINA
SUITED FOR DOMESTIC PURPOSES
OF ENGLISH MANUFACTURE

Recently consigned from the Manufactory for actual sale, and high deserving the attention of Persons of Fashion and Private Families.

It comprises

A large assortment of complete table and dessert services, composed of a strong and serviceable material, painted in imitation of the rich Japan and other Oriental Patterns; Breakfast, tea and coffee equip-

ages, ornamental Dejeunes and vases for flowers and essence, including about twelve of noble size, suited to fill niches or recesses in
Drawing Rooms, superbly ornamented . . .

It will be observed that Mason's name is not mentioned, nor is Ironstone
China; but there can be no doubt that the 'strong and serviceable material
painted in imitation of the rich Japan' was Mason's Ironstone China. The
inclusion of 'Twelve (vases) of noble size suited to fill niches or Recesses
in Drawing Rooms' confirms this, as does the description of service patterns
which match existing marked specimens.

The later sale, held in June 1822, was of a fourteen-day duration. It was
held at 11 Albemarle Street, the London retail shop of George and Charles
Mason, '*Sole patentees, manufacturers and sellers of Patent Ironstone China*'
[London Directories 1820–4], and was sold by Mr. Harry Phillips, the
auctioneer. The catalogue, together with many others of the same period,
has been preserved by successive generations and is now published by kind
permission of the present Directors of Messrs. Phillips, Son & Neale Limited,
Blenstock House, Blenheim Street, London, W.1.

According to the catalogue, the sale was occasioned by the death of Miles
Mason; but as he had assigned the business to his sons in 1813, it is difficult
to believe that his death was the real reason for the sale. Whatever the reason,
the sale and its catalogue descriptions are of the greatest value to present-day
collectors, showing the objects and designs produced at the Fenton Patent
Ironstone China Manufactory in or just prior to 1822. By comparing objects
mentioned in the 1818 Christie catalogue with those in Phillips' of 1822,
one can gauge the progress made in the intervening four years. The catalogue
descriptions are reproduced on pages 115 and 123.

It should be noted that several lots of glass were included in the 1822 sale.
As was the practice of the period, manufacturers and retailers often dealt
in related objects—glass sellers sold china, china dealers stocked glass, papier
mâché trays, etc. The glass items have been deleted here to avoid confusion,
leaving 1,538 lots of Mason's earthenware. Of these lots, 1,148 were 'bought
in', having failed to reach their 'reserve' or the auctioneer's valuation—so
only 390 of the 1,538 lots of earthenware offered in 1822 were sold, for a total
of £1,119. 1. 6.

The rest of this chapter describes the objects and patterns produced in
Ironstone China—first with dinner and dessert services, which are the most
important products and also those most often encountered (if one includes
odd dishes, plates, etc. originally forming part of such services). The remaining articles are listed in alphabetical order, with quotations from the catalogues
of 1818 and 1822. In the case of items included in the 1822 sale, the reserve
prices are given (when only one object or set of articles was included), but
in the majority of cases the reserve was not reached and the lot was 'bought
in'.

DINNER SERVICES

The Times advertisement of December 1813, quoted on page 21, stresses the main selling points of the newly introduced Patent Ironstone China: ' . . . the durability of the composition is beyond any other yet produced, and not being so liable to chip or break . . . will prove a recommendation for its general utility . . .' It is not surprising, therefore, that the earliest Ironstone ware was gaily decorated dinner and dessert services. Surviving specimens prove their general durability but can perhaps be faulted, by present standards, on their thick potting and consequent heaviness. In reality, however, this apparent fault is an asset in dinner ware, for heated ironstone plates, vegetable dishes, etc. retain their heat for far longer than a modern thinly-potted plate—a fact that can readily be proved by experiment.

In December 1814, Messrs. Chamberlain—the Worcester porcelain manufacturers—purchased from 'G. & C. Mason, Lane Delph', a dinner service of Patent Ironstone China, pattern 'Birds & flowers'. This purchase is listed in the *Chamberlain Wholesale & Retail Journal* covering the period 1811 to 1816. The entry is most fortunate as it sets out the individual components of the service, with their prices.

2 Tureens (& covers) & Stands	@ 11/–	£1.	2. 0.
4 Sauce tureens & Stands	4/2		16. 8.
4 Square covered (vegetable) dishes	5/–	£1.	0. 0.
1 Sallad bowl	5/6		5. 6.
1 20-inch Gravy (dish with well)			13. 0.
1 20-inch dish			10. 6.
2 18-inch dishes	7/6		15. 0.
1 (pierced) Drainer to 18-inch dish			7. 6.
2 16-inch dishes	4/6		9. 0.
1 (pierced) Drainer to 16-inch dish			4. 8.
2 14-inch dishes	3/6		7. 0.
4 12-inch dishes	2/–		8. 0.
4 10-inch dishes	1/3		5. 0.
1 12-inch Baker (deep oval baking dish)			2. 8.
1 10-inch ,, ,, ,, ,, ,,			1. 4.
60 Table (dinner) plates	6½	£1.	12. 6.
24 Soup	6½		13. 0.
24 Twifflers (middle size plates)	5½		11. 0.
24 6-inch plates	5		10. 0.

The sale held by Mr. Christie in December 1818 contained several 'table' or dinner services. Lot 5 describes the contents of a typical service:

One table service, India pheasant pattern; viz. 2 soup tureens, covers and stands, 4 sauce ditto, 4 square vegetable dishes, 1 salad ditto, 1 fish ditto, 18 dishes in sizes, 72 table plates, 24 ditto soup and 24 pie ditto (150 separate pieces).

The pattern 'India pheasant' is a typical Anglo-Chinese Mason design and is probably the same as the 'Birds & flowers' sold to Chamberlain in 1814 (see Plates 20 and 24 for patterns of this type). The basic composition of the 1818 service is much the same as that of the 1814 Chamberlain set. The 'fish ditto' (dish) is the same article as the 'drainer' in the Chamberlain set. It is an oval, flat, pierced dish which fits into one of the several large dishes or platters, the surplus liquids draining through to the dish below. The typical sizes of the '18 dishes in sizes' are given in the Chamberlain list. These are 20, 18, 16, 14, 12 and 10 inches in length. The number of plates in a dinner service could be adjusted to the customer's requirements, but there are always very many more dinner plates than soup plates—in a ratio of about three to one.

The 1818 Christie sale included dinner services in the following patterns, all with the same composition as that listed above:

'Chinese Landscape pattern' (Plate 31)
'Blue and gold border'
'Table and flowerpot pattern' (Plates 17, 19, and 39)
'India grasshopper* pattern' (Plate 21)
'Pagoda pattern in mazarine, red and gold'
'Mogul pattern'
'Basket Japan'
'India gold jar'
'India Water Melon'
'Richly coloured figure pattern'
'Blue pheasants' (Plates 20 and 24)
'Blue Chinese landscape'
'Rose and rock pattern a la Chinoise'
'Old Japan pattern in green, pink, mazarine, red and richly gilt'
'Richly Japanned in red, blue, green and gold' (Plate 22).

All of these patterns owe their origin to eighteenth-century Chinese export porcelain—the type that Miles Mason originally dealt in at London before he started manufacturing porcelain (see Chapter I). The 'Blue Chinese landscape' design is of willow-pattern type printed in underglaze blue. The 'Blue pheasants' was also produced by means of an underglaze blue print, sometimes with added gilt borders, gilt handles, etc. and sometimes in the less expensive plain version. Most Mason patterns were 'richly Japanned in red, blue, green and gold', with bold areas of red, and a rich, dark, underglaze 'mazarine' blue. Some of these typical and traditional designs were based

---

* This pattern (see Plate 21) is still produced, but under the name 'Regency' or 'Regency Ducks'.

on a printed outline which was filled in by semi-skilled painters, so reducing the cost of the finished article.

A table service, Chinese Figures, gold edge	R. £18. 0. 0.
A table service, very richly Japanned, hexagonal tureens, gold burnished tops	R. £26. 0. 0.

Several others similar to those in the 1818 sale, decorated with 'rich old Japan pattern' (with reserves of about £25), were also included in the 1822 sale.

The normal soup tureen and sauce tureen shapes are based on Chinese export market prototypes, being of elongated octagonal form (see Plates 17 and 20–2). This form is repeated in the dishes, of various sizes, with the plates of regular octagonal form (see Plates 28 and 31).

A second basic dinner service design has hexagonal tureens (see Plates 24, 26 and 28). Some sets listed in the 1822 catalogue are described as 'hexagon shape', and oval tureens are very occasionally found (see Plates 19 and 23). The other sets, and those in the 1818 sale, must be presumed to be of the standard octagonal forms.

In the 1822 sale, dinner services were also included. The 'R' prices are the reserves as marked in the original catalogue:

A Table service, white (142 pieces)	R. £6. 6. 0.
A dinner service, dragon pattern, 142 pieces as per label on tureen	R. £9. 9. 0. Unsold at £7. 10. 0.
A Dinner service, in boquet, 142 pieces	R. £12. 12. 0.
A Dinner service, gilt and ornamented with flowers, 142 pieces	R. £21. 0. 0.
A Dinner service, rich Japan pattern, sumptuously gilt	R. £35. 0. 0.
A Table service, gilt Japan	R. £26. 0. 0.
A ditto, common Japan	R. £14. 0. 0.
A dinner service, hexagon shape, blue birds and flowers (Plate 24)	R. £11. 11. 0.
A Dinner service, Dresden sprig	R. £26. 5. 0.
A Dinner service, peacock & flowers, 142 pieces	R. £14. 14. 0.
A handsome Table service, rich India devices, hexagon tureens	R. £21. 0. 0.
A table service, green flowers, only 1 tureen	R. £13. 13. 0.
A dinner service, nosegay pattern	R. £12. 0. 0.
A table service, Chinese characters on mazarine ground	R. £40. 0. 0.
A blue table service, Willow (Plate 31)	R. £9. 4. 6.
A very rich coloured and gilt table service, 142 pieces	R. £35. 0. 0. Unsold at £31. 10. 0.
A Dinner service, Tourney Sprig	R. £11. 11. 0.
A Dinner service, hexagon shape, grass hopper pattern	R. £15. 0. 0.

DESSERT SERVICES

As explained at the beginning of the dinner service section, the durability of the new Patent Ironstone China was its most important attribute, and dinner and dessert services represented the bulk of the early productions.

The sale catalogue of December 1818 gives the composition of standard Mason dessert services, although this was sometimes modified to suit customers' requirements.

> One dessert service, Mogul pattern [see Colour Plate III], viz. 1 centre piece, 2 cream tureens and stands, 12 fruit dishes and 24 plates (Sold for £5. 18. o.).

The shapes of these dessert ware units are shown in Plates 35 to 42. Of the twelve fruit dishes, four are usually oblong, four are shaped long dishes with a moulded handle at one end, and four are shaped dishes with a moulded handle at one side. The plates are basically of circular form, with a slightly shaped edge, the rim divided into twelve divisions by slight ribs (see Plate 35). The early centre pieces and cream and sugar tureens (now generally known as sucriers or sauce tureens) are of two basic forms—one with open arch in the foot, the other with solid, rather lower bases to the centre piece and tureens (see Colour Plate II and Plates 35 to 37). A later dessert ware form is shown in Plate 42. A very rare moulded dessert set is shown in Plate 41; the handles are formed as goats' heads, and a reclining cow is used on the tureen covers. A plate from this service bears the rare impressed Royal Arms mark.

In general, the types of patterns found on dessert services match those on dinner ware (see page 25). The 1818 sale catalogue contained the following dessert sets, each matching in composition that listed above:

> 'Old Japan pattern' (Colour Plate II)
> 'Pheasants in colours and gold'
> 'Japan, red, purple and gold'
> 'India, gold vase pattern'
> 'India flower basket Japan'
> 'Rock and Rose, Japan and gilt' (perhaps as Plate 36)
> 'Gold Thorn'
> 'India Grass Hopper'

The June 1822 sale contained further dessert services, but these were not always fully listed as the full composition was placed 'on the largest or principal' piece in each service.

A dessert service, beautifully painted in flowers and green ground   R. £18. 18. o.

A dessert service, gilt and painted in flowers, centre (piece),   R. £7. 10. 0.
12 compotier (fruit dishes) and 24 plates   Unsold at £6. 15. 0.
A dessert service, blue and gold flower border   R. £9. 10. 0.
A dessert service, blue birds and flowers, 43 pieces   R. £3. 0. 0.
A dessert service, blue sprig, 43 pieces   R. £5. 5. 0.
A rich Japan dessert service, 43 pieces   R. £8. 8. 0.
A dessert set, blue   R.   63/–
A dessert service, Japan   R. £5. 5. 0.
A dessert service, white   R.   36/–
A dessert service, roses and gold edge, 41 pieces   R. £6. 6. 0.
A dessert service, Dresden flowers, 37 pieces   R. £7. 7. 0.
A handsome dessert service, painted in boquets, relieved by R. £15. 15. 0.
sea green and gold devices   Unsold at £14. 14. 0.
A dessert service, Indian landscape, 43 pieces   R. £4. 0. 0.
A very beautiful, painted landscape dessert service by
S. Bourne [for notes on Bourne, see page 43]   R. £30. 0. 0
A costly dessert service, exquisitely painted in select views
by S. Bourne, enriched with burnished gold   R. 35 gns.

ALPHABETICAL LIST OF OBJECTS LISTED IN THE 1818 AND 1822 SALE CATALOGUES WITH SAMPLE DESCRIPTIONS AND PRICES

The prices prefixed 'R' are those written in the auctioneer's catalogue before the sale either as a 'reserve', under which the lot should not be sold, or as an indication of the estimated value. In practice, few lots exceeded their reserve or estimated values, and many were sold for less than these figures. The significance of the reserve prices lies in the fact that they were given either by Mason's, as an indication of the value, or by the auctioneer, who would have been familiar with the worth of the articles. Being the estimate of one person (Mason's or the auctioneer) the prices are perhaps a better indication of the relative values of each lot than the realised prices—for, owing to the unpredictable conditions of auction sales, a lot may fetch far more or less than its true market value.

It will be observed that many articles were sold 'with shades'. These were the glass domes normally associated with the Victorian era but which, in fact, came into fashion quite early in the nineteenth century. In November 1821, Messrs. Pellatt & Green, the London retailers, supplied:

$$24 \text{ French Shades } 3\tfrac{1}{2} \times 3\tfrac{1}{2} \quad @ \quad 4/–$$
$$18 \quad ,, \quad ,, \quad 4\tfrac{1}{2} \times 5\tfrac{1}{2} \quad 6/6$$
$$6 \quad ,, \quad ,, \quad 6\tfrac{1}{2} \times 6\tfrac{1}{2} \quad 9/–$$
$$2 \text{ Large oval shades} \quad 16/–$$

and E. Ring & Co. of Bristol were supplying 'glass shades' at 2/9d and 3/6d in 1819.

Baskets

1822 SALE

Pr. fruit baskets, rich Japan	R.	18/-
2 violet baskets (see Plate 43)		—
2 fruit baskets, on feet	R.	20/-
2 fruit baskets and stands, Oriental designs	R.	35/-
A violet basket painted in landscape (with a pair of toy jars, gilt and painted in flowers)	R.	25/-
2 richly painted flower baskets (and 2 lavender bottles and shades)	R.	27/-

Basins

1822 SALE

6 basins, covers & stands, painted in flowers	R.	£2. 2. 0.
4 basins, covers & stands, gilt edge	R.	£1. 0. 0.
2 broth basins, covers and stands, Japan (and 4 soup plates)	R.	30/-

Beakers

1818 SALE

. . . 2 flower beakers . . .		—
2 dragon octagonal beakers		—

1822 SALE

A pair of beakers, painted in flowers and a Japan vase	R.	£1. 0. 0.
A pair of green dragon beakers	R.	£1. 1. 0.

Bottles

1818 SALE

2 fine large bottles, ornamented, à la Chinoise		—
2 flat formed bottles		—

1822 SALE

2 Bottles, mazarine (ground), white figures with shades (and a centre jar, ditto)	R.	£3. 3. 0.
2 small hexagon bottles, mazarine, with shades (and 2 small candlesticks, red ground, with ditto)	R.	27/-
2 bottles, India figures and landscape	R.	£1. 10. 0.
2 Lavender bottles and shades (and 2 richly painted flower baskets)	R.	27/-

Bowls

1818 SALE

2 Trentham bowls, highly finished		—
1 very large dolphin-headed bowl, richly embellished in colours and gold, damaged		—
2 dolphin-head bowls, rich in colours and gold		—

1822 SALE

A salad bowl (and centrepiece with cover)	R.	25/-
1 large sideboard bowl, Indian pattern	R.	£5. 5. 0.
5 punch bowls, blue	R.	30/-

A large sideboard bowl	R.	£4. 4. o.
A flower bowl, mazarine (ground) and delicate sprigs	R.	£1. 10. o.
A conservatory bowl		Sold for £2.
2 sugar bowls, covers & stands, Japanned	R.	£1. 4. o.
A beautiful flower bowl, mazarine (ground)	R.	18/–
5 punch bowls, blue	R.	£1. 10. o.
2 punch bowls, blue iron-stone	R.	15/–
A fine flower bowl and shade	R.	£3. 13. 6.

Breakfast Sets

'Breakfast Sets' were enlarged tea services, often with large cups, egg cups, covered muffin or toast dishes (see Plate 47) and sometimes with plates (not included in standard tea services). Other breakfast ware is listed under 'Tea Sets', on page 38, as combined 'tea and breakfast' or 'breakfast, tea and coffee sets' were catalogued.

It should be noted that the term 'breakfast set' is now often applied to covered dishes—(four segmented and one centre piece (see Plate 84)—which fitted into a wooden tray. In contemporary accounts, these sets were termed 'supper sets' q.v. or 'sandwich sets'.

1822 SALE

A breakfast set, white, 82 pieces	R.	£2. o. o.
A breakfast set, white & gold, 76 pieces	R.	£5. 10. o.
A breakfast service, neat sprig, 100 pieces		—
A breakfast service, dragon pattern, 70 pieces	R.	£4. 10. o.
A breakfast set, coloured flowers, 61 pieces	R.	£3. 15. o.
12 breakfast cups and saucers, white & gold	R.	30/–
A breakfast service, green scroll and gold border, 77 pieces	R.	£5. 5. o.
A breakfast set, Indian coloured sprigs, 70 pieces, gold edge	R.	35/–
A breakfast service, enamelled roses, 77 pieces	R.	£3. 3. o.
A breakfast service, rock pattern, 94 pieces	R.	£8. 8. o.
A breakfast set, 55 pieces, dragon, ironstone	R.	30/–

Broth Basins

1822 SALE

A pair of broth basins, covers & stands, Japanned blue compartments	R.	30/–
6 broth basins and stands, grass hopper, Japan	R.	24/–

Candlesticks

1818 SALE

2 taper candlesticks, coloured and gilt		—
4 card candlesticks		—
2 tall taper candlesticks		—

1822 SALE

A pair of hand candlesticks with extinguishers and glass shades	R.	£2. 2. o.
2 candlesticks, flowers and orange ground, with shades	R.	£2. o. o.
2 candlesticks, buff ground, with shades	R.	£2. 2. o.
2 small candlesticks, red ground, with shades (with 2 small hexagon bottles, mazarine)	R.	27/–

4 Japan candlesticks, mazarine	R.	16/-
4 candlesticks and extinguishers, mazarine, Japan	R.	15/-
2 large flat candlesticks, mazarine, with shades	R.	£2. 2. 0.
A pair of handsome candlesticks, painted in flowers and glass shades	R.	30/-
A pair of reading candlesticks, Dresden flowers, a pentray and an inkstand with glass shade	R.	£1. 10. 0.
A pair of flat candlesticks and extinguishers, mazarine	R.	25/-
2 candlesticks, green and flowers, with shades	R.	28/-
2 shell candlesticks (with a small ewer & basin, 2 Toy watering cans)	Sold for £1. 3. 0.	

Card Racks/Cases
1822 SALE

2 card racks, mazarine (ground) (Plate 49)	R.	£1. 0. 0.
A pair of card cases, mazarine and white embossed figures	R.	24/-
A pair of card racks, and a pentray, mazarine	R.	28/-

Cheese Stands
N.B. Low, circular cheese dishes were sometimes included in dinner services.

1822 SALE

A Stilton cheese stand and cover	R.	£2. 4. 0.
3 cheese stands (and 6 bakers), rich Japan	R.	£2. 0. 0.

Chocolate Cups and Stands
1822 SALE

2 very rich chocolate cups and stands	R.	£1. 10. 0.
2 cups & covers, moths on mazarine ground with shades (and two sprinkling bottles)	R.	£1. 10. 0.
2 rich cups, covers & stands, painted in landscapes and shades	R.	£2. 18. 0.

Coffee Pots
1818 SALE

1 coffee pot, antique pattern and shape	—	

1822 SALE

2 antique coffee pots, with glass shades	R.	35/-
2 beautiful antique coffee pots, with shades	R.	35/-
A coffee ewer, richly gilt, from the antique, and glass shade	R.	25/-
A blue and gold coffee ewer and 2 tea cannisters	R.	26/-

Cornucopia
1818 SALE

2 flower horns (see Plate 48, for a later example)	—	

Cups and Saucers
1818 SALE

2 handsome tulip (shape?) cups & saucers	—	
. . . 2 cabinet coffee biggins . . .	—	

1822 SALE

2 beautiful caudle cups and shades   R.   £4. 4. 0.

Other normal cups and saucers were components of tea, coffee and breakfast services.

Custard Cups
1822 SALE

12 Custard cups and covers, basket pattern	R.	14/–
12 Custard cups and covers, grasshopper	R.	14/–

Essence Bottles
1822 SALE

A pair of blue essence bottles   —

Essence Bowls
1822 SALE

A pair of Grecian form essence bowls, with handles, sumptuously gilt and glass shades   R.   £6. 0. 0.

N.B. Essence bowls were probably what are now called pot pourri bowls, containing sweet smelling leaves, dried flowers, etc. Such objects are listed under 'Pot Pourri', on page 37, and include 'a large essence jar . . .'

Ewer and Basin (see also Toilet Sets)
1822 SALE

An ewer and basin, Indian sprig, gilt edge	R.	£1. 0. 0.
An ewer & basin, enamelled moths & flowers . . .		
2 rich toilet ewers and basins	R.	£3. 3. 0.
A mazarine toilet, ewer & basin, with shades	Unsold at £1.	2. 0.
3 ewers, blue dragon, from the antique	R.	11/–

Fireplaces or Mantels
These important objects were not included in the 1818 and 1822 sale catalogues, probably because the manufacture and firing of such large pieces had not been mastered by this period. Several firms made ceramic slabs or tiles which were built into fireplaces, but Mason's appear to be the only firm to have produced purely ceramic mantels.

Examples are illustrated in Plates 54 to 58. These range in size from miniature models only twelve inches high (perhaps made as samples for retail shops or travellers) to the huge examples six feet in width. Mason fireplaces bear a large printed mark comprising the pre-Victorian Royal Arms and supporters with the wording 'China Chimney piece. Mason & Co., Patentees, Staffordshire Potteries' arranged above; but this mark (Plate 56) is not visible on examples which are built into the wall.

Flower Pots

1818 SALE

2 garden flower pots and stands. —

1822 SALE

A pair of hexagon flower pots and stands, mazarine ground and gold edges	R.	£5. 5. 0.
2 large flower pots and stands, mazarine (ground)	R.	£4. 0. 0.
2 blue large flower pots and stands	R.	£2. 0. 0.
4 small flower pots and stands, mazarine and delicate sprigs	Unsold at £1. 18. 0.	
A pair of flower pots and stands, painted in moths (and an accurate sun dial, with glass shades)	R.	25/-
A pair of beautiful hexagonal, flower pots & stands	R.	£3. 10. 0.
A pair of flower pots and stands, painted in birds, with glass shades and 2 match cases	R.	£1. 8. 0.

Foot Baths

1822 SALE

2 foot pans, white	R.	25/-
2 foot pans, blue	R.	£1. 0. 0.

Large oval foot baths also occur with typical 'Japan' patterns and these sometimes still have the matching large water jug.

Goblets

1822 SALE

2 exquisitely painted satyr goblets	R.	£5. 0. 0.
2 beautiful painted goblets	R.	£4. 4. 0.
A pair of very richly painted goblets	R.	£4. 14. 0.

Inkstands

1818 SALE

2 inkstands (Plate 61)	—
2 vase shaped ink stands	—
2 cabinet inkstands	—

1822 SALE

2 Inkstands, green ground and flowers, gilt	R.	24/-
A shell ink stand, red ground (1 toy watering can and 2 teapots with glass shades)	R.	£1. 12. 0.
A shell ecritoire and pair of match cases, blue and gold	R.	32/-
A shell ink stand and 2 paper cases, flower border	R.	23/-

Jardinieres (see also Flower Pots)

1818 SALE

2 Jardinieres & Stands	13/-

Jars

N.B. Some articles described here as jars would today be termed vases.

1818 SALE

2 elegant mitre shaped jars & covers, sumptuously gilt (see Plate 59)		—
1 handsome sideboard jar, dragon handles and sumptuously gilt (see Plate 90)		—
2 large bottle shaped perfume jars	R.	£1. 4. 0.
2 tall octagonal embossed Chinese covered jars		—
1 drawing room lions-head perfume jar		—
1 splendid dragon jar, à la Chinoise		—
2 small griffin octagonal jars		—
2 tall Roman shaped jars	R.	£1. 0. 0.
1 costly Hall jar, elegant Chinese design		—
2 strawberry jars and covers		—
1 fine hexagonal hall jar and cover, enamelled in compartments and sumptuously gilt		—
1 richly executed jar, Chinese subjects, on mazarine ground		—
2 curious antique formed jars, handsomely gilt, etc.		—
2 octagonal jars & covers		—
1 ditto embossed jar & cover		—
2 rose and apple jars and covers, octagonal bronze and gold		—
2 costly jars, à la Chinoise, beautifully pencilled and gilt		—
2 bells jars, lions heads		—
2 small griffin octagonal jars		—
2 three handle jars		—
2 rose and apple handled octagonal perfume jars		—
2 strawberry jars and covers		—

1822 SALE

A pair of jars, Chinese landscape and figures	R.	25/–
A pair of jars and covers, Japanned flower and gilt ram's head and edges	R.	£3. 10. 0.
A pair of shaped jars and covers, Japanned and gilt flowers	R.	£5. 0. 0.
A noble lofty jar with cover surmounted with griffins and blue ground, beautifully enamelled in bird and flowers	R.	£9. 9. 0.
A lofty essence jar and cover, dragon handles, and top painted in flowers	R.	£3. 3. 0.
A pair of shaped jars and covers, gilt and painted flowers	R.	£2. 2. 0.
A pair of essence jars and covers	R.	30/–
A pair of jars with dragon handles	R.	35/–
A handsome essence jar, green ground and flowers (and 2 match cases in landscapes)	R.	£3. 3. 0.
3 jars, mazarine and gold chased figures, with shades		£5. 5. 0.
1 fine hexagonal Hall jar	R.	£7. 10. 0.
1 superb square very large hall jar, mazarine and Indian devices	R.	£17. 17. 0.
(auctioneer's note 'chipd a little but may be regilt')		
A Trentham plaid jar	R.	35/–
2 elegant griffin jars, painted in fruit and flowers, sumptuously gilt	R.	£6. 6. 0.
A rose and apple Jar	R.	£2. 2. 0.
2 Indian flower Jars, mazarine	R.	£2. 2. 0.
A large hydra top jar, mazarine, birds and flowers	R.	£9. 9. 0.
2 Chinese jars & covers, no reserve, sold for		17/–
2 hexagon tall jars and covers, Japan	R.	£2. 2. 0.
2 Jars, sprigs, on mazarine (ground), one faulty		Unsold at £1. 1. 0.

A fine Hall jar, Oriental design	Unsold at £6. 10. 0.
A hall jar, lion head handles	R. £2. 10. 0.
2 serpent handled jars	R. 42/–
A splendid hall jar, from an improved Indian model	R. £16. 16. 0.
A pair of jars neat sprig, on blue ground	R. £3. 3. 0.
A pair of jars, painted in landscape and glass shades	R. £2. 0. 0.
A noble essence jar, painted in flowers on a celeste ground relieved by burnished gold	R. £21. 0. 0.
A pair of blue jars, raised figures on blue ground, and glass shades	R. £2. 0. 0.
A pair of Jars, Japanned, flower and dragon handles	R. £1. 4. 0.
A rich pagoda formed hall jar	R. £6. 6. 0.
A very fine hall jar, mazarine hydra top	R. £9. 9. 0.
A handsome mantle jar, beautifully painted in shells	R. £2. 10. 0.

Jugs

1822 SALE

A handsome jug, painted in landscape and hunting subject	R. £2. 2. 0.
4 Antique shape jugs	R. 14/–
5 Jugs from the Antique and 5 Kitchen jugs	R. 16/–
2 large jugs, gold plaid and flowers	R. 30/–
6 jugs, pheasant and flowers from the Antique (see Plate 69)	R. 14/–
6 jugs, blue ironstone	R. 13/–
6 jugs, blue earthenware	R. 13/–
8 stone figured jugs	R. £1. 0. 0.
3 jugs from the Antique fancy patterns	R. 30/–
A suite of 4 jugs in flowers	R. 30/–
8 Jugs, blue bird & flower	—
12 Jugs and covers, blue bird, etc.	R. 30/–
4 Antique form jugs, grasshopper pattern	R. 11/–
5 large jugs, embossed flower	R. 15/–
6 coloured jugs (and 12 mugs)	R. 27/–
3 rich India pattern jugs	R. 25/–
8 uncovered jugs and 5 covered ditto, blue	R. 35/–
6 hunting jugs (and 5 mugs)	R. 24/–
6 Jugs, gold jar pattern	R. 25/–
3 Jugs, Japan	R. 25/–
4 hexagon jugs, mazarine and gold bands	R. £2. 10. 0.
6 jugs, gold jar, and 4 ditto, grass hopper	R. 26/–
2 large jugs, richly Japanned	R. £2. 2. 0.
2 very rich water jugs	Sold for £1. 3. 0.
10 jugs, embossed flowers and figures	R. £1. 3. 0.
Fine hunting jugs, stone	R. 12/–
Fine jugs from a beautiful Chinese original	R. 30/–
Six jugs, blue ironstone	R. 13/–
12 ditto, blue earthenware	R. 13/–
A pair of water jugs, mazarine and broad gold edge	R. 32/–

Lunch Service

1822 SALE

A lunch set, of basket pattern, gold edge, 68 pieces (the Plates are not gilt)	R. £4. 10. 0.
35 Lunch plates, rich brown and gold border	R. £4. 10. 0.

Match Boxes/Cases/Pots
1822 SALE

2 match boxes (and 3 paper cases) mazarine ground	R.	30/-
A pair of match cases, Dresden flowers and glass shades	R.	£1. 0. 0.
2 match pots, roses on black ground (and an antique coffee pot with shade)	R.	£1. 12. 0.
2 match cases, delicately finished, with shades	R.	£1. 7. 0.
A pair of match cases, blue and gold (with a shell ecritoire)	R.	32/-
2 match cases and shades, mazarine	R.	22/-

Mugs
1822 SALE

9 hunting Mugs	R.	12/-
12 mugs, ironstone	R.	14/-

Myrtle Pots
1822 SALE

2 large Myrtle pots and stands, mazarine	£4. 4. 0.

Ornaments
1818 SALE

2 low bat-head ornaments	—
2 Pan's head ornaments, landscapes in compartments of mazarine (ground) and splendidly gilt	—

Paper Cases
1822 SALE

2 paper cases, cases, raised figures on mazarine	R.	15/-
3 paper cases, rich, with shades	R.	38/-
3 richly painted paper cases, with shades	R.	£2. 10. 0.
3 paper cases, rich landscapes	R.	30/-
3 paper cases, painted birds	R.	£2. 0. 0.

Pastille Jars or Burners
1818 SALE

2 Etruscan jars for pastiles	—
2 essence burners	—
2 Etruscan jars for pastiles	—

1822 SALE

A pair of essence jars, gilt and painted in birds and flowers, faulty	R.	30/-
2 pastile burners, with glass shades	R.	55/-
A pair of essence burners, mazarine	R.	32/-
A pair of ditto (blue & Gold) essence burners and 2 cups and covers	R.	30/-

Pen Trays
1822 SALE

2 shell pen trays (2 hand candlesticks and 2 glass shades)	R.	24/-

Plates

1822 SALE

6 very rich plates	R.	£4. 12. 0.
12 plates, richly painted in various arms & crests	R.	£6. 0. 0.
7 handsome dessert plates, Melange	R.	35/-
22 Lunch plates, gilt Japan	R.	25/-
35 Lunch plates, rich brown and gold border	R.	£4. 10. 0.
12 rich Melange plates, no reserve—sold for		9/-
17 ice plates, Japan	R.	£2. 10. 0.
6 plates, birds and shells on gold border	R.	30/-
8 rich plates, arms	R.	£2. 0. 0.

Pot Pourri

1822 SALE

A pot pourri, ram's head, mazarine	R.	£2. 2. 0.
A large essence jar, Japanned & gilt (see Plate 78)	R.	£2. 2. 0.
A rich pot pourri	R.	36/-
1 pot pourri, rich Japan (see Plate 78)	R.	38/-

Ragout Dish and Cover

1822 SALE

A very rich ragout dish & cover	R.	£2. 10. 0.

Sprinklers (see also Watering Cans)

1822 SALE

A pair of blue sprinklers, gilt handles, embossed figures and glass shades	R.	£2. 0. 0.

Sprinklers were small watering-can-like objects of toy size, intended for sprinkling lavender water, etc.

Sundial

1822 SALE

An accurate sundial (and a pair of flower pots and stands painted in moths, with glass shades)	R.	25/-

Supper Sets

Supper sets, made up of four covered dishes which fit round a central covered bowl, are today often called breakfast services in error. A typical example is illustrated in Plate 84. Such sets were also known as 'sandwich sets'. Although supper, or sandwich, sets were not included in the 1818 sale, such articles were made by 1815 as is evidenced by Messrs. Chamberlain's (of Worcester) account books:

'A Table service and Sandwich, white Patent Ironstone. £12. 14. 0.' purchased from George & Charles Mason in February 1815.

1822 SALE

A white supper set	R.	20/-

A supper service, centre and 4 quadrants and covers, Japanned flower, gilt	R.	£4. 0. 0.
A supper set, richly gilt, 10 pieces	R.	£3. 10. 0.
A supper set, rich Japan, gold edge	R.	30/–
A blue supper set (see Plate 84)	R.	25/–
An oval set, Japan, gilt, with mahogany tray	R.	£2. 12. 0.
A square supper set, rich Japan	R.	£2. 10. 0.
A square supper service, finished Japan	R.	£3. 10. 0.
A square supper set, 8 pieces, snipe pattern	R.	£2. 0. 0.
A square supper set, willow Japan, 12 pieces	R.	£3. 10. 0.
A supper set, 5 pieces and tray, Rose Japan	R.	£3. 3. 0.

Tea Caddies

1818 SALE

2 square caddies		—
2 tea caddies, groups of flowers and gold lace border		—
2 caddies, mazarine ground & gold		—

1822 SALE

4 square canisters (tea caddies?) Japan, with shades	R.	£2. 0. 0.
A pair of Chinese tea caddies	R.	30/–
2 rich caddies and shades	R.	42/–

Tea Kettles

1818 SALE

2 Cabinet tea kettles   —

Teapots

1818 SALE

1 Cabinet teapot (perhaps as Plate 85)   —

Tea Sets, etc.

1818 SALE

One breakfast, tea and coffee service, corn flower sprig and gold lines, viz. 12 bowls and saucers, 12 tea cups and saucers, 15 coffee cans, 12 breakfast plates, 1 teapot and stand, 1 salt (sugar) box, 1 cream ewer, 1 pint basin, 2 bread and butter plates, and 2 butter tubs and stands   —

1 breakfast, tea and coffee set, vine embossed   —

1822 SALE

A tea and breakfast set, 56 pieces		—
A tea service, Dresden sprig, 68 pieces		—
A dejeune (tea set) gold edge, Japan	R.	£2. 2. 0.
A dejeune (tea set) festoon flowers & sprig	R.	15. 0.
A teaset, Japan, 57 pieces	R.	£4. 4. 0.
A teaset, coloured flowers, 45 pieces	R.	30/–
A breakfast & tea service, India sprig, 111 pieces	R.	£4. 4. 0.
A dejeune, Indian garden	R.	50/–
A breakfast service, dragon pattern, 70 pieces	R.	£2. 15. 0.
A tea service, white, 45 pieces	R.	15/–
A ditto, yellow & gold border, 45 pieces	R.	£1. 5. 0.

Toilet Sets

1818 SALE

1 elegant toilet ewer and basin, antique form & pattern   —

1822 SALE

2 chamber sets, white	R.	26/–
2 blue and white pheasant toilet suites, 16 pieces	R.	10/–
6 ditto jugs and a toilet suite, dragon pattern	R.	10/–
A ditto (pheasant and flowers) toilet suite, 8 pieces		—
A chamber slop pail and cover, painted in flowers, gilt edges and ornaments	R.	£2. 0. 0.
A chamber slop pail & cover, blue birds and flowers	R.	16/–
A chamber service, Chinese figures, with (glass) carafe and tumblers	R.	25/–
2 chamber sets, white, with (glass) carafes and tumblers	R.	25/–
2 new form blue chamber sets, with (glass) carafes and tumblers	R.	£2. 0. 0.
2 chamber sets, green leaf border, with (glass) carafes and tumblers	R.	35/–
A chamber service, very richly Japanned, with carafes and tumblers (glass?)	R.	£2. 2. 0.
A chamber set, basket Japan, with carafe and tumbler (glass)	R.	£1. 0. 0.
2 chamber sets, jar pattern	Sold for £1. 11. 6d.	
2 chamber services, gold jar pattern	R.	35/–

Toy or Miniature Pieces (see Colour Plate IV)

1818 SALE

1 toy ewer, basin, jug and mug, for a cabinet	—
4 toy Dresden pattern cups and saucers	—
2 toy tea kettles	—
2 toy jars & covers	—

1822 SALE

2 toy ewers and basins, mazarine, with shades	R.	27/–
4 toy spouted mugs, rich Japan (and 2 candlesticks, Tourney sprigs and shades)	R.	35/–
1 toy watering can (a shell inkstand, red ground and 2 teapots with glass shades)	R.	£1. 12. 0.
A pair of toy chamber candlesticks and 2 buckets with glasses	R.	23/–
A pair of toy hand candlesticks, a pen tray and sprinkling pot, gold edges and flowers	R.	25/–
A pair of toy jars, gilt and painted in flowers (and a violet basket painted in landscape)	R.	25/–
A toy jug (with a violet basket painted in landscapes, an ink stand and sprinkler)	R.	£1. 0. 0.
2 toy jugs and a sprinkler, Japan flowers, 3 glasses and 4 toy candlesticks	R.	£2. 0. 0.
A toy ewer and basin, painted in landscape, 2 pairs of candlesticks and glass shades	R.	25/–
1 toy teapot, 2 inks and 3 shades	R.	24/–
A small ewer & basin, 2 toy watering cans and 2 shell candlesticks	Sold for £1. 3. 0.	

Tureens

Tureens were normally part of dinner services, two being included in most sets. They were rarely sold as individual pieces.

1822 SALE

2 soup tureens and stands, rich brown and gold border	R. £3. 10. 0.

Urns

1822 SALE

A pair of handsome urns on pedestals, richly gilt and glass shades	R. £2. 0. 0.
A pair of flower urns, richly gilt and painted and 2 glass shades	R. 35/–
A set of fine Grecian shape urns, painted in birds and flowers, sumptuously gilt and 5 shades	R. £6. 10. 0.
A handsome essence urn, blue ground, enriched by moths, flowers and gilt decoration	R. £4. 4. 0.
A ditto, its companion	R. £4. 4. 0.
A pair of urns, beautifully painted in landscapes, and glass shades	R. £2. 2. 0.

Vases (see also Jars and Bottles)

1818 SALE

2 Lizard-handled vases	18. 0.
2 Three handled fluted vases	—
1 sideboard vase, dragon handles, sumptuously gilt	—
2 oak leaf low vases and covers	—
2 Three handle dragon vases	—

1822 SALE

A pair of hexagon vases, gilt Chinese buildings, figures, flowers and moths	R. £2. 15. 0.
A pair of biscuit vases, with bandeau of flowers and glass shades	R. 35/–
A suite of 3 ditto, with shades	R. 45/–
A splendid Neapolitan vase, painted by S. Bourne (see Plate 94)	R. £30. 0. 0. Unsold at £25. 4. 0.
2 Hexagon vases, mazarine, 1 faulty	R. £10. 0. 0.
2 Chimney vases, Chinese pattern	R. £1. 0. 0.
2 ditto, Japanned	R. 25/–
A set of 3 vases, fruit and green ground, with shades	R. £3. 15. 0.
2 vases, views in Rome	R. £4. 4. 0.
A very beautiful Italian formed vase, painted by S. Bourne, superbly gilt and burnished (see Plate 94)	R. 35 gns. Unsold at 33 gns.
A Pagoda vase, Japan	R. £5. 15. 6.
A set of 5 vases, painted shells and landscapes, red ground	R. £8. 8. 0.
A splendid hall jar, mazarine and oriental devices	R. £12. 12. 0.
An Italian formed vase, superior painting, richly burnished and finely modelled	R. £18. 18. 0.
5 two handle vases, enamel sprig, on mazarine ground	R. £2. 10. 0.
A hexagon temple jar	R. £1. 8. 0.
A dragon vase and cover, Indian devices	R. £3. 13. 6.

A two handled Etruscan formed flower vase, highly finished
    in flowers and gold, with shade — Unsold at £2. 14. 0.
A Pagoda vase, for vestibule — Unsold at £3. 12. 0.
2 vases, green ground, fruit, and shades — R. £4. 4. 0.
A pair of handsome vases, richly gilt and painted in flowers,
    and 2 blue bottles in birds, and glass shades — R. 30/–
A noble vase, formed from the antique, beautifully painted in
    landscapes and figures by Bourne, and sumptuously gilt — R. £21. 0. 0.
    (see Plate 94) — Unsold at £17. 6. 6.
A pair of ornaments in the style of the Portland vase and
    shades — R. £2. 10. 0.
3 handsome vases, painted in landscape, and shades — R. £4. 4. 0.
2 vases, flies [painted] on mazarine [ground], and shades — R. 28/–
Five vases and covers, Japan — R. 40/–
2 vases and covers, green dragon — R. 30/–
2 vases, views in Rome — R. £4. 0. 0.
3 vases, painted in landscapes — R. £3. 10. 0.
A vase, painted in shells — R. £2. 10. 0.
2 Grecian shape vases, flowers and green ground, with
    shades — R. £3. 3. 0.
A handsome two-handle vase, mazarine and shade — R. £2. 2. 0.
2 handsome Satyr vases, painted in landscapes and shades — R. £4. 10. 0.
A handsome one-handled vase, fruit and green ground — R. 30/–
2 rich vases, fruit and green ground — R. £2. 10. 0.
A pair of four-handled vases, mazarine — R. £2. 2. 0.
2 Spanish (shape?) vases, mazarine — R. £2. 2. 0.
2 Satyr vases, flowers and red ground — R. £3. 3. 0.

Vegetable Dishes

Ordinary covered vegetable dishes were included in dinner services (Plates
25 and 26). The 'vegetable dishes for hot water' listed here are rarely found.
The base is deep and was intended to be filled with hot water. A shallow
dished section fitted over this to hold the vegetables, the middle section
was kept hot by contact with the hot water in the base, and a cover fitted
over the middle section enclosing the heat.

1822 SALE
2 vegetable dishes for hot water — R. £3. 0. 0.
2 vegetable dishes, Japan — R. 30/–
2 vegetable dishes for hot water, gold jar pattern (and a rag-
    out dish & cover) — R. £2. 2. 0.
2 vegetable dishes for hot water (2 cheese stands and 6
    bakers) grasshopper, Japan — R. 28/–
2 hexagon vegetable dishes for hot water and 6 bakers,
    nosegay pattern — R. 30/–

Wafer Cup

1822 SALE
Wafer cup and cover (with 2 inkstands) — —

Watering Cans

1818 SALE
2 Watering cans — —

1822 SALE

1 Toy watering can (1 shell ink and 2 teapots with glass
   shades)   R.   £1. 12. 0.
2 sprinkling bottles (2 cups and covers, moths on mazarine
   ground, with glass shades)   R.   30/-

Wine Coolers

1822 SALE

2 white ice pails   R.   16/-
A pair of wine coolers, gilt mask heads and ornaments (see
   Plate 100)   R.   £2. 2. 0.
A pair of Ice pails, covers and liners, gilt and painted in
   flowers   R.   £3. 0. 0.
A wine cooler, gilt and Japanned flowers   R.   30/-
Pair of blue Ironstone coolers   R.   14/-
2 ice pails, covers and liners, grass hopper and flowers, gilt
   edge   R.   £2. 2. 0.
2 fluted top wine coolers, willow (and 2 Stilton cheese stands) R.   £2. 0. 0.
2 ice pails, richly gilt   R.   £3. 10. 0.
2 wine coolers, elegantly gilt   R.   £2. 2. 0.
A pair of ice pails, Japan   R.   £3. 0. 0.
2 ice pails, flowers in compartments, on blue border, richly
   gilt   R.   £4. 4. 0.
2 porous wine coolers and 24 (glass) wines   R.   30/-
2 ice pails, blue, and 2 wine coolers, white   R.   25/-
2 richly gilt ice pails   R.   £4. 0. 0.
2 ice pails, peacock Japan   £2. 0. 0.
A pair of ice Pails, very richly Japanned   R.   £3. 3. 0.
Two ice pails, rich Japan   R.   £4. 4. 0.
2 coolers, plaid Japan   R.   £2. 10. 0.
A pair of blue Ironstone coolers   R.   14/-
A pair of wine coolers, rich Japan   R.   £2. 10. 0.

Sundries

   Many lots comprised 'Sundries', presumably small or inexpensive utilitarian objects

1822 SALE

69 sundry pieces, peacock Japan   R.   £4. 10. 0.
38 articles of useful ware, white   R.   £2. 2. 0.
27 pieces of useful articles, white   R.   £1. 0. 0.

SUMMARY OF MASON PATTERNS
LISTED IN 1818 AND 1822 SALE CATALOGUES

The colourful Chinese-styled 'Japan' patterns, with their rich underglaze
blue and overglaze reds and greens and gilt enrichments, were the designs
most favoured for the many dinner and dessert services listed in the catalogues
of 1818 and 1822. Typical examples were:

Mogul pattern (Colour Plate III)
Table and flower pot (Plate 17)
India grasshopper (Plate 21)
India gold vase pattern
Rose and rock pattern (Colour Plate II)

and others listed as 'Old Japan' or merely as 'Japan, red, purple and gold'.

These and similar bold, colourful designs were the staple patterns employed by the Masons on their Patent Ironstone China, not only on dinner and dessert ware but also on a host of other objects: jugs in sets of graduating sizes (Plates 63 to 71); spill vases (Plate 82); punch bowls (Plates 45 and 46); vases, and so on.

A popular design based on a Chinese original was the dragon pattern, which was produced in different colours—blue, green, red, etc.—and used to decorate services, jugs and vases.

Another popular style had a deep underglaze blue ground with gilt floral designs added over the glaze, producing a very rich effect and showing the fine quality of the Mason gilding. Some very fine blue-ground ware was delicately enamelled with birds, etc., in place of the formal gilt floral designs. Such objects were far more expensive than the repetitive 'Japan' patterns with their broad areas of colour. Lot 55, on the first day of the 1822 sale, must have been a good example of this style—'A Noble lofty jar with cover, surmounted with griffins and blue ground, beautifully enamelled in birds and flowers', and again, Lot 887—'A handsome Essence Urn blue ground, enriched with Moths, flowers and gilt decoration'. Very many objects are listed in the 1818 and 1822 catalogues as having a rich mazarine blue ground (see Plates 49, 66, 67, 90, 91 and Colour Plate V).

Many objects were painted with flowers, ranging from simple, inexpensive sprig patterns—'A breakfast service, neat sprig, 100 pieces'—to the finer, naturally-depicted flowers described as 'Dresden flowers'—'A dessert service, Dresden flowers, 37 pieces'.

Ware was sometimes decorated to special order, rare examples having regimental arms and similar devices. The '12 plates, richly painted with various arms and crests' may well have been samples kept in the London shop so that the various styles could be viewed by the customer. Apart from special orders taken at the London shop or sent direct to the manufactory, it must be remembered that some untypical designs could have been added by London decorators or by other manufacturers—for the sales included several lots of white ware, and Messrs. Chamberlain of Worcester purchased white ironstone direct from the Mason factory at Fenton.

The only artist mentioned by name in the catalogues of the 1818 and 1822 sales is Samuel Bourne, and the references relate to landscape subjects:

'A very beautiful, painted landscape dessert service, by S. Bourne.' (Lot 309, 1822, sale. Reserve £30. unsold at £29. 18. 6.).
'A costly dessert service exquisitely painted in select views by S. Bourne,

enriched with burnished gold.' (Lot 837, 1822 sale. Reserve £36. 15. 0. but sold for £31. 10. 0.). 'A noble vase, formed from the antique, beautifully painted in landscapes and figures by Bourne, and sumptuously gilt.' (Lot 866, 1822 sale. Reserve £21., unsold at £17. 6. 6.).

There is a further lot, but no subject is mentioned:

'A splendid Neapolitan vase, painted by S. Bourne.' (Lot 240, 1822 sale. Reserve £30., unsold at £25. 4. 0.).

The very high price of these lots painted by S. Bourne, compared with the prices of the standard dessert services and vases listed on pages 27 to 41, should be noted. The superb vase illustrated in Plate 94 is almost certainly by Bourne.

The first edition of L. Jewitt's *Ceramic Art of Great Britain*, 1878, gives some information on this little known artist:

Mr. Samuel Bourne, of Norton-in-the-Moors, Staffordshire, who had been apprenticed to Messrs. Wood & Caldwell [this partnership terminated in July 1818], to learn the art of enamel-painting, and who had attained by his industry and talents a high reputation, entered the service of Mr. Minton, in 1828, as chief designer and artist, and continued to render the firm occasional services until 1860 [this date is corrected to 1863 in the 1883 revised edition] when the infirmities of increasing years necessitated his retirement.

The Fenton 1851 census return describes 'Samuel Bourne, Painter-artist' as aged sixty-two, and his place of birth as Norton, Staffordshire. (His son, also Samuel Bourne, is listed as having been born at Fenton and aged twenty-nine in 1851.) The place of birth tallies with Jewitt's information, and there can be little doubt that this Samuel Bourne is the S. Bourne referred to in the 1822 Mason sale catalogue. The census return shows that he was born in or about 1789, so at the time of the 1822 sale he would have been approximately thirty-three.

It is possible that Samuel Bourne may have been employed by Miles Mason, decorating his porcelain (as opposed to the post-1813 Ironstone china), from perhaps the age of twenty in about 1809. The rather free landscape painting on post-1813 Ironstone ware, such as the two-handled pot shown in Plate 93, may have been executed by Bourne. Some of the more elaborately decorated articles included in the 1822 sale could well have been painted by this artist, like 'A set of 5 vases, painted shells and landscapes, red ground.'

Chapter IV

Mason Marks and Dating

Miles Mason porcelain rarely has a mark. When one does occur, it comprises the initial and name M. MASON impressed, sometimes placed on the bottom of the footrim and thus easily overlooked. Identification is not made easier by the fact that cups and saucers do not appear to have ever been marked, and in some tea services only one or two pieces bear the impressed mark. Luckily, however, some Mason forms seem to be unique to this manufactory, so we can confidently regard unmarked specimens which exactly match in form those illustrated in Plates 3 to 16 as authentic.

Some authors have quoted as a mark the full name MILES MASON, but I have seen this only on blue-printed willow-pattern styled designs of the 1810–13 period, in conjunction with a mock-Chinese seal mark, all printed in underglaze blue. On some of these patterns, the seal appears without a name. As other manufacturers also used seal devices of this type, the shapes should be closely compared with the marked forms.

As for dating, all Mason porcelain—as opposed to the later opaque Ironstone and earthenware—was produced between c. 1800 and c. 1813, pattern numbers 1 to 100 probably having been introduced before 1805.

The printed mark W. MASON appears on a fine blue printed earthenware platter formerly in the Meigh Collection (see my *Illustrated Encyclopaedia of British Pottery and Porcelain*, 1966, Plate 389). This and other similarly marked specimens belong to the period 1811 to 1824 (see page 11).

It must also be remembered that Miles Mason and his sons produced the normal run of earthenware, of pearlware type. Blue-printed ware including large dinner services was made and may bear the printed marks

SEMI-CHINA

WARRANTED

and, rarely, the name MASON'S is placed in a curved line above the standard marks.

When the brothers George M. Mason and Charles James Mason formed a working partnership on the retirement of their father in 1813, they used many different marks incorporating the initials 'G. & C.J.M.' or the fuller particulars 'G.M. & C.J. Mason'. Examples relate to the 1813–26 period, but such marks do not often occur on Ironstone ware.

From 1813, various 'Patent Ironstone' marks were used. On plates and large articles, the full description 'Mason's Patent Ironstone China' normally appears in one or in two lines; on small items, the name 'Mason' is often omitted and the words 'Patent Ironstone China' are arranged in circular form. Although within a few years the description 'Ironstone China' was taken up by other manufacturers, the word 'Patent' should only occur on Mason ware or on ware made after 1850 by succeeding firms, such as Ashworth's (see page 53). The use of these impressed Mason marks would seem to have ceased by about 1825, and so such a mark always indicates an early example.

In carrying out the research needed to prepare this volume, I have been astounded to discover how high a proportion of seemingly Mason Ironstone ware does not bear a factory mark. In some services, only a few pieces are marked. Consequently, when the services are divided, many individual pieces may be found unmarked. Many vases and other ornamental articles are also without marks, and yet other pieces are marked in unusual and easily overlooked positions such as inside covers and inside the top flange of vases.

Apart from the normal 'Mason's . . .' or 'Patent Ironstone China', the following more unusual marks of identification may be found on some rare pieces, especially dinner service tureens: an ornate printed Royal Arms mark (see Plate 18); an impressed Royal Arms device with the word 'Patent' in the central shield (see Plate 22A); 'Mason's Cambrian Argil', on the printed earthenware apparently of the 1820s (see Plate 32); and occasionally the inscription 'Patent Ironstone Warranted' is found printed in blue or black.

The standard blue or black printed Mason's 'Patent Ironstone China' mark with the crown was in use by 1815, but the impressed marks are those normally found on pre-1820 Ironstone. For a few years, the impressed marks and the new crowned printed marks were used concurrently, the two marks occurring on the same piece; but by 1820 or 1825 the use of the printed mark would seem to have superseded the former impressed markings completely.

Early version of printed mark with impressed 'Patent Ironstone China' mark.

This printed mark was used over many years with several variations, on Ironstone ware. In some specimens from the 1840's the word 'Improved' was introduced (replacing the word 'Patent'), and in the 1840s the outline of the crown became angular. This basic mark was also used by Messrs. G. L. Ashworth & Bros. Ltd. in the latter part of the nineteenth century and on twentieth-century pieces (see pages 53–5).

Earlier Mason printed mark with rounded outline to crown.

Printed marks of the 1840s with angular outline to crown.

Other late marks, with ribbon-like crown or word 'Improved'.

The words FENTON STONE WORKS appear printed within an octagonal double-lined frame on ware from c. 1825 onwards, with a painted pattern number normally added below the main printed mark. Specimens bearing this mark are not of the finest quality and are normally purely utilitarian pieces decorated with standard gay 'Japan' patterns based on printed outlines.

In 1826, the partnership of G. M. & C. J. Mason was terminated and the firm of C. J. Mason & Co. came into being. Several printed marks were used incorporating the initials 'C.J.M. & Co' or, more rarely, 'C.J. Mason & Co'. The elevation of the factory is sometimes incorporated in these marks, which belong to the 1826–45 period. One of two addresses might be included —'Fenton Stone Works', describing the works depicted, or 'Lane Delph'. The description 'Granite China' is incorporated in several marks of this period. The mark 'Mason's Bandana Ware' probably relates to this period, but Charles J. Mason's exhibits shown at the 1851 Great Exhibition also included this ware.

From 1845 to his bankruptcy in 1848, Charles James Mason continued the Fenton Stone China Works, producing Ironstone ware on the old traditional lines. The basic printed crowned mark was also used, and it is difficult, if not impossible, to distinguish the ware made in this final period from that made by C. J. Mason & Co. from 1829 to 1845. As explained on page 19, Mason survived the bankruptcy to continue until c. 1853 on a limited scale. These late products, including the ware shown in the 1851 Exhibition, were in all probability indistinguishable from the ware of the 1840s.

Late printed Mason's mark. Note angular outline of crown, with registration mark (see page 20) of April 1849.

It is noteworthy that the early impressed marked specimens of 'Mason's Patent Ironstone China' do not have painted pattern numbers. As a general rule, it may be considered that specimens bearing a printed pattern number are post-1830.

With regard to other marks incorporating the name 'Mason', the reader should bear in mind the fact that Messrs. G. L. Ashworth & Bros. (Ltd.) used this name in the latter part of the nineteenth century and up to 1968, when the firm was retitled Mason's Ironstone China Ltd. As successors to the original firm, they were—and are—quite entitled to use this registered trade-name, although it is confusing to some new collectors.

Chapter V

Mason-Type Ware and Other Manufacturers

I have already explained on page 7 that the Masons were by no means the first potters to produce a durable compact earthenware, but there can be no doubt that they publicised and popularised the material—in much the same way that Josiah Wedgwood's perfecting of the creamware body and marketing of it under the new name 'Queen's Ware' caught the public's fancy some forty-five years earlier.

Just as other potters copied Wedgwood's Queen's Ware, so numerous manufacturers strove to produce ware similar to Mason's new Ironstone. It has been stated that Mason's were protected by their patent rights; but in practice, very similar bodies could be produced from materials differing from Mason's patent specification. There being no copyright on the Mason style of colourful 'Japan' patterns, the only real protection that Mason's patent gave them was over the use of the words 'Patent Ironstone' in describing and marking their ware. The most valuable aspect of the patent was to give publicity to Mason's ware and to suggest to the public that the body was entirely new.

In the following pages, details are given of some of the firms that are known to have Ironstone-type ware. This alphabetically arranged list is probably not complete. Examples by little known potters may come to light as interest in this ware increases.

Before Charles James Mason introduced the description 'Ironstone' for his new ware in 1813, the standard name for this type of heavy, compact and durable body was 'Stone China', a description used in the marks of Messrs. Spode, Davenport, Hicks & Meigh, Ridgway's and some lesser known firms. The term 'Opaque China' was also widely used, but this body is normally a standard white earthenware unrelated to the heavy Stone China. 'Opaque China' and similar descriptions were merely sophisticated and accurate trade terms for earthenware.

The term 'Ironstone' was first used by C. J. Mason in 1813. When this name is preceded by the word 'Patent' on early pre-1830 objects, it may be considered to relate to genuine Mason ware; but existing examples prove that other potters soon adopted the new description, without the prefix 'Patent', to describe their own ware made in the Mason tradition.

The term 'Granite' China was adopted before 1842, as it occurs on marked 'Brameld' ware (see page 59). The name 'Granite' became very popular, especially on ware exported to North America. It was much used by late nineteenth-century manufacturers and occurs with great frequency in trade advertisements.

A check-list of trade terms for Ironstone-type ware is given on page 108.

The address 'Staffordshire' in the following list refers to the district known as the Staffordshire Potteries. This was made up of seven separate towns— **Burslem, Cobridge, Fenton, Hanley, Longton, Stoke** and **Tunstall**— all now combined to form the city of Stoke-on-Trent.

William Adams & Sons (Potters) Ltd., Tunstall and Stoke, Staffordshire 1769 to present day

This well-known firm produced a wide range of good quality ceramics: basalt, jasper, creamware, parian, porcelain and standard earthenware, as well as Ironstone-type ware. Various marks were used on the Ironstone-type ware from about 1830 onwards. These normally comprise or incorporate the name 'ADAMS' or the initials 'W.A. & S'. However, the firm changed its title from time to time and from c. 1866 to 1899 traded as William & Thomas Adams, during which period the marks incorporated the name 'W. & T. Adams' or the initials 'W. & T. A.' The addition of the word 'England' on any Adams mark (or other mark) signifies a date after 1891. The date '1657' incorporated in several Adams marks is the claimed date of the firm's establishment. In 1851, Messrs. William Adams employed 165 men, 71 women, 65 boys and 26 girls. Sample marks are reproduced below.

E

Henry Alcock & Co. (Ltd.), Cobridge, Staffordshire
c. 1861–1910

Jewitt, writing of Messrs. Henry Alcock & Co. in the revised 1883 edition of his *Ceramic Art of Great Britain*, noted:

> At these extensive works, which have recently been much enlarged (formerly carried on by John Alcock), Henry Alcock & Co. manufacture white Granite ware, under the names of 'Ironstone china' and 'Parisian porcelain', exclusively for the American markets, and also the common descriptions of printed wares.

The Henry Alcock ware bears marks incorporating the initials 'H.A. & Co.' or the name in full. From 1910 to 1935 the firm was retitled **The Henry Alcock Pottery,** and the marks include this new title.

John & George Alcock, Cobridge, Staffordshire
c. 1839–46

This partnership produced good quality Ironstone-type ware.
 Impressed mark:

ORIENTAL
STONE
J. & G. ALCOCK

Other printed marks incorporated the initials 'J. & G.A.'

John & Samuel Alcock (Junr.), Cobridge, Staffordshire
c. 1848–50

This firm succeeded John & George Alcock (see above) and continued the old lines and patterns, which included 'flowing blue' designs. Marks include 'J. & S. Alcock Jr.', and the description 'Oriental Stone' was favoured.

Samuel Alcock & Co., Cobridge and Burslem, Staffordshire
c. 1828–59

Messrs. Samuel Alcock & Co. manufactured a large range of decorative and fine quality porcelain and earthenware. The name has not, in the past, been associated with Ironstone but recent finds on the factory site include fragments marked:

ALCOCK'S
INDIAN IRONSTONE

with, in some cases, other standard Alcock marks which incorporate the initials 'S.A. & Co.' or the name in full. One site fragment bearing the impressed 'Alcock's Indian Ironstone' mark has also the date '1839'.

G. L. Ashworth & Bros. (Ltd.), Hanley, Staffordshire

c. 1861–1968 (subsequently continued under the new style 'Mason's Ironstone China Ltd.')

Messrs. Ashworth have been the largest producers of Ironstone since 1861. The firm acquired Mason's original moulds, patterns, etc., through the partnership between Taylor Ashworth and Francis Morley, the latter having purchased them—some on his own account and some through his later partnerships, the last of which, between Morley and Taylor Ashworth (c. 1858–61), led to the formation of the G. L. Ashworth & Bros. firm.

The April 1861 Hanley census returns show that at that period Taylor Ashworth, then aged only twenty-two, employed 250 men, 100 women, 50 boys and 50 girls. These figures may have been approximate, as the numbers are strangely even, but they do show that the Ashworth concern was quite large. There is no mention of a partner with Ashworth, a fact that suggests that the Morley–Ashworth partnership had terminated by this period—that is, prior to 1862, the date which has been given by other authorities.

The original Mason engraved designs, incorporating the 'Mason's Patent Ironstone' printed marks, have been extensively used to the present day. Various new marks have also been issued, but these still retain the original wording. Some 'Mason' marks had the name 'Ashworth' added, but these are rather rare. The addition of the word 'England' to a 'Mason' mark indicates an Ashworth parentage after 1891. The wording 'Made in England' is a twentieth-century variation (see Plate 101). Some Ashworth–Mason ware of early twentieth-century date has month and year numerals impressed to show the date of potting. These date numerals take the form 6·07 for June 1907, 7·08 for July 1908, and so on.

Messrs. Ashworth also produced earthenware other than Ironstone, bearing various printed marks incorporating the initials 'G.L.A. & Bros.' or 'A. Bros.'. Sample Ashworth marks are reproduced below.

The *Art Journal* featured an article on Mason and his Ironstone China, in 1867, which included a review of the current Ashworth products:

> . . . Messrs. Ashworth Brothers continue, to the fullest extent, the manufacture of the 'Patent Ironstone China' . . . and produce all Mason's best patterns in services, etc. from the original moulds . . . These they produce in immense quantities, both for home and foreign markets, about one-third of their whole productions being export . . . The 'Ironstone China', from its extreme hardness and durability . . . is specially adapted, in its simpler styles of decoration, for services used in large steamship companies, hotels, clubs, colleges, and other places where hard usage has to be undergone; while in its more elaborate and rich style—and it is capable of the very highest degree of finish—it is eminently fitted for families of the highest ranks. It is much used in the houses of the nobility and higher classes. No climate affects this ware . . .

The largest proportion of Messrs. Ashworth's output comprises useful ware—dinner, dessert or tea services, with some jugs, vases, etc., decorated with traditional Mason-style designs. A notable exception occurred just before the outbreak of the 1914–18 war when experiments were carried out to produce decorative glaze effects after the Chinese 'rouge flambé' ware. An Austrian chemist, Dr. Basch, was engaged by the then Managing Director, Mr. J. V. Goddard. Numerous experimental pieces were produced and the new ware was christened 'Lustrosa'—but, reputedly, not a piece was marketed due to the outbreak of the war, Dr. Basch's return to Austria and Mr. Goddard's entry into the armed forces. Experimental pieces of Ashworth 'Lustrosa' ware are still preserved in the works museum. Examples were shown at an exhibition held in the Louvre in 1914, and the official catalogue states that these pieces were designed by J. V. Goddard.

On a recent visit to the Ashworth–Mason factory, I was shown all of the numerous processes of manufacture and the production of the traditional Mason Ironstone designs. In some cases, these designs have been slightly simplified or amended to bring them into line with modern taste; but in all cases, the spirit of the original design has been preserved. Many will regret, however, the retirement of the old bottle-shaped kilns in favour of the smaller gas-fired ovens into which trolley loads of ware are run without the need of the old protective saggars.

Passing as one does from one process to another, seeing the various skilled hands through which the clay forms must progress before they become fit objects for the table, the ultimate reaction is one of bewilderment that the finished articles can be sold so cheaply. In this world, so many objects seem grossly overpriced; but no one who has seen a pottery in action can ever regard fine ceramics as anything but an inexpensive luxury.

As I have stated previously, the Ashworth firm adopted the new name 'Mason's Ironstone China Ltd.' in the summer of 1968.

W. Baker & Co. (Ltd.), Fenton, Staffordshire
c. 1839–1932

The early ware of this firm was often unmarked, and the marks 'W. Baker & Co.' or 'Baker & Co.' are rarely found. A late printed mark of the post-1893 period, when 'Ltd.' was added to the firm's title, is reproduced below. The firm was a large one, employing over five hundred people in 1851, and six hundred and fifty in 1861.

Barker & Son, Burslem, Staffordshire
c. 1850–60

The impressed mark 'BARKER & SON' is recorded on Ironstone-type ware, and the initial mark 'B. & S.' occurs on a printed design 'Missouri', registered at the Patent Office on 5th June 1850 in the name of Barker & Son, Hill Works, Burslem. The partnership employed two hundred and sixty-five people in 1851 and was, consequently, a large concern.

Bates & Bennett, Cobridge, Staffordshire
c. 1868–95

The first printed mark reproduced may have been used by this firm, but the initials could relate to any one of sixteen other Staffordshire partnerships of the 1820-80 period. An earlier 'B.B.' mark with the pre-Victorian Royal Arms is also reproduced.

Batkin, Walker & Broadhurst, Lane End, Staffordshire
c. 1840-5

Good quality Ironstone-type ware was made by this short-lived firm under the description 'Stone-China'. Printed marks incorporate the initials 'B.W. & B.'

Beardmore & Edwards, Longton, Staffordshire
c. 1856-8

The initial mark 'B. & E.' occurs, rarely, on blue printed ware. No other Staffordshire partnership used these initials before Messrs. Bradbury & Emery of c. 1889-1902.

J. & M. P. Bell & Co. (Ltd.), Glasgow, Scotland
c. 1842-1928

Messrs. Bell produced a very large range of earthenware and porcelain. Their exhibits at the 1851 Exhibition included:

> Dinner services in stoneware: Blue printed . . .
> Toilet services in stoneware . . .
> Tea services and jugs in stoneware and porcelain . . .

Patterns mentioned by name include 'Italian lakes'; 'Warwick Vase'; 'Diana'; 'Convolvulus'.

Most of Bell's ware bears marks incorporating the initials 'J.B.' or 'J. & M.P.B. & Co.'; 'Ltd.' was added to the firm's style, and initial marks, from 1881. A bell device was also used as a mark, and it occurs impressed or printed.

Further information on this important firm may be found in Jewitt's *Ceramic Art of Great Britain* or in J. A. Fleming's *Scottish Pottery*, 1923.

Belleek Factory, Co. Fermanagh, Ireland
c. 1863 to present day

This factory is mainly known for its delicate, thinly potted porcelain ware, often based on marine forms: objects vastly different from one's image of Ironstone. However, Ironstone or Granite-type ware was made and L. Jewitt in the first, or 1878, edition of his *Ceramic Art of Great Britain* especially notes:

> Besides the speciality of these works (the 'Belleek China') Messrs. McBirney & Armstrong manufacture to a large extent white granite ware services of every variety, and of excellent quality both in body, in glaze, and in printed, painted, enamelled, and gilt decorations. Many of the patterns are of more than average excellence, and in every respect the Irish earthenware equals the ordinary commercial classes of Stafford-shire wares . . .

Belleek earthenware is rare. It may be marked with the words 'BELLEEK Co. FERMANAGH' and a crowned harp device or with the standard hound, tower and harp mark with the name 'BELLEEK' below. A catalogue of Belleek ware, dated 1904, includes useful earthenware but no Ironstone.

Birks Brothers & Seddon, Cobridge, Staffordshire
c. 1877–86

This firm employed the Royal Arms device above the wording 'IMPERIAL IRONSTONE CHINA, BIRKS BROS. & SEDDON'.

Bishop & Stonier, Hanley, Staffordshire
c. 1891–1939

This partnership succeeded Messrs. Powell, Bishop & Stonier (c. 1880–90), and various types of earthenware, including Ironstone, were produced. The marks incorporate the name 'Bishop & Stonier' or the initials 'B. & S.'.

Edward F. Bodley & Co. (& Son), Burslem, Staffordshire
c. 1862–98

Edward F. Bodley & Co. worked the Scotia Pottery at Burslem from 1862 to 1881. Various kinds of earthenware were produced and marked with the name or initials 'E.F.B. & Co.' or 'E.F.B.'. The name 'Scotia Pottery' also occurs. Much Bodley Ironstone was exported.

In 1881, the firm's style was amended to **Edward F. Bodley & Son** and the New Bridge Pottery at Burslem was taken over. Advertisements feature 'Genuine Ironstone China', which was manufactured between 1881 and 1898 and would bear marks incorporating the initials 'E.F.B. & Son' or 'E.F.B. & S'. A further mark incorporates the address, 'New Bridge Pottery', arranged in a Staffordshire knot as below.

T. & R. Boote Ltd., Burslem, Staffordshire
c. 1842 to present day

Messrs. Boote made a wide selection of earthenware and parian ware in the middle of the nineteenth century; but by 1880, the firm had confined its attention to tiles (now its only concern) and to Ironstone or 'Granite ware' marketed under the title 'Royal Patent Ironstone'. The printed marks incorporate the firm's name or the initials 'T. & R.B.'. Much of Boote's Ironstone and Granite ware was made for the overseas markets, and a great quantity was made for North America.

Booth & Meigh, Lane End, Staffordshire
c. 1828–37

The mark $\frac{\text{IRONSTONE}}{\text{B \& M}}$ is recorded, and some writers have attributed it to Bagshaw & Meir of c. 1802–8—but the name 'Ironstone' could not have been used at so early a period. These initials probably relate to Booth & Meigh, c. 1828–37, or to Brougham & Mayer of Tunstall, c. 1853–5.

Thomas Booth & Co. (& Sons), Tunstall, Staffordshire
c. 1868–76

T. Booth & Co. produced earthenware and Ironstone-type bodies, as did their successors Thomas Booth & Son, c. 1872–6. Initial marks were used: 'T.B. & Co.' or 'T.B. & S.', 'T.G.B.' or 'T.G. & F.B.'.

G. F. Bowers (& Co.), Tunstall, Staffordshire
c. 1842–68

George Frederick Bowers is mainly known for his good quality porcelain and standard earthenware, but Ironstone-type ware was made and is marked:

IRONSTONE
CHINA
G.F. BOWERS

Brameld (& Co.), Swinton, Yorkshire
c. 1806–42

The Bramelds owned and managed the Swinton pottery (more popularly called **'Rockingham'**) from 1806 to its closure in 1842. The pottery is mostly known for its standard earthenware and fine porcelain, but Ironstone bodies were also made (see Plate 105). Printed marks incorporate the name of the printed pattern with the description 'GRANITE CHINA' (an early use of this term), 'STONE CHINA' or 'FINE STONE'. The initial 'B' occurs rarely in these printed marks. The impressed name 'BRAMELD' or 'BRAMELD & CO.' may also appear on this Swinton or Rockingham ware. For further information see *The Rockingham Pottery* by A. A. Eaglestone and T. A. Lockett, 1964, and Dr. D. Rice's *Illustrated Guide to Rockingham Porcelain* (London and New York, 1970).

Bridgwood & Clarke, Burslem & Tunstall, Staffordshire
c. 1857–64

Messrs. Bridgwood & Clark produced Ironstone or 'Granite' ware mainly for the American market. Their ware bears the names in full or the initials 'B. & C.' with descriptions such as 'Opaque China' or 'Porcelain Opaque'. This firm was continued by Edward Clarke (& Co.).

Sampson Bridgwood & Son, Longton, Staffordshire
c. 1805 to present day

The early Bridgwood earthenware is unmarked. In the middle of the nineteenth century, a large range of earthenware and porcelain was produced. In Jewitt's account of this firm, written in or before 1878 (*The Ceramic Art of Great Britain*), he records:

> In earthenware they produce largely the white granite for the United States, Australian and Canadian trade, and they also produce for the home market. One of their specialities is what is technically called 'Parisian granite' (stamped as 'Limoges'), which is of fine, hard, durable body and excellent glaze. In this ware tea, breakfast, dessert, dinner and toilet services are largely produced; many are of excellent design . . . The Parisian granite bears the impressed stamp, an oval, with the word 'Limoges', and in the centre P.G. (for Parisian granite). It also bears the printed mark of an elaborate shield of arms with mantling, sceptres, etc. and the words 'Porcelaine Opaque, Bridgwood & Son'.

Initial marks were also used:

Brougham & Mayer, Tunstall, Staffordshire
c. 1853–5

The printed mark of the words 'Ironstone' and 'Brougham & Mayer' occurs, rarely, with a garter-shaped device.

William Brownfield (& Son(s)), Cobridge, Staffordshire
c. 1850–91

William Brownfield produced large quantities of fine earthenware (and porcelain from 1871), and over four hundred and fifty people were employed in 1861. The Brownfield pottery is not known for its Ironstone, but such ware was certainly produced. William Brownfield's son was taken into partnership in 1871 and from this period '& Son' was added to the firm's style and marks. The plural form dates from 1876. Marks comprise the name 'Brownfield', the initials 'W.B.', or 'W.B. & S.' (after 1871). From 1891 to 1898, the firm was titled Brownfields Guild Pottery Society Ltd.; and from 1898 to 1900, Brownfields Pottery Ltd.

Thomas & John Carey, Lane End, Staffordshire
c. 1823–42

John Carey started potting at Lane End in about 1813. The Careys produced very good quality standard earthenware, often decorated with fine blue printed designs. The standard mark is the word 'CAREY'S' with or without an anchor; but one mark incorporates the description 'SAXON STONE CHINA'. A finely printed tureen stand is shown in Plate 106.

Cartwright & Edwards (Ltd.), Longton & Fenton, Staffordshire
c. 1869 to present day

Messrs. Cartwright & Edwards worked the Borough Pottery at Longton from c. 1869. The Victoria Works were taken in 1912 and the Heron Cross Pottery at Fenton in 1916. Advertisements of the 1880s mention 'IRONSTONE CHINA, AND EARTHENWARE of every description for the home, colonial and foreign markets'. Marks feature or include the initials 'C. & E.'; 'Ltd.' was added to the firm's style and to some marks from c. 1907. A wide range of ware has been produced, including bone china.

Edward Challinor, Tunstall, Staffordshire
c. 1842–67

Edward Challinor worked the Pinnock Pottery at Tunstall (and the Unicorn Pottery from 1862 to 1867). Good quality earthenware, including Ironstone-type ware, was produced and marked with the initials 'E.C.' or the name 'E. CHALLINOR'. This pottery should not be confused with **E. Challinor & Co.** of Fenton (see next entry), although there were firms having this style at Tunstall in 1851 and in 1853–4.

E. Challinor & Co., Fenton, Staffordshire
c. 1853–62

This firm produced good quality blue printed earthenware, examples of which are recorded with the name mark 'E. CHALLINOR & CO.' Messrs. E. & C. Challinor succeeded (see next entry).

E. & C. Challinor, Fenton, Staffordshire
c. 1862–91

This firm succeeded E. Challinor & Co. (1853–62). Printed or impressed marks incorporate the name 'E. & C. CHALLINOR' or the initials 'E. & C.C.', sometimes below the Royal Arms.

Chamberlain & Co., Worcester
c. 1786–1852

I have already shown, on page 24, that as early as 1814—one year after the original Ironstone patent was granted—Messrs. Chamberlain & Co., the Worcester porcelain manufacturers, had ordered Ironstone ware from Messrs. Mason.

It would appear that at least by the 1840s they had themselves commenced the manufacture of a similar type of hard, durable ware which they sold under the popular term 'Stone-china'. However, this is now extremely scarce and was perhaps only made for a short period as an experiment.

A special mark has been recorded incorporating the name of an American importer:

MR. BILLSLAND, IMPORTER, 447 BROADWAY.
CHAMBERLAINS
WORCESTER
MANUFACTURERS TO THE ROYAL FAMILY.
STONE—CHINA

This printed mark would appear to be of the 1840–50 period. The Chamberlain firm was succeeded by Messrs. Kerr & Binns in 1852.

Edward Clarke (& Co.), Burslem & Tunstall, Staffordshire
c. 1865–87

This firm succeeded Messrs. Bridgwood & Clarke (see page 59). Similar ware was produced, and the marks incorporate the name 'EDWARD CLARKE' or 'EDWARD CLARKE & CO'. A Tunstall address indicates a date prior to 1878, a Burslem address a date between 1878 and 1887.

Clementson Bros. (Ltd.), Hanley, Staffordshire
c. 1865–1916

Messrs. Clementson Bros. succeeded Joseph Clementson, 1839–64 (see next entry). Good quality Ironstone and 'Royal Patent Stoneware' was made and sold with several marks incorporating the style 'Clementson Bros.'. 'England' was added to most marks between 1891 and 1916. Much Clementson Ironstone was exported to Canada, and from the 1840s Francis Clementson had an important retail establishment in Canada.

Joseph Clementson (Shelton), Hanley, Staffordshire
c. 1839–64

Good quality Ironstone and standard earthenware was made by Joseph Clementson. One design registered in 1842 has a printed mark incorporating the initials 'J.C.' and the description 'GRANITE WARE'. Other ware is marked with the name in full, with or without the word 'IRONSTONE' or 'STONE CHINA'. In 1861, Joseph Clementson employed 149 men, 63 women, 146 boys and 76 girls.

Clementson, Young & Jameson (Shelton), Hanley, Staffordshire
1844

This short-lived partnership produced Ironstone, as is proved by a design registered in October 1844. The mark incorporates the initials 'C.Y. & J.' and the description 'Ironstone'. Messrs. **Clementson & Young** (c. 1845–7) succeeded, and probably made Ironstone-type ware marked with their name or initials.

James & Ralph Clews, Cobridge, Staffordshire
c. 1818–34

This partnership produced very good quality earthenware, often blue printed and intended for the American market. Stone china was also produced and this description is incorporated in several marks with the name 'Clews'. The term 'Dresden Opaque China' was also used.

Cochran & Fleming, Glasgow, Scotland
c. 1896–1920

This Scottish firm produced 'ROYAL IRONSTONE CHINA', using this description with their name and the Royal Arms device or the seated figure of Britannia.

Cockson & Chetwynd (& Co.), Cobridge, Staffordshire
c. 1867–75

Ironstone ware, marked with the Royal Arms and having the description 'Imperial Ironstone China' and the names of the partnership, was produced between 1867 and 1875. Similar ware and marks were used by the succeeding partnership of **Cockson & Seddon** (c. 1875–7) with, of course, the new name replacing the former.

Cork & Edge, Burslem, Staffordshire
c. 1846–60

This firm produced a large range of ornamental and useful earthenware, much of which was exported to North America. Trade terms 'STAFFORD-SHIRE STONE WARE' and 'PEARL WHITE IRONSTONE' were employed on marks with the names 'CORK & EDGE' or with the initials 'C. & E.'. This partnership was succeeded by Messrs. **Cork, Edge & Malkin** (c. 1860–71). Marks were employed with these names or with the initials 'C.E. & M.'.

W. & E. Corn, Burslem, Longport, Staffordshire
c. 1864

Messrs. W. & E. Corn traded from Burslem from c. 1864 to 1891 and at the Top Bridge Works, Longport, from 1891 to 1904. Early ware was marked with the initials 'W. & E.C.' or 'W.E.C.'. Jewitt, writing in or before 1878 (*Ceramic Art of Great Britain*), noted that 'Messrs. W. & E. Corn, are exclusively devoted to the production of white graniteware for the United States and other foreign markets'. From c. 1900, printed marks incorporating the trade name 'Porcelaine Royale' were employed.

H. & R. Daniel, Stoke and Shelton, Staffordshire
c. 1823–41

Messrs. Daniel produced very fine quality porcelain, richly decorated, of which few examples are marked. The firm also produced Ironstone and stone china. The rare impressed mark 'DANIEL'S REAL IRONSTONE' has been recorded. Simeon Shaw, in his *History of the Staffordshire Potteries*, 1829, stated that in 1826 Messrs. Daniel produced their stone china in Shelton: 'the shapes and patterns being of the improved kind, so much preferred by the public . . .'

An existing pattern and price book confirms that Daniels produced 'Stone China' dinner and dessert and tea services, as well as toilet sets. Recorded patterns reach Number 1946. A typical entry reads:

> 1925 Japan Groups [of flowers] blue outlines, blue & green leaves, gold fibres & gold lines.

Printed tea ware patterns mentioned by name include Birds; Broseley; Indian figure; Peacock; Swiss Girl; Barbeaux; Gothic; Fruit & Flowers; Strawberry.

Printed dinner ware designs were termed Chinese Scenery; Oriental Vases; Birds; Fruit & Flowers; Strawberry & Barbeaux.

It is interesting to note that articles made in 'Stone China' were more expensive than the same object in the standard earthenware body.

Davenport (Ltd.), Longport, Staffordshire
c. 1793–1887

Messrs. Davenport produced a very fine range of porcelain, earthenware, stoneware and even glass. Neatly potted and tastefully decorated 'Stone China' was produced from c. 1805 to about 1820 (see Plate 109). Direct copies of the later Mason Ironstone ware were seldom attempted, although a variation of the standard Mason jug shape does occur with the Davenport name mark (see Plate 107). Advertisements show that Davenport Ltd. produced Ironstone-type ware up to the 1880s. Early marks incorporate the names 'REAL STONE CHINA', 'STONE CHINA', 'REAL IRON-STONE CHINA', or 'IRONSTONE'. An impressed mark of the 1840–60 period has the words 'Davenport. Ironstone China' surrounding the anchor device. The date of manufacture of much of the mid-nineteenth century Davenport earthenware can be discovered by careful examination of the standard impressed 'Davenport' and anchor mark, for the last two numerals of the year were placed each side of the anchor. The plate shown in Plate 108 is dateable to 1844 by this device (see sample mark below). Other pieces sometimes have the month and year of manufacture impressed, i.e. 6·67 for June 1867.

L. L. Dillwyn, Swansea, Wales
c. 1831–50

Lewis Llewelyn Dillwyn owned the famous Swansea Pottery in Wales from 1831 to 1850. Among the varied pottery he produced was some Ironstone-type ware which bears descriptive marks 'CYMRO STONE CHINA'. Other printed marks use the term 'STONE WARE' with the initial 'D' or the name 'DILLWYN & CO.' The standard reference book on Swansea ceramics is E. Morton Nance's *The Pottery and Porcelain of Swansea and Nantgarw*, 1942.

Thomas Dimmock & Co. (Shelton), Hanley, Staffordshire
c. 1828–59

Messrs. Dimmock were important producers of a large range of earthenware, but this is little known today. Ironstone-type ware was made under the description 'Stone Ware'. Printed marks incorporate the initial 'D' and can be mistaken for similar 'D' marks as employed by Davenport's and by L. Dillwyn of Swansea. However, some Dimmock ware also bears an impressed monogram device which is a great help in identifying this Company's products. The device is reproduced below.

Basic Dimmock
mark, found impressed
or incorporated in
printed marks.

Dunn, Bennett & Co. (Ltd.), Burslem, Staffordshire
c. 1875 to present day

This firm, originally of the Boothen Works, Hanley, produced good Ironstone ware. Jewitt, writing in the revised 1883 edition of his *Ceramic Art of Great Britain*, noted:

> Messrs. Dunn, Bennett & Co. here manufacture earthenware and ironstone china in all the usual services, both for the home and American markets. Their productions are of a high quality, and having houses both in London and New York, they are in a position to cater successfully for both countries.

The firm's advertisement of the 1890s mention 'IRONSTONE CHINA', specially adapted for ships, hotels, restaurants and coffee house use. Early marks incorporated the initials 'D.B. & Co.', often with a beehive device; 'Ltd.' was added to marks late in 1907. Subsequent marks include the term 'Vitreous Ironstone' with the Company's name in full. Their ware enjoys a large sale at the present time. In 1968, the Company was merged with Messrs. Doulton's.

Edge, Malkin & Co. (Ltd.), Burslem, Staffordshire
c. 1871–1903

Messrs. Edge, Malkin & Co. succeeded Cork, Edge & Malkin (see page 63).

Advertisements of the 1880s mention 'IRONSTONE-CHINA AND EARTHENWARE, plain, printed, enamelled and gilt dinner, tea and toilet ware, in white ivory and other coloured bodies . . .' The standard printed mark incorporates the initials 'E.M. & Co.' on a ribbon under a dog device. The full name or initials also occur as impressed marks.

James Edwards (& Son), Burslem, Staffordshire
c. 1842–82

From 1842, James Edwards traded under his own name until, in 1851, '& Son' was added to the style. Good class Ironstone-type ware was manufactured and sold under the descriptions 'Ironstone China' or 'Stone China', with the name of the firm or the initials 'J.E. & S.'.

John Edwards (& Co.), Fenton, Staffordshire.
c. 1847–1900

John Edwards first potted at Longton, moving to Fenton in about 1853. In 1861, 170 persons were employed. Marks on Ironstone-type ware include the name John Edwards, 'England' being added after 1891. Jewitt noted in 1878 (*Ceramic Art of Great Britain*): 'The goods now produced are semi-porcelain and white granite for the American market.'

Elsmore & Forster, Tunstall, Staffordshire
c. 1853–71

This firm worked the Clayhills Pottery at Tunstall, where general earthenware as well as Ironstone-type ware was produced. One of the best known lines has a raised wheat design. This basic pattern was registered in November 1859. Marks incorporate the name of the partnership, often with the Royal Arms. Messrs. Elsmore & Son succeeded this firm c. 1872–87.

Ferrybridge Pottery, Nr. Pontefract, Yorkshire
c. 1792 to present day

Prior to 1804, this pottery was known as the Knottingley Pottery. A succession of owners worked it and many different marks were used, basic details of which are given in my *Encyclopaedia of British Pottery and Porcelain Marks*, 1964.

F

In 1856, Lewis Woolf purchased the Ferrybridge Pottery, and in the following year his sons built the adjoining Australian Pottery—both works trading under the style 'Lewis Woolf & Sons'. Several printed marks incorporate the initials 'L.W.' or the addresses 'Ferrybridge and Australian Potteries'. The name 'Ferrybridge' also occurs as a mark, sometimes with the 'd' reversed.

Jewitt, writing in or before 1878 (*Ceramic Art of Great Britain*), stated that the marks included 'a shield, with the words OPAQUE GRANITE CHINA in three lines, supported by a lion and unicorn, and surmounted by a crown. This mark is also impressed . . . The mark at the present time (that is, in the late 1870s) is that of the lion and unicorn with shield and crown and the words "Ferrybridge and Australian Potteries" sometimes impressed, and at others printed on the goods, with the names of the bodies, as "granite", "stone china", etc.' The first mark mentioned would seem similar, apart from the crown, to that found on fragments at the Swillington Bridge Pottery (see page 94). Jewitt also records that the two factories employed some five hundred hands.

In c. 1884 the works passed to Poulson Brothers, then to Sefton & Brown (c. 1897–1919) and from then to Messrs. T. Brown & Sons (Ltd.).

Stephen Folch, Stoke, Staffordshire
c. 1819–30

A long but damaged Folch Ironstone china dinner service was sold at Christie's in 1967. The shapes were very similar to the standard Mason Ironstone dinner ware shapes as depicted in Plate 17.

The mark, printed in underglaze blue on this service, took three forms. Firstly, the key mark comprised an elaborate version of the Royal Arms with the Prince of Wales feathers behind and, under this device, the wording 'GENUINE FOLCH'S STONE CHINA' appeared in a ribbon. Other pieces bore the same arms mark with two different styles of wording below— either 'IMPROVED IRONSTONE CHINA' or 'IMPᵈ IRONSTONE CHINA, STOKE WORKS'. These do not include the key word 'Folch's', but all pieces were clearly from the same service and the work of one manufacturer—so these marks can be added to those used by Stephen Folch during the period c. 1819–30.

According to a trade account dated October 1819, Folch's ware was moderately priced: covered soup tureens and stands at 11/–, plates at 3½d. However, it would seem that Folch's Stoke factory produced a wide range of decorative Mason-style ironstone china, much of which has not been correctly attributed to this manufacturer.

Jacob Furnival & Co., Cobridge, Staffordshire
c. 1845–70

Ironstone-type ware occurs with the initial mark 'J.F. & Co.', which may relate to this firm.

Jacob & Thomas Furnival (Shelton), Hanley, Staffordshire
c. 1843

Ironstone-type 'Stone China' made by this firm bears the Royal Arms device with the initials 'J. & T.F.'. The partnership was succeeded by **Thomas Furnival & Co.** (c. 1844–6) and this later ware bears initial marks 'T.F. & Co.'. Thomas Furnival's ware was, to a great extent, exported to America. Some American authorities have attributed the 'T.F. & Co.' marks to Thomas Ford & Co., but the Patent Office registration mark and the contemporary records prove that the firm concerned was Thomas Furnival & Co.

Thomas Furnival (& Sons), Cobridge, Staffordshire
c. 1851–90

Thomas Furnival's early ware bears the impressed name mark 'FURNI-VAL'. From c. 1871, '& SONS' was added to the firm's style. Various marks incorporate the initials 'T.F. & Sons' or the name in full. Ironstone-type ware was made, advertised as 'white granite', as well as standard earthenware.

Furnivals (Ltd.), Cobridge, Staffordshire
c. 1890–1968

Messrs. Furnivals succeeded Thomas Furnival & Sons (see above entry); 'Ltd.' was added to the firm's style and to most marks in 1895. In January 1919, the style was changed to 'FURNIVALS (1913) LTD.'. Good quality Ironstone-type ware was made by all these firms, using marks similar to the four examples reproduced.

Godwin Rowley & Co., Burslem, Staffordshire
c. 1828–31

Blue printed Ironstone-type ware appears bearing the description 'STAF-FORDSHIRE STONE CHINA' with a crown device and the initials 'G.R. & Co.'.

Thomas Godwin, Burslem, Staffordshire
c. 1834–54

Good quality 'Stone China' ware occurs with the name 'THOS. GODWIN, BURSLEM'.

Thomas & Benjamin Godwin, Burslem, Staffordshire
c. 1809–34

Messrs. T. & B. Godwin manufactured a wide range of earthenware decorated with fine quality transfer printed designs. Some Ironstone-type ware was made under the description 'Stone-China', and printed marks incorporate the initials 'T. & B.G.'.

Thomas Goodfellow, Tunstall, Staffordshire
c. 1828–59

Thomas Goodfellow made general earthenware, including Ironstone-type ware bearing the name mark 'T. GOODFELLOW'.

Griffiths, Beardmore & Birks, Lane End, Longton, Staffordshire
c. 1830

This partnership is listed in the Lane End (Longton) rate record for March 1830. The names match the initials 'G.B. & B.' found on 'STAFFORD-SHIRE IRONSTONE CHINA' with the pre-Victorian Royal Arms device.

W. H. Grindley & Co. (Ltd.), Tunstall, Staffordshire
c. 1880 to present day

Messrs. W. H. Grindley & Co. Ltd. represent one of the later manufacturers of Ironstone-type ware. Their ware is clearly marked.

Hackwood, Shelton & Hanley, Staffordshire

Several potters with the surname **Hackwood** worked in the Staffordshire Potteries in the nineteenth century producing good quality earthenware of various descriptions. A printed mark of an urn with swag containing the words 'IRONSTONE CHINA' occurs on ware bearing the impressed name mark HACKWOOD, c. 1830–40.

Ralph Hall (& Co.) or (& Son), Tunstall, Staffordshire
c. 1822–49

Ralph Hall produced a range of very good quality earthenware bearing fine printed designs, sometimes expressly made for the American market. Marks from 1822 to 1841 incorporate the name 'R. Hall' or 'R. Hall & Son'. From c. 1841 to 1849 the style became Ralph Hall & Co., during which time marks included the initials 'R.H. & Co.' or the fuller name 'R. Hall & Co.' Messrs. Podmore, Walker & Co. succeeded this firm (see page 82).

Ralph Hammersley (& Son), Burslem & Tunstall, Staffordshire
c. 1860–1905

Ralph Hammersley's advertisements list 'IRONSTONE CHINA & GENERAL EARTHENWARE . . . specially adapted to the home and colonial trade, also the United States of America and continental markets. Real Ironstone china in shapes suitable for Hotels, ships, etc. etc. . . .' Early marks incorporated the initials 'R.H.'. In 1883, the firm's style was amended to Ralph Hammersley & Sons, and marks then incorporated the initials 'R.H. & S.'.

C. & W. K. Harvey (Charles Harvey & Sons), Longton, Staffordshire
c. 1835–53

Messrs. Harvey made good quality earthenware, including Ironstone. The Ironstone often bears the Royal Arms device with the description 'REAL IRONSTONE CHINA' and the initials 'C. & W. K. Harvey'. Messrs. Holland & Green succeeded this firm (see page 73).

Joseph Heath, High Street, Tunstall, Staffordshire
c 1841, 1845–53

A Joseph Heath is recorded at the Newfield Pottery, Tunstall, in 1841 and at High Street, Tunstall, from 1845–53. Ironstone-type ware bearing the name 'J. Heath' probably relates to this Tunstall potter.

Joseph Heath & Co., Newfield Pottery, Tunstall, Staffordshire
c. 1828–41

Good quality general earthenware was made, sometimes with North American transfer printed views. Marks include 'J. Heath & Co.'; 'J.H. & Co.' or 'I.H. & Co.'. (In many nineteenth-century marks the initial 'J' appears as 'I', which was normal practice of the period.)

Hicks & Meigh (Shelton), Hanley, Staffordshire
c. 1804–22

Messrs. Hicks & Meigh were among the first producers of 'Stone China' as made by Davenport and Messrs. Spode. The ware is of good quality, boldly decorated on fine imposing shapes (see Plates 110–17). The name mark was rarely used. Most of their stone china bears the pre-Victorian Royal Arms device with the wording 'Stone China' below. A numeral is often added below these words.

Hicks, Meigh & Johnson (Shelton), Hanley, Staffordshire
c. 1822–35

This partnership, which succeeded Hicks & Meigh (see previous entry), produced the same class of good quality 'Stone China'. In 1833, this firm employed some six hundred work people. Marks include the following two devices. The firm's initials 'H.M. & J.' (appearing as 'H.M. & I.') were rarely used on printed marks.

Holland & Green, Longton, Staffordshire
c. 1853–82

Messrs. Holland & Green succeeded C. & W. K. Harvey (see page 71). Their Ironstone-type ware was marked with the Royal Arms and the firm's name or 'H. & G., late Harveys'. The descriptive term 'Real Ironstone china' was used.

Thomas Hughes, Burslem (& Longport), Staffordshire
c. 1860–94

Thomas Hughes produced 'GRANITE' and 'IRONSTONE CHINA' largely for the North American market. His ware was marked with the name in full.

Thomas Hughes & Son (Ltd.), Longport, Staffordshire
c. 1895–1957

This firm produced a good range of Ironstone ware over a long period. Their ware is normally plainly marked with the name; 'Ltd.' was added to the firm's title in about 1910.

Reuben Johnson, Hanley, Staffordshire
c. 1817–38

Printed marks occur depicting the name $\begin{array}{c} \text{JOHNSON} \\ \text{HANLEY} \end{array}$ over the description 'stone china'. These are believed to relate to this potter and to Phoebe Johnson, who continued from c. 1823–c. 1838. A typical jug is shown in Plate 118.

Johnson Bros. (Hanley) Ltd., Hanley, Staffordshire
c. 1883 to present day

Messrs. Johnson Bros. (Hanley) Ltd. are among the largest producers of twentieth-century Ironstone-type ware. Their marks are clear and self-explanatory.

J. K. Knight, Foley, Fenton, Staffordshire
c. 1846–53

John King Knight succeeded the Knight, Elkin & Co. (c. 1826–46) partnership. He made 'Stone China' as well as other earthenware. Marks incorporate the initials and name 'J. K. Knight', or sometimes 'I. K. Knight'.

Liverpool

The 'Herculaneum' factory may well have produced good quality 'Stonechina'-type ware during the closing years of its existence—during the management of Messrs. Case & Mort (c. 1833–6) and then of Messrs. Mort & Simpson (c. 1836–40). This Liverpool stone china ware may bear the impressed 'Liver bird' mark, and specimens will probably be found in North America and in the other export markets enjoyed by this great seaport factory. The full story of the important Herculaneum Pottery is given in Mr. Alan Smith's *Illustrated Guide to Liverpool Herculaneum Pottery*, 1970.

Livesley Powell & Co., Hanley, Staffordshire
c. 1851–66

Livesley Powell & Co. produced a good range of earthenware and china. The firm was an important one, employing over four hundred and eight persons in 1861. Some marks incorporate the description 'Ironstone China' with the name in full or the initials 'L.P. & Co.'. Messrs. Powell & Bishop succeeded this Company in 1866.

J. Maddock, Burslem, Staffordshire
c. 1842–55

John Maddock succeeded the Maddock & Seddon (c. 1839–42) partnership. Good quality earthenware was produced, with tasteful printed motifs. Various fancy printed marks occur with the initial 'M' introduced to one side. The description 'Stone China' occurs below the main mark (see example below).

John Maddock & Sons (Ltd.), Burslem, Staffordshire
c. 1855 to present day

This important firm produced a large range of durable earthenware. Jewitt, in *Ceramic Art of Great Britain*, records that the firm 'manufacture white graniteware for the American markets to a large extent'. Various marks have been employed incorporating the name 'Maddock' or 'John Maddock & Sons'; 'Ltd.' was added to the firm's style after 1896—a fact which assists in dating specimens. Trade names include 'Ironstone China', 'Royal Vitreous' and 'Stone China', as well as other descriptions for different non-ironstone bodies.

Maddock & Seddon, Burslem, Staffordshire
c 1839–42

This firm produced good quality ware, including 'Stone China'. Marks incorporate the initials 'M. & S.', often placed one above the other at the side of a mark—similar in position to the 'M' on the later J. Maddock mark reproduced.

Masons

See Chapters 2 and 3 for history, and Chapter 4 for marks.

Mason's Ironstone China Ltd.

From the summer of 1968, the new trading title adopted by the former firm of G. L. Ashworth & Bros. Ltd. (See pages 5 to 7).

J. Maudesley & Co., Tunstall, Staffordshire
c. 1862–4

Printed marks occur on 'Stone ware' incorporating the initials 'J.M. & Co.', which are believed to relate to this firm.

NOTE: The following three entries refer to English potters and should not be confused with American firms bearing the name 'Mayer', several of which produced Ironstone ware.

Thomas Mayer, Stoke and Longport, Staffordshire
c. 1826–38

Many different Mayers were potting in Staffordshire from the late eighteenth century onwards. Thomas Mayer of the Cliff Bank Works at Stoke (c. 1826–1835) and then at Brook Street, Longton (c. 1836–8), produced very good quality earthenware, often transfer-printed with tasteful designs, many of which were made for the American market. The American eagle appears in several marks. Ironstone-type ware was also made. Marks include the name 'T. Mayer', sometimes with the place name 'Stoke'.

Thomas & John Mayer, Longport (Burslem), Staffordshire
c. 1841

Thomas & John Mayer are recorded at the Dale Hall Works, Longport, in 1841; but the partnership may well date back to 1838, when Thomas Mayer entries ceased at Longport. The partnership may have continued until 1843. The name mark 'T. & J. Mayer, Longport' occurs on Ironstone.

T. J. & J. Mayer, Longport (Burslem), Staffordshire
c. 1842–55

Thomas, John & Joseph Mayer succeeded Thomas & John Mayer. A wide range of ware, including good parian, was produced and shown at the exhibitions of 1851, 1853 and 1855. Ironstone-type articles bear marks 'T. J. & J. Mayer' or 'Mayer Bros.', often with the address 'Dale Hall Pottery, Longport'. Succeeding firms working this famous pottery were:

> Mayer Bros. & Elliott (c. 1856–8);
> Mayer & Elliott (c. 1858–61);
> Liddle, Elliott & Son (c. 1862–70);
> Bates, Elliott & Co. (c. 1870–5);
> Bates, Walker & Co. (c. 1875–8);
> Bates, Gildea & Walker (c. 1878–81);
> Gildea & Walker (c. 1881–5) and
> James Gildea (c. 1885–8).

Meakin & Co., Cobridge, Staffordshire
c. 1865–82

The products of this firm (also known as Meakin Brothers & Co.) were, according to Jewitt (*Ceramic Art of Great Britain*), confined to white granite ware for the American market. He records that the works were capable of producing about 2,500 crates of ware per year.

Alfred Meakin (Ltd.), Tunstall, Staffordshire
c. 1875 to present day.

Alfred Meakin's advertisements of the 1880s feature 'IRONSTONE CHINA, WHITE GRANITE, suitable for North America, South America, West Indies, the Colonies, etc.'. Various self-explanatory marks were employed, and 'Ltd.' was added to the title in about 1897. Marks include the trade description 'Royal Ironstone China'. From c. 1913 the firm was retitled 'Alfred Meakin (Tunstall) Ltd.' but marks record only the name 'Alfred Meakin'.

Charles Meakin, Burslem & Hanley, Staffordshire
c. 1876–89

Charles Meakin worked the Trent Pottery at Burslem from c. 1876 to 1882. From 1883 to 1889, Charles Meakin potted at the Eastwood Pottery at Hanley. His Ironstone-type granite ware was exported to North America. The mark comprises his name below the Royal Arms; 'Hanley' was added below the name from 1883.

Henry Meakin, Cobridge, Staffordshire
c. 1873–6

Henry Meakin made Ironstone-type earthenware which was marked with his name and initial below the Royal Arms device and the words 'IRON-STONE CHINA'.

J. & G. Meakin (Ltd.), Hanley, Staffordshire
c. 1851 to present day

This important firm produced in the second half of the nineteenth century (245 persons were employed in 1861) a good range of Ironstone-type granite ware which was largely exported to North America. The marks are self-explanatory, including the firm's name and the description 'Ironstone China'. The registered trade name 'SOL' with a rising sun dates from 1912 and is used on many modern marks.

Charles Meigh (& Son), Hanley, Staffordshire
c. 1835–49 and 1851–61

Charles Meigh succeeded his father Job in 1835, although he had managerial command over the 'Old Hall Works' before this date. A vast quantity of good quality earthenware, which included Ironstone-type ware, was produced by Charles Meigh. Various marks incorporate the name or the initials 'C.M.'. An impressed mark incorporates the description 'Improved Stone China' (see below).

From 1849 to 1851, Charles Meigh was in partnership under the style 'Charles Meigh, Son & Pankhurst'. This partnership was succeeded in 1851 by Charles Meigh & Son. Marks then included the initials 'C.M. & S.' or the name in full. In March 1861, the firm became *Old Hall Earthenware Co. Ltd.* (see page 80).

Impressed mark

John Meir & Son, Tunstall, Staffordshire
c. 1837–97

Messrs. John Meir & Son produced a wide range of good quality earthenware, often decorated with underglaze blue printed designs. The marks are numerous and incorporate the name 'MEIR', 'MEIR & SON', 'J. MEIR & SON' or the initials 'I.M. & S.'. or 'J.M. & S.'. Descriptions such as 'Stone China' or 'Ironstone' were used in the marks. The son was Henry Meir (born c. 1812), who ran the firm for the greater part of its duration. In 1851, two hundred people were employed.

Mellor, Taylor & Co., Burslem, Staffordshire
c. 1881–1904

L. Jewitt, in the revised 1883 edition of his *Ceramic Art of Great Britain*, wrote of this firm ' . . . Mellor, Taylor & Co., who continue to produce the usual articles in hard durable "granite" or "Ironstone china" for the American markets. Goods are also to some extent, produced for the home trade.' The mark of the firm was 'the royal arms in plain shield, with crown and wreath, exactly copied from the reverse of the half crown of Queen Victoria, surrounded by the words MELLOR, TAYLOR & CO. ENGLAND, WARRANTED STONE CHINA'. A further mark is reproduced below.

Mellor, Venables & Co., Burslem, Staffordshire
c. 1834–51

Messrs. Mellor, Venables & Co. produced a fine range of printed earthenware, including Ironstone-type ware. Much was exported to North America,

and several designs—including the Arms of the different American States
—were engraved.

Many different marks were employed incorporating the name 'Mellor,
Venables & Co.' or the initials 'M.V. & Co.' with descriptions such as 'Royal
Patent Ironstone'. The firm was succeeded by Venables & Baines, c. 1851–3.

Henry Mills, Hanley, Staffordshire
c. 1892

The mark below is believed to relate to the shortlived works of Henry Mills,
although it could have been used by a Henry Mills who potted at Shelton
from 1841 to 1850.

Minton's (various titles), Stoke, Staffordshire
c. 1793 to present day

The Minton firms are mainly known for their superb porcelain, but many
different types of earthenware were also produced. During the Minton &
Boyle period (c. 1836–41), marks incorporated the initials 'M. & B.'. The
initials 'M. & H.' occur on marks during the Minton & Hollins period
(c. 1845–68), but 'M. & Co.' was widely used from c. 1841 to 1873. The
later Minton ware does not include the Ironstone body.

Morley & Ashworth, Hanley, Staffordshire
c. 1846–61

As related on page 20, the Morley & Ashworth partnership succeeded
Francis Morley & Co. (see below). This partnership is a vital link in the
preservation of the original Mason moulds, designs, etc., which Francis
Morley had acquired. Messrs. Ashworth succeeded this partnership in 1861.
The standard marks incorporate the name in full or the initials 'M. & A.'.

Francis Morley (& Co.), Shelton, Hanley, Staffordshire
c. 1845–58

Francis Morley had great experience of the pottery trade. He married the daughter of William Ridgway, and a link exists between Francis Morley and Messrs. Hicks, Meigh & Johnson, the celebrated producers of 'Stone China' (see page 20). Francis Morley acquired the Mason designs, moulds, etc., and passed them on to the succeeding Morley & Ashworth partnership (see previous entry). The many marks incorporate the initials 'F.M.', or 'F.M. & Co.', or the name in full.

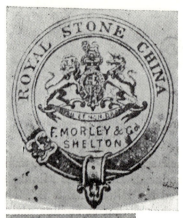

New Bridge Pottery

See Edward F. Bodley & Co. (page 58).

Old Hall Earthenware Co. Ltd., Hanley, Staffordshire
1861–86

This firm, the first limited liability company in the ceramic industry, was formed in March 1861, succeeding Charles Meigh & Son (see p. 77). Good earthenware was produced. Trade descriptive names used include 'Indian Stone China'—sometimes arranged in triangular form reading 'Stone China Indian'—'Imperial Parisian Granite' and 'Opaque Porcelain', the last name being used on normal earthenware and not on Ironstone ware. Marks incorporate the initials 'O.H.E.C.' or 'O.H.E.C.(L)', the name 'Old Hall', or the full title of the company.

The firm was succeeded by the **Old Hall Porcelain Works Ltd.** (c. 1886–1902).

J. W. Pankhurst & Co., Hanley, Staffordshire
c. 1850–82

James Pankhurst and John Dimmock traded as J. W. Pankhurst & Co. from 1852. Good quality Ironstone-type stone china was made, mainly for the American market, and was marked with the Royal Arms above the description 'Stone China' and the firm's name.

George Phillips, Longport, Staffordshire
c. 1834–48

This potter produced good earthenware between 1834 and 1848. Marks often include his name with the place name 'LONGPORT'. The example reproduced relates to the pattern 'Friburg', registered in November 1846.

Thomas Phillips & Son, Burslem, Staffordshire
c. 1845–6

The name 'T. PHILLIPS & SON, BURSLEM' occurs on some marks found on earthenware of Ironstone-type. Other potters with this surname include Edward Phillips of Shelton (c. 1855–62), Edward & George Phillips, Longport (c. 1822–34), and George Phillips, Longport (c. 1834–48).

Pinder, Bourne & Co., Burslem, Staffordshire
January 1862–82

Messrs. Pinder, Bourne & Co. succeeded Messrs. Pinder, Bourne & Hope (c. 1851–62) of Nile Street, Burslem. A large range of earthenware includes Ironstone-type stoneware. The name 'IMPERIAL WHITE GRANITE' occurs on some marks, sometimes with the American eagle. The full name or the initials 'P.B. & Co.' was incorporated in marks. Messrs. Doulton purchased the firm in 1878, but it was continued under the old style until 1882.

Plymouth Pottery Co. Ltd., Plymouth, Devon
c. 1856–63

Jewitt, in his *Ceramic Art of Great Britain* mentions this firm and the mark —the Royal Arms with the initials 'P.P.Coy.L.' and the description 'STONE CHINA'—but he was far from enthusiastic about the products.

Podmore, Walker & Co., Tunstall, Staffordshire
c. 1834–59

The products of this important firm were often marked with the name 'WEDGWOOD'. Enoch Wedgwood was, indeed, a partner and his name was found to be most useful. Good earthenware, including Ironstone-type ware titled 'IMPERIAL IRONSTONE CHINA' and 'PEARL STONE WARE', was made and exported to many countries. Many marks were employed with the initials 'P.W. & Co', 'P.W. & W.', 'WEDGWOOD' or 'WEDG-WOOD & CO.'. A large export market was enjoyed by this firm. The firm was large, employing 164 men, 133 boys, 60 women and 57 girls in 1851. From c. 1860 the firm was retitled WEDGWOOD & CO. (see page 97).

This 'Wedgwood' mark occurs on ware registered by Podmore, Walker & Co. in 1849. It proves that the name 'Wedgwood' was then used by this firm.

Pountney & Co, (Ltd.), Temple Backs, Bristol
c. 1849 to present day

Messrs. Pountney & Co. were preceded by Pountney & Allies (c. 1815–35) and by Pountney & Goldney (c. 1836–49). These Bristol firms produced a fine range of decorative earthenware, including 'stone china' and 'Granite'. Marks used include 'BRISTOL POTTERY', 'P', 'P. & A.', 'P. & Co.' or the firms' names in full; 'Ltd.' was added to the style and marks from c. 1889.

Powell & Bishop and Powell, Bishop & Stonier, Hanley, Staffordshire
c. 1876–91

The partnership of Messrs. Powell & Bishop was of short duration, c. 1876–8, being then succeeded by Powell, Bishop & Stonier. Two factories were in use. The Church Works at High Street, Hanley, were devoted to the manufacture of Ironstone-type granite ware which, according to Jewitt in *Ceramic Art of Great Britain*, 'they produce of excellent quality and in every variety of style, both plain, embossed, and otherwise decorated . . . for the United States and Canadian markets'. Marks incorporate the initials 'P. & B.' or 'P.B. & S.', the names of the partnership, or one of the two trade marks reproduced below.

Pratt & Simpson, Fenton, Staffordshire
c. 1878–83

This firm's advertisements feature 'semi-porcelaine, white Granite, printed, and all kinds of earthenware, suitable for Colonial and foreign markets'. Printed marks incorporate the initials 'P. & S.'.

Read & Clementson (Shelton), Hanley, Staffordshire
c. 1833–5

This Shelton partnership produced good quality richly-decorated stone china ware (see Plate 119). Printed marks like the one following incorporate

G

the initials 'R. & C.'. Messrs. Read, Clementson & Anderson continued in 1836, their marks incorporating the initials 'R.C. & A.'.

J. Reed, Mexborough, Yorkshire
c. 1839–73

James Reed, of the Rock Pottery (renamed Mexborough Pottery in c. 1849), produced a wide range of useful earthenware, often bearing the impressed 'REED' name mark; but various printed marks also occur incorporating the description 'STONE CHINA' and the name 'REED'. John Reed succeeded his father in c. 1849. Messrs. Sidney Woolfe & Co. worked the Pottery from 1873 to 1883.

Registration Marks

Many items of English pottery (and porcelain) produced between 1842 and 1883 will be found to bear an impressed, or printed, upright diamond-shaped device containing in the centre the letters 'R^d'. Numerals and letters are contained in the inner angles of the diamond.

 This device indicates that the basic shape or added design was registered at the Patent Office in London and was thereby protected from copying for an initial period of three years. Contrary to general opinion, it does *not* show the date of production of such article but, when decoded, only the date of registration and therefore the *earliest possible* date of production. The date decoding key is reproduced on page 86.

 From January 1884, a new system of numbering consecutively registered designs was started: 'R^d. No. 1.' in January 1884, 'R^d. No. 351202' in January 1900, etc. These registered numbers can be a most useful guide to dating later Ironstone and other ceramic designs.

 The official files contain thousands of drawings of registered shapes, and drawings of added patterns. More importantly, hundreds of entries contain pulls taken direct from the engraved copper-plates. One such design is reproduced below—a print which was used by John Ridgway in the 1840s. This particular print would appear to depict a North American scene and was probably one of the many designs engraved especially for this important market.

Table of Registration Marks
1842–1883

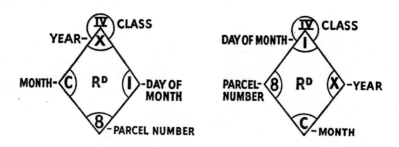

Above are the two patterns of Design Registration Marks that were in current use between the years 1842 and 1883. Keys to 'year' and 'month' code-letters are given below.

The left-hand diamond was used during the years 1842 to 1867. A change was made in 1868, when the right-hand diamond was adopted.

INDEX TO YEAR AND MONTH LETTERS

YEARS

1842–67 *Year Letter at Top*		1868–83 *Year Letter at Right*	
A = 1845	N = 1864	A = 1871	L = 1882
B = 1858	O = 1862	C = 1870	P = 1877
C = 1844	P = 1851	D = 1878	S = 1875
D = 1852	Q = 1866	E = 1881	U = 1874
E = 1855	R = 1861	F = 1873	V = 1876
F = 1847	S = 1849	H = 1869	W = (Mar. 1–6)
G = 1863	T = 1867	I = 1872	1878
H = 1843	U = 1848	J = 1880	X = 1868
I = 1846	V = 1850	K = 1883	Y = 1879
J = 1854	W = 1865		
K = 1857	X = 1842		
L = 1856	Y = 1853		
M = 1859	Z = 1860		

MONTHS (BOTH PERIODS)

A = December	G = February	M = June
B = October	H = April	R = August (and
C or O = January	I = July	September 1st–
D = September	K = November (and	19th 1857)
E = May	December 1860)	W = March

Table of Design Registration Numbers
Found on Ware from 1884

These numbers are normally prefixed by 'R^d N^o':

1–19753	registered in 1884
19754–40479	registered in 1885
40480–64519	registered in 1886
64520–90482	registered in 1887
90483–116647	registered in 1888
116648–141263	registered in 1889
141273–163762	registered in 1890
163767–185712	registered in 1891
185713–205239	registered in 1892
205240–224719	registered in 1893
224720–246974	registered in 1894
246975–268391	registered in 1895
268392–291240	registered in 1896
291241–311657	registered in 1897
311658–331706	registered in 1898
331707–351201	registered in 1899
351202–368153	registered in 1900
368154–385087	registered in 1901
385088–402912	registered in 1902
402913–424016	registered in 1903
424017–447547	registered in 1904
447548–471458	registered in 1905
471486–493486	registered in 1906
493487–518414	registered in 1907
518415–534962	registered in 1908

This system is continued to the present time.

Job Ridgway & Sons (Shelton), Hanley, Staffordshire
c. 1808–13

Job Ridgway was the founder of several 'Stone China' firms, which subsequently all produced very fine Ironstone and stone china as well as other earthenware and porcelain. The sons mentioned in the firm's title were John and William, each of whom later owned separate factories (see subsequent entries).

The early Job Rigway & Sons ware was rarely marked. The impressed name 'RIDGWAY & SONS' occurs, and also the initials 'J.R. & S.', sometimes with a beehive device.

John & William Ridgway (Shelton), Hanley, Staffordshire
c. 1814–30

Job Ridgway's two sons, John and William, took over their father's Cauldon Place works, and also the Bell Works. Their various kinds of ware are difficult to fault in design or workmanship (see Plates 120, 121 and 123). Many marks incorporate the initials 'J.W.R.', 'J. & W.R.', or 'J. & W. Ridgway'.

John Ridgway (& Co.) (Shelton), Hanley, Staffordshire
c. 1830–55

John Ridgway separated from his brother, c. 1830, and continued his father's celebrated Cauldon Place Works, where the finest porcelain and earthenware was produced (Plate 122). Many printed marks were used, often featuring the Royal Arms and the initials 'J.R.', 'J.R. & Co.' (from c. 1841) or the name in full. The descriptions 'Real Ironstone China', 'Superior Stone China' or 'Imperial Stone China' were sometimes used, and high pattern numbers are normally found on John Ridgway pieces—numbers often in excess of 1,000.

William Ridgway (& Co.) (Shelton), Hanley, Staffordshire
c. 1830–54

William Ridgway, after the separation from his brother John, worked the Bell Works and the Church Works. Fine earthenware and stoneware was produced. The hand-painted ornamental ware was often unmarked, but the transfer-printed useful ware bears marks, including the name 'W. Ridgway' or 'W. Ridgway & Co.' (from c. 1834), or the initials 'W.R.' or 'W.R. & Co.' (from c. 1834). Descriptive names 'OPAQUE GRANITE CHINA' and 'QUARTZ CHINA' were used. An impressed mark occurs comprising the Royal Arms, supporters and a shield, similar to that reproduced on page 94 but with the initials 'W.R. & Co.' and sometimes with the printed Royal Arms reproduced below (see also Plates 124 and 125).

William Ridgway, Son & Co., Hanley, Staffordshire
c. 1838–48

This variation of the William Ridgway Company produced the same type of ware as the parent firm. Marks incorporate the initials 'W.R.S. & Co.' or the firm's style in full.

Ridgway, Morley, Wear & Co. (Shelton) Hanley, Staffordshire
c. 1835–42

This firm succeeded the Shelton Works of Hicks, Meigh & Johnson (see p. 72). The new partnership continued to produce very good quality stone china, richly decorated in the Mason style. Many different marks incorporate the initials 'R.M.W. & Co.' or the name in full. The description 'Improved Granite China' was used.

FLORENCE ROSE

Ridgway & Morley (Shelton), Hanley, Staffordshire
c. 1842–5

Messrs. Ridgway & Morley succeeded Ridgway, Morley, Wear & Co. (see previous entry). Good quality earthenware was produced, which included 'Improved Granite China' and 'stone ware'. Marks incorporate the initials 'R. & M.' or the name of the firm in full. Francis Morley continued on his own from 1845. He purchased most of Mason's moulds and designs, passing them on through the Morley & Ashworth partnership of c. 1849–62 to the present holders, the Ashworth firm recently retitled 'Mason's Ironstone China Ltd.). Several original Mason engraved copper plates are still preserved through Francis Morley's far-sighted purchase in the 1840s.

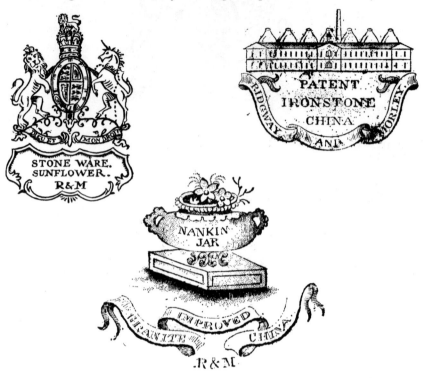

N.B. Succeeding Ridgway firms

Ridgways c. 1879–1920
Ridgways (Bedford Works) Ltd. c. 1920–52
Ridgways & Adderley Ltd.
Booths & Colcloughs Ltd.   } 1952–5
Ridgway, Adderley, Booths & Colcloughs Ltd.
Ridgways Potteries Ltd. c. 1955 to present day

have from time to time reissued some of the old Ridgway patterns, which sometimes bear versions of the original mark. Later reissued marks should include the words 'England' or 'Made in England', not found on the originals.

Seacombe Pottery, Seacombe, near Liverpool
c. 1851–70

This little-known pottery was established by the Staffordshire potter John Goodwin in 1851. The first kiln was fired in June 1852 and good general earthenware as well as 'Ironstone China' was produced, mostly decorated with underglaze blue prints in the Staffordshire tradition. In fact, Goodwin took with him to Liverpool engraved copper plates he had previously used in Staffordshire. The works had closed by October 1871. Marks include the name 'J. Goodwin' or 'Goodwin & Co.' with the address 'Seacombe Pottery, Liverpool'. A typical Ironstone mark is reproduced, and it is interesting to see that the registration mark relates to a printed design registered by John Goodwin in 1846, while he was working the Crown Pottery at Longton. This fact suggests that similar Ironstone-type ware was produced by John Goodwin in Staffordshire prior to 1851—but such examples would not, of course, bear the Liverpool address. A large export business was carried on, and in the 1850s the firm had a retail establishment in Toronto. The printed design 'Lasso' was a very popular one in the American markets.

Anthony Shaw (& Sons), Tunstall and Burslem, Staffordshire
c. 1850–1900

Jewitt, writing in his *Ceramic Art of Great Britain*, revised 1883 edition, noted:

> The Mersey Pottery was established in 1850 by Anthony Shaw, and is now, since 1882, carried on as 'Anthony Shaw & Sons'. Goods, specially adapted for the various American markets are made, the specialities being white graniteware and cream-coloured wares for the United States . . . In 1855 Mr. Shaw was awarded a medal at the Paris Exhibition. The mark formerly used was the Royal Arms, with ribbon bearing the words STONE CHINA, and beneath, in three lines,

WARRANTED. ANTHONY SHAW, BURSLEM. That at the present time has the words WARRANTED. ANTHONY SHAW & SONS, OPAQUE STONE CHINA, ENGLAND. The works were rebuilt on a very extensive scale in 1866.

Various name marks were used: 'SHAWS', 'A. SHAW', or 'ANTHONY SHAW'. From 1882, '& Son' or '& Sons' may be added to the name; but from c. 1898 to 1900 '& Co.' takes the place of '& Sons'.

South Wales Pottery, Llanelly, Wales
c. 1839–58

W. Chambers established the South Wales Pottery in 1839, producing a wide range of earthenware, including 'PEARL WHITE IRONSTONE'. Marks include the name 'Chambers', 'South Wales Pottery' or the initials 'S.W.P.'. From 1854 to 1858 the pottery was continued by Coombs & Holland, then by Holland & Guest, and finally by Guest & Dewsberry to c. 1927.

Spode, Stoke, Staffordshire
c. 1784–April 1833

Josiah Spode was possibly the second potter to have produced 'Stone China'. He is said to have purchased Turner's patent rights on the then new body in about 1805 (see page 97); but Leonard Whiter, in his recent work *Spode: A History of the Family, Factory and Wares from 1733–1833*, 1970, suggests that this Spode body was newly introduced in 1814—a view partly supported by an account of a royal visit to the firm's London showroom as reported in *The Times* of 4th July 1817. My own view—at present, supported only by the style of the ware, the patterns and the shapes—is that it was first produced several years before the royal visit of 1817, and before 1814.

Be this as it may, the Spode firm produced very fine 'stone china', proving that this hard, durable body could be finely potted and decorated in tasteful designs fit for any drawing rooms and dining rooms. Superb dessert and dinner services were made by Spode and decorated with Chinese-type patterns (see Colour Plate VIII and Plates 127–131). One gains the impression that Spode was striving to capture the vast market formerly served by imported Chinese porcelain, the importation of which certainly fell sharply as the new English 'Stone China' came into prominence. It must be admitted that this change was assisted by the raising of import duties on Chinese porcelain; but at the same time, Spode 'Stone China' was finer in the potting and far less liable to chip than the Oriental porcelain. Messrs. Spode made many replacements and additions to Chinese porcelain services, and these have withstood the passing of time better than the originals.

No 'Stone China' is as fine in quality as the Spode examples, which are thinly-potted and excellently finished. Many fine pieces were made: ice pails, trays, baskets and bowls, as well as the more normal components of dinner, dessert and tea services.

As noted above, Spode was favoured with royal patronage. Wedgwood's salesman, Josiah Bateman, reported in October 1817 of the effect of the royal visit:

> ... Since the Queen went to Mr. Spode, the Stone China is much inquired for and is got more into repute—indeed a dealer cannot be without it, and a great deal is sold.

The Wedgwood firm acted on this intelligence and itself introduced a similar body (see page 99).

The standard printed mark is reproduced below. On plates and dishes the mark is often found under the flange or edge, not in the centre. The impressed mark $\frac{\text{SPODES}}{\text{NEW STONE}}$ is also often found, as are the impressed initials 'N.S.', both of which date from c. 1822. Messrs. Copeland & Garrett succeeded from March 1833 to 1847 (some Spode pieces will be found bearing a printed mark of this partnership), when the present firm of W. T. Copeland (& Sons Ltd.) was established.

A standard reference book is *Spode and his Successors* by A. Hayden, 1924—a work recently superseded by Leonard Whiter's tour-de-force *Spode: A History of the Family, Factory and Wares from 1733–1783* (1970).

Stone-China

Stevenson & Williams, Cobridge, Staffordshire
c. 1825

Printed marks incorporating the initials 'R.S.W.' or 'R.S. & W.' are believed to relate to the partnership between Ralph Stevenson and Williams, which is mentioned in a mortgage deed of 1825.

A fine tureen from a dinner service bearing the Royal Arms, the description 'ROYAL STONE CHINA' and the initials 'R.S. & W.' is illustrated in Plate 132, and a moulded-edge plate is shown in Plate 133.

Swift & Elkin, Longton, Staffordshire
c. 1840–3

This Staffordshire partnership produced 'Staffordshire Stone China' as well as normal earthenware. Printed marks include the initials 'S. & E.'.

Swillington Bridge
c. 1820–50

Recent excavations by Mr. Christopher Gilbert on the site of the Swillington Bridge pottery, some six miles south-east of Leeds, has shown that this small Yorkshire pottery produced 'Ironstone China' and 'Opaque Granite China' during the 1820–50 period.

Good quality blue printed ware was made, as well as brown printed and enamelled earthenware. Excavated factory wasters show that an impressed crown mark was used, as well as a shield mark incorporating the words 'Opaque Granite China', the shield supported by a lion and a unicorn. The same basic mark, but with the initials 'W.R. & Co.', was used by William Ridgway of Shelton.

Blue printed Ironstone bears the printed mark reproduced below, left. The discovery of these fragments on the site of the small, little-known factory suggests that other small Yorkshire potteries may well have made Ironstone ware.

John Tams (& Son) (Ltd.), Longton, Staffordshire
c. 1875 to present day

John Tams worked the Crown Pottery at Longton from c. 1875. Early marks incorporate the name 'J. Tams' or 'Tams' with a crown above and the description 'ROCK STONE'. Other marks incorporate the initials 'J.T.', often joined. Several marks incorporating the initials 'J.T.' with the descriptive term 'stone ware' are believed to relate to John Tams, and the name of the patterns—'Orleans', 'Peacock', etc.—are also included. From 1903 to 1912 '& Son' was added to the firm's style, and initial marks 'J.T. & S.' occur. From 1912 the style has been John Tams Ltd., but most marks include only the name 'Tams'.

William Taylor, Hanley, Staffordshire
c. 1860–73

L. Jewitt, writing in *Ceramic Art of Great Britain* of William Taylor and the Pearl Pottery, Brook Street, Hanley, stated: 'In 1860 the works passed into the hands of William Taylor, who commenced making white Granite and common coloured and painted ware, but he discontinued, and confined himself to white graniteware for the United States and Canadian markets, of both qualities—the bluish tinted for the provinces, and the purer white for the city trade. He was succeeded in 1881 by Wood, Hines & Winkle . . .'

John Thomson (& Son), Glasgow, Scotland
c. 1816–97

John Thomson worked the Annfield Pottery, Glasgow, where a wide range of earthenware was produced, including 'STONE WARE'. Printed marks include the initials 'J.T.' or 'J.T. & Sons' (from c. 1865), sometimes with the name 'Annfield' or 'Glasgow'.

Thomas Till & Son(s), Burslem, Staffordshire
c. 1850–1928

Thomas Till & Son of the Sytch Pottery, Burslem, exhibited at the 1851 Exhibition and their ware included 'pearl white Granite':

> Albany shape dishes, baker and plates; pearl white granite.
> Virginia shape set, teapot, sugar, cream (jug), cup and saucer, in pearl white Granite.
> Set of jugs, pearl white granite.
> Albany shape soup tureen, complete, and sauce tureen, complete, white granite, gold bands . . .
> Virginia shape, set tea cup and saucer and teapot, white granite, gold band.

At that period, 61 men, 34 women, 46 boys and 33 girls were employed.

Messrs. Till's various earthenware pieces are normally marked with the name in full.

George Townsend, Longton, Staffordshire
c. 1850–64

Printed marks occur showing the Royal Arms, the description 'Staffordshire Ironstone China' and the name 'G. Townsend'.

Turner, Goddard & Co., Tunstall, Staffordshire
c. 1867–74

The description 'Royal Patent Ironstone' occurs on marks with the Royal Arms and the name 'TURNER, GODDARD & CO.'

ROYAL . PATENT.
IRONSTONE.
TURNER . GODDARD & Cᵒ

John Turner (Turner & Co.), Lane End, Staffordshire
c. 1762–1806

John Turner produced extremely fine earthenware—cream-coloured ware, Wedgwood-type jasper and basalt ware, and, later, fine stoneware-type jugs, etc. with relief motifs—as well as porcelain. The standard reference book on John Turner and his ware is *The Turners of Lane End—Master Potters of the Industrial Revolution* by Bevis Hillier, 1965.

For the purposes of this book, the most important section of Turner's varied products is his 'patent' stone-china-type body, which bears the painted mark 'TURNER'S PATENT' or the impressed mark 'TURNER'.

The abstract of the patent (No. 2367 of January 1800) is in the names of William and John Turner and reads:

> A new method, or methods of manufacturing porcelain and earthenware, by the introduction of a material not heretofore used in the manufacturing of these articles. The material is known in Staffordshire by the names 'Tabberner's Mine Rock', 'Little Mine Rock' and 'New Rock'. It is generally used as follows: ground, washed, dried in a potter's kiln, commonly called a slip kiln, afterwards mixed with a certain proportion of growan or Cornish Stone, previously calcined, levigated, and dryed, a small quantity of flint similarly prepared is also added, but in different proportions, according to the nature of the ware, and the heat required in burning it.

The resulting ware bears the painted mark 'Turner's Patent' and, although the first of the stone chinas, it is often slightly translucent. Fine dessert services, mugs, jugs, bowls, etc. were made, the favourite pattern being a neat but bold formal floral pattern in the Chinese style (see Plate 137), similar in general effect to the later Mason 'Japan' patterns. Other rarer examples show finer styles of decoration (see Plates 135 and 136).

In 1803, John Glover and Charles Simpson joined the Turners; but the new partnership was of short duration, for in November 1804 John Turner withdrew, and in March 1806 the remaining partners dissolved their association. In July 1806 the Turners were declared bankrupt, and in June 1807 'a large and elegant assortment of Earthenware and china, comprising the different articles . . . consisting of cream colour, china glazed blue edge, china glaze printed and painted, Egyptian black (basalt), Cane, Stone, Jasper, Pearl and Patent China . . . of Messrs. Turner & Co. . . .' was offered for sale.

According to tradition, Josiah Spode purchased the rights to the 'Turner Patent' body. However, no reference is made to it in the marks used by Spode on his own 'Stone China', which was probably a new variation of Turner's patent, using the basic raw materials with additions. For Spode's ware, see page 92.

Turner's-Patent

Venables & Baines, Burslem, Staffordshire
c. 1851–3

This short-lived partnership succeeded Mellor, Venables & Co. at Nile Street, Burslem, and produced some blue printed Ironstone-type ware. Marks incorporate the name or initials of the partnership. Messrs. Venables, Mann & Co. (also termed J. Venable & Co.) succeeded c. 1853–5.

Thomas Walker, Tunstall, Staffordshire
c. 1845–51

Thomas Walker worked the Lion Pottery at Tunstall. A good range of earthenware was produced, much of which was intended for the American markets. Marks include the name 'T. WALKER' or 'THOS. WALKER'. In some instances, the place name 'Tunstall' was added to distinguish the ware from that produced by other potters of this name—Thomas Walker of Longton, c. 1856–7 and Thomas Henry Walker of Longton, c. 1846–9.

Edward Walley, Cobridge, Staffordshire
c. 1845–56

Edward Walley produced general earthenware, including Ironstone which bears the impressed mark 'Ironstone china. E. Walley'. Bold hand-painted designs were employed as well as printed patterns.

Wedgwood & Co. Ltd., Tunstall, Staffordshire
c. 1860 to present day

This firm succeeded Podmore, Walker & Co.—a firm which had already used the name Wedgwood in its marks (see page 82). Quotations from

Jewitt's standard work *Ceramic Art of Great Britain* show the standing of the Company and its products in the 1870s:

> The works, which are very extensive, and give employment to six or seven hundred persons, occupy an area of about an acre of ground, and are among the most substantially built and best arranged in the pottery district. The goods produced are the higher classes of earthenware ... The quality of the 'Imperial Ironstone China'—the staple production of the firm, is of remarkable excellence, both in body and in glaze, and the decorations are characterized by pure taste, artistic feeling, and precision of execution ... they associate durability of quality in body and a perfect glaze with purity of outline in form, chasteness of decoration, and clearness and harmony of colour, adapting their designs and styles of decoration to the National tastes of the people in the various climes to which the goods are sent. One of the most successful of their original ordinary printed designs is the pattern known as 'Asiatic Pheasants', which has become so popular as to be considered one of the standard patterns of this country and the colonies. They also supply large quantities of ironstone china specially made for the use of ships, restaurants, hotels, etc. ... The Unicorn Works (as opposed to the Pinnox Works) is entirely devoted to the production of plain white granite ware for the American trade ...

The 'Asiatic Pheasants' pattern referred to is shown in Plate 138. It was indeed popular, for I have seen the design and special 'Asiatic Pheasants' mark with the name or initials of more than twenty firms.

The Wedgwood firm continues to the present time, but with changes in its title. Owing to the confusion between Josiah Wedgwood & Sons Ltd, and Wedgwood & Co. Ltd., the latter was changed to Enoch Wedgwood (Tunstall) Ltd. in 1965.

The various marks incorporate the name 'Wedgwood & Co', and 'Ltd.' was often added from c. 1900. The use of the '& Co.' distinguishes the marks from the one word 'Wedgwood' impressed into the ware made by Josiah Wedgwood & Sons Ltd. Standard descriptive names include 'Stone-Ware', 'Stone China', 'Imperial Ironstone China' and 'Patent Paris White Ironstone'. Sample marks are reproduced below.

Basic Wedgwood & Co. mark, not to be confused with the simple 'Wedgwood' name marks used by Josiah Wedgwood & Sons Ltd.

Josiah Wedgwood (& Sons Ltd.), Etruria (now at Barlaston) Staffordshire
c. 1759 to present day

This famous firm should not be confused with Messrs. Wedgwood & Co. Ltd:
(see previous entry). Josiah Wedgwood & Sons Ltd. are mainly known for
their fine coloured jasper ware with white relief motifs and for their fine
cream-coloured or 'Queen's' ware.

In 1819, experiments were begun to produce 'Stone China' to compete
with Spode's successful body marketed under this name. A letter of 1817
from Josiah Bateman, Wedgwood's salesman, is quoted on page 93, and
this may have sparked off the experiments. Examples are plainly marked in
underglaze blue WEDGWOOD'S STONE CHINA but examples are rarely found today. A
dessert set with typical 'Japan' style design is illustrated in Plate 139. Factory
records suggest that production of their 'Stone China' started in 1827 and
ceased in 1861.

A. J. Wilkinson Ltd., Burslem, Staffordshire
1885 to present day

Messrs. Wilkinson Ltd. (formerly Wilkinson & Hulme) produced good
quality 'Royal Patent Ironstone' for the home and American markets from
the 1880s onwards. Marks are full and self-explanatory.

Wood & Brownfield, Cobridge, Staffordshire
c. 1838–50

This partnership produced good quality earthenware, including 'Stone Ware'.
Various marks incorporate the initials 'W. & B.'. Messrs. W. Brownfield
succeeded (see page 60).

Wood & Hawthorne, Cobridge, Staffordshire
c. 1882–7

This partnership produced white granite ware or Ironstone exclusively for
the American market. The standard mark includes the description 'Ironstone
china' and the names 'WOOD & HAWTHORNE, ENGLAND' beneath
the Royal Arms.

H

John Wedg(e) Wood, Burslem and Tunstall, Staffordshire
c. 1841–60

This potter used misleading marks reading 'J. Wedgwood', as the example reproduced below. The marks of Josiah Wedgwood & Sons Ltd. do not include the initial 'J'. John Wedg(e) Wood's marks sometimes have a slight space or dot between 'WEDG' and 'WOOD' but in some cases this distinction is not apparent.

Wood & Son(s) (Ltd.), Burslem, Staffordshire
c. 1865 to present day

Messrs. Wood & Son produced good quality general earthenware and Ironstone ware. Marks are clear and self-explanatory. From c. 1907 '& Son' became '& Sons', and from 1910 'Ltd.' was added to the firm's official title but not to all marks. Sample marks are reproduced below. The firm still enjoys a large export trade in Ironstone ware.

G. Wooliscroft, Tunstall, Staffordshire
c. 1851–2 and 1860–4

George Wooliscroft (also spelt Woolliscroft) potted at High Street and Well Street, Tunstall, during the 1851–3 period, and at the Sandyford Potteries, Tunstall, c. 1860–4. Marks normally incorporate the name of the body— 'Ironstone', etc.—the pattern, and the potter's name.

John Yates, Fenton, Staffordshire
c. 1784–1835

John Yates produced a wide range of earthenware. The early examples would seem to have been unmarked, but ware of the 1820–35 period occurs with the mark 'J.Y. Warranted Stone China, Fenton'. The initials are believed to relate to this potter.

Ynysmedw Pottery, Nr. Swansea, Wales
c. 1840–70+

Recent excavations by Mr. D. Harper on the site of this little-known Welsh pottery have proved that its production included 'Ironstone' china. A fragment with a printed Ironstone mark is shown in Plate 141 with a blue printed platter of the same 'Rio' design.

Marks include the impressed initials 'Y.M.P.' or 'Y.P.' or the name in full, 'YNISMEDW POTTERY. SWANSEA VALE' (note alternative spelling of Ynysmedw). Printed marks incorporate the name WILLIAMS (c. 1854–60) the initials 'L. & M.' (c. 1860–70) or the initials 'W.T.H.', denoting the last proprietor, W. T. Holland, c. 1870+.

This last entry underlines the point that Ironstone-type ware was made by potteries large and small throughout the British Isles, and it was by no means limited to the Staffordshire potteries.

Unidentified Marks Found on Ironstone-type Ware

The ornate version of the pre-Victorian Royal Arms mark occurs on very fine quality Ironstone China, often decorated with extremely colourful designs. The wording below the Royal Arms reads 'IMP. (Improved) IRON STONE CHINA, Stoke Works'. The use of the word Ironstone suggests a date after 1813, but the identity of the manufacturer has not as yet been discovered. William Adams had works at Stoke (as well as at Tunstall) from 1811 to 1830, and he may be regarded as a possible producer of the fine early Ironstone ware which bears this printed mark. These same ornate Arms, with the Prince of Wales' feathers above and the motto 'Ich Dien' below, are shown in Plate 18, and the same ornate design occurs with the words 'Genuine Folch's Stone China' (see page 68).

Britannicus Dresden China

This wording occurs printed in underglaze blue on good quality Ironstone-type ware of the 1820 period, but the maker has, as yet, not been identified.

F. Primavesi (& Son)

Many examples of English earthenware can be found with ornate printed marks including this name, with various addresses—Cardiff, Swansea, etc. This was a firm of retailers and shippers, not manufacturers.

The name-marks of hundreds of retailers may be found on nineteenth-century English ceramics which were made to their special order. The names and periods of the more important retailers are given in my *Encyclopaedia of British Pottery and Porcelain Marks*, 1964. Messrs. Primavesi operated from c. 1850 to 1915; '& Son' would seem to have been added to marks from about 1860.

Real Stone China

This wording occurs on printed marks with crown above (see example below). It would appear to have been first used by Hicks, Meigh & Johnson (c. 1822–35) but can also occur on ware made by John Ridgway in the 1830s.

Tonquin China

Blue printed marks incorporating the description 'Tonquin China' occur on good quality Ironstone-type ware of the 1820 period (see Plate 140). The name of the manufacturer is, as yet, not known.

Wrekin Ironstone China

No ware has so far been discovered with this name; but newspaper advertisements mention Wrekin or Shropshire Ironstone china, which suggests that it was produced before Mason's introduced their Patent Ironstone.

The Wrekin is a high hill in Shropshire—a prominent landmark visible for many miles—and it would appear that Wrekin Ironstone was of Shropshire manufacture. Many potteries were in the neighbourhood of Coalport. In November 1816 T. Brocas, the Shrewsbury retailer, advertised in the *Salopian Journal* ' . . . Wrekin Ironstone which they have sold for many years, and which lately has been so highly approved of . . .'; and in November 1815, Thomas Brocas begged 'leave to observe there lately being an amazing improvement in the British Manufacture of china, both in material, shape and pattern, he now has by him a number of tea and breakfast services also Table (Dinner) services of the WREKIN or SHROPSHIRE IRONSTONE CHINA, etc . . .'

Details of many of the small British manufacturers can be found in L. Jewitt's *Ceramic Art of Great Britain* (J. Virtue & Co., 1878, revised edition 1883). The basic marks and working periods of many potters are recorded in my *Encyclopaedia of British Pottery and Porcelain Marks* (Herbert Jenkins Ltd., 1964). Some details of scenic patterned English Ironstone-type ware are given in Sam Laidacher's *Anglo-American China*, Part II (privately published in the U.S.A., 1951), but there are some errors of attribution and dating.

The British potters were not left entirely alone to enjoy the North American market for their popular Ironstone and Granite ware. The marks used by many American producers are given in C. Jordan Thorn's *Handbook of Old Pottery and Porcelain Marks* (Tudor Publishing Co., New York, 1947) and R. M. & T. H. Kovel's *Dictionary of Marks—Pottery and Porcelain* (Crown Publishers Inc., New York, 1953). Many American marks follow the standard English mark forms in style (even including versions of the British Royal Arms!) and the ware can consequently be mistaken for British Ironstone.

GENERAL NOTES

IRONSTONE IN 1866

In 1866, a Canadian—James Torrington Spencer Lidstone—published a collection of poems under the title *The Thirteenth Londoniad, giving a full description of the principal establishments in the (Staffordshire) Potteries* . . .

This rare booklet gives interesting information on the products of many large and small manufacturers of the 1860s. The poems are set out below the firm's title, specialities and address—information probably gleaned from letter-headings. These headings are interesting in themselves.

The following extracts relate to the manufacture of Ironstone-type ware. Many of the poems are lengthy, and only the relevant lines are quoted here.

William & Thomas Adams

Manufacturers of General Earthenware, Granite, Etc.
Tunstall, Staffordshire.

> . . .
> White Ironstone-china, lovely in form,
> Dinners, Toilets in ditto, that must ever charm.
> . . .
> See also page 51.

Mr. Taylor Ashworth

Messrs. Geo. L. Ashworth & Bros. Manufacturers of Ironstone China, etc.
Hanley, Staffordshire Potteries.

> . . .
> Who knows not th' illustrious House of Ashworth,
> Is famed in every region of the earth.
> . . .
> The only house that represents 'Old Mason'.
> They bought the moulds and drawings and they stand,
> Like Pharos in Time's sea, a light to every land.
> For Teas, Dinner sets, nations assign a
> Station high as for their Patent Ironstone-China;
> . . .
> See also page 53.

Edward F. Bodley & Co.

Manufacturers of Genuine Ironstone China and Earthenware.
Scotia Works, Burslem, Staffordshire Potteries.

. . .

Here I beheld the fairy boudoir sets,
and arts-creations, wondrous toilets.
Great, varied, in his gen'ral enchanting line a
Thousand contours rise in Granite, Ironstone china.
Not only to the public of the world they're sent,
But he makes for Princes all over the Continent.

. . .

See also page 58.

T. & R. Boote

Manufacturers of Earthenware, Stone, Parian, etc.
Patentees of Royal Mosaic Ware, also Patentees and Manufacturers of
Mosaic and Ornamental Pavements.
Waterloo Potteries, Burslem.

. . .

And are famous o'er the globe on all its lands and seas.
Yes; their Granite or Opaque Porcelain,
Otherwise Iron-stone china, doth attain
To Empire throughout the bounds of Nature's reign.

. . .

See also page 58.

George Frederick Bowers

Manufacturer of Improved Porcelain, Ironstone, Earthenware, and white
Granite, and other Dinner, dessert, Toilet, Tea, and Breakfast Ware, Gilded
and Ornamented.
Brownhills Works, Tunstall, Staffordshire Potteries.

. . .

Every thing in his varied line hath to solar heights been borne;
And he does a large business with the Empires of the Morn.

. . .

See also page 58.

William Brownfield

Manufacturer of Improved Ironstone and Earthenware.
Cobridge, Staffordshire Potteries.

. . .

Our age him hails prime Manufacturer
Of Improved Ironstone and Earthenware.
The taste display'd, the vigour he imparts
Have carried his works up to the Fine Arts;

. . .

See also page 60.

Edward Clarke

Manufacturer of White Ironstone China, Chemical and
Apothecaries ware. . . .
Phoenix Works, Tunstall.

. . .
Best Granite, none better, famed in all lands;
. . .
See also page 62.

Holland & Green

Earthenware Manufacturers, Longton, Staffordshire.

In other lands, 'midst many another scene,
I had often heard of Messrs. Holland and Green;
Nor the perception of the Art-Student escapes
Their variety of designs, the colour and the shapes.
. . .
On th' Ironstone-china, and Earthenware manufacturers.
See also page 73.

John Meir & Son

Manufacturers of Earthenwares, etc.
Green Gates Pottery, Tunstall, Staffordshire.

. . .
Here many thousand articles, most lovely in form,
Toilets, whose contours and design might well th'
              Art-Student charm;
Here are Breakfasts, Dinners, and Teas, here Granite
              and Willow,
. . .
Pioneers of Art! we trace them **thro'** all the radiant lines
Of Science, in their Collieries, and in their Iron-
              stone Mines;
Of Flint-stones, and Cornish stones, they ever
              grind their own,
. . .
See also page 78.

PRODUCERS OF IRONSTONE AND GRANITE WARE
ADVERTISING IN POTTERY GAZETTE 1885 DIARY

Geo. L. Ashworth & Bros., Hanley.
Sole manufacturers of Real Ironstone-china and Mason's
Patent Ironstone-china Patterns and shapes.

Baker & Co., Fenton . . . Manufacturers of white Granite . . .

E. F. Bodley & Son, New Bridge Pottery, Longport.
Manufacturers of Genuine Ironstone china and earthenware . . .

T. G. & F. Booth, Tunstall . . . Best Ironstone for Hotels
and Ship's use . . .

E. & C. Challinor, Fenton . . . Manufacturers of Ironstone,
white Granite . . .

Clementson Bros., Phoenix & Bell Works, Hanley . . .
Earthenware and Ironstone china . . .

Davenports Limited, Longport . . . Ironstone ware, plain and decorated, in
china patterns, suitable for barracks, clubs, hotels and ship uses. White
Granite, in great variety suitable for home trade, North & South America
and the Colonies . . .

J. Dimmock & Co., Albion Works, Hanley . . . Earthenware and Ironstone
china, for home, colonial and Export . . . originators of the celebrated flowing
blue . . .

Edge, Malkin & Co., Newport Works, Burslem . . . Ironstone china and
earthenwares . . .

John Edwards, Fenton, Manufacturer of Porcelaine de Terre,
Ironstone-china and white Granite . . .

Thomas Furnival & Sons, Cobridge . . . Manufacturers of white Granite . . .

W. H. Grindley & Co., Tunstall, Manufacturers of plain and embossed
Ironstone china . . .

Ralph Hammersley & Son, Overhouse Pottery, Burslem.
Manufacturers of Ironstone china and general earthenware . . .
Real Ironstone china in shapes suitable for Hotels,
Restaurants, Steamships, etc. with crests or monograms . . .

Alfred Meakin, Tunstall . . . Manufacturers of Ironstone china, white
Granite . . .

Powell, Bishop & Stonier, Hanley, Manufacturers of china and earthenware . . . White Granite for the United States . . .

Wedgwood & Co., Unicorn & Pinnox Works, Tunstall . . . white Granite . . .

The list for the year 1900 is substantially the same:

'Ltd.' is added to Baker & Co.'s style.
Messrs. T. G. & F. Booth are restyled 'Booths Ltd.'
Messrs. Thomas Furnival & Sons are restyled 'Furnivals Ltd.'
'Ltd.' is added to A. Meakin's style

and the following firms were listed as producers of 'Ironstone china' or 'White Granite':

Cockran & Fleming, Britannia Pottery, Glasgow . . . Manufacturers of Royal Ironstone china and Porcelain Granite . . .
W. & E. Corn, Longport . . . white Granite.

Dunn Bennett & Co., Burslem . . . Ironstone china, specially adapted for ships, hotels, restaurants and coffee house use . . .

Thomas Hughes & Son, Longport . . . White Granite.

Anthony Shaw & Co., Burslem, Earthenware and Ironstone china.

T. Till & Sons, Burslem . . . ironstone china . . .

Wood & Son, Burslem . . . white granite . . .

CHECK LIST OF DESCRIPTIVE NAMES 'STONE CHINA', ETC., FOUND ON IRONSTONE-TYPE WARE

Generous spacing has been provided in this section so that collectors can add to this alphabetical list as new marked specimens are discovered. Further details on the manufacturers will be found between pages 51 and 101.

Cymro Stone China   Dillwyn

Dresden Opaque China   J. & R. Clews

Fine Stone   Brameld & Co.

Granite China	Brameld & Co., J. Clementson, Ferrybridge Pottery, T. Hughes, Pountney & Co.
Imperial Ironstone (China)	Birks Bros. & Seddon, Cockson & Chetwynd, Morley & Ashworth, Podmore, Walker & Co., Wedgwood & *Co. Ltd.* (see also page 101)
Imperial Parisian Granite	Old Hall Earthenware Co.
Imperial White Granite	Pinder Bourne & Co.
Improved Granite China	Ridgway, Morley, Wear & Co., Ridgway & Morley
Improved Stone China	C. Meigh
Indian Ironstone	J. & G. Alcock
Indian Stone China	Old Hall Earthenware Co.
New Stone	Spode (also found on pieces decorated after 1833 by Messrs. Copeland & Garrett)
Opaque China	Bridgwood & Clarke

Opaque Granite China	Ferrybridge Pottery, W. Ridgway & Co., Swillington Bridge Pottery
Opaque Porcelain	Bridgwood & Clarke
Opaque Stone China	A. Shaw
Oriental Stone	J. & G. Alcock, J. & S. Alcock
Parisian Porcelain	H. Alcock
Patent Ironstone China	G. L. Ashworth, Mason's
Patent Paris White Ironstone	Wedgwood & Co. Ltd.
Pearl White Granite	Thomas Till & Son
Pearl White Ironstone	Cork & Edge, South Wales Pottery
Pearl Stone Ware	Podmore, Walker & Co.
Porcelain Opaque	S. Bridgwood & Son

Quartz China   W. Ridgway (& Co.)

Real Ironstone China   Davenport, Hicks, Meigh & Johnson,
                                        Alfred Meakin, John Ridgway

Real Stone China   Davenport,
                                        C. & W. K. Harvey

Rock Stone   J. Tams

Royal Ironstone China   Cockran & Fleming

Royal Patent Ironstone   T. & R. Boote Ltd.,
                                        Mellor, Venables & Co.,
                                        Turner, Goddard & Co.,
                                        A. J. Wilkinson Ltd.

Royal Patent Stoneware   Clementson Bros.

Royal Stone China   Stevenson & Williams

Royal Vitreous   J. Maddock & Son

Saxon Stone China   T. & J. Carey

Staffordshire Ironstone China Griffiths, Beardmore, & Birks,
                                        G. Townsend

Staffordshire Stone China   Godwin, Rowley & Co.,
Swift & Elkin

Staffordshire Stone Ware   Cork & Edge

Stone China   Batkin, Walker & Broadhurst,
Brameld & Co., J. Clementson,
J. & R. Clews, Davenport,
J. Edwards, Ferrybridge Pottery,
Hicks & Meigh, Hicks, Meigh &
Johnson, R. Johnson,
J. Maddock (& Sons),
Maddock & Seddon, J. Meir & Son,
Mellor, Taylor & Co.,
J. W. Pankhurst & Co.,
Plymouth Pottery Co., J. Reed,
J. Ridgway & Son,
J. & W. Ridgway, Ridgway & Morley,
A. Shaw, Spode, J. Thomson,
Wedgwood & Co. Ltd., J. Yates,
J. Wedgwood & Sons Ltd., etc.

Stone China Indian   Old Hall Earthenware Co.

Stone Ware   Dillwyn, J. Maudesley & Co.

Tonquin China   See page 103

Wrekin Ironstone China   See page 103

Appendix I

Mason Factories
And Subsequent Owners
Being Lists Based on the Researches of
The Late Alfred Meigh

VICTORIA POTTERY
LANE DELPH, FENTON

c. 1800	*Miles Mason* & George Wolfe
c. 1800–6	*Mason & Co.*
c. 1806–43	Samuel Ginder & Co.
c. 1844–5	Samuel & Henry Ginder
c. 1847–57	James Floyd
c. 1860	Wathen & Hudden
c. 1862–4	Wathen & Lichfield
c. 1864–9	James Bateman Wathen
c. 1870–1948	James Reeves

MINERVA WORKS
LANE DELPH, FENTON

c. 1800–5	John Lucock
c. 1806–16	*Miles Mason*
c. 1818–26	Felix Pratt & Co.
c. 1826–34	Pratt, Hassall & Gerrard
c. 1834–47	Green & Richards
c. 1848–59	Thomas Green (died 1859)
c. 1860–75	Mary Green & Co.
c. 1876–90	T. A. & S. Green
c. 1891 to present day	Crown Staffordshire Porcelain Co. Ltd.

SAMPSON BAGNALL'S WORKS
at angle of the road below
MINERVA WORKS

c. 1811–22	*William Mason* (works probably run by George and Charles Mason while William was dealing in china, see page 11).
c. 1822–5	*Miles Mason* (executors of)
c. 1825–6	*George & Charles Mason*
c. 1827	Void (or empty according to rate records; works may have been dismantled and combined with the FENTON STONE WORKS).

FENTON STONE WORKS
PATENT IRONSTONE MANUFACTORY
HIGH STREET
LANE DELPH, FENTON

c. 1780–1805	Sampson Bagnall
c. 1805–15	Josiah Spode
c. 1815–29	*George & Charles Mason*
c. 1829–39	*Charles James Mason*
c. 1841–3	*Mason & Faraday* (or 'C. J. Mason & Co.')
c. 1845–8	*Charles James Mason* (bankrupt February 1848)
c. 1849–52	Samuel Boyle (& Son)
c. 1853–60	E. Challinor & Co.
c. 1862–91	E. & C. Challinor
c. 1891–6	C. Challinor & Co.
c. 1897–1932	William Baker & Co. (Ltd.)

DAISY BANK WORKS
LONGTON

c. 1797–1802	Samuel Hughes
c. 1803–11	Peter & Thomas Hughes
c. 1812	Drury & Co.
c. 1815–17	John Drury (or 'Drury & Co.')
c. 1818–30	Thomas Drury & Son
c. 1831–7	Ray & Tideswell
c. 1838–46	Richard Tideswell
c. 1851–3	*Charles James Mason*
c. 1853–68	Hulse, Nixon & Adderley
c. 1869–73	Hulse & Adderley
c. 1876–85	William Alsager Adderley
c. 1886–1905	William Alsager Adderley & Co.
c. 1906 to recent years	Adderley's Ltd.

[Appendix II appears after the plates]

1. Unglazed wasters from the Wolfe-Mason Liverpool factory site, showing parts of pre-1800 blue-printed patterns (see page 3). *Liverpool Museums.*

2. A blue-printed Wolfe-Mason Liverpool porcelain teabowl and saucer, shown with a pre-1800 waster from the factory site (see page 3). *Liverpool Museums.*

3. A pair of impressed-marked 'M. Mason' porcelain plates decorated in the Chinese fashion. The mark has been arrowed for clarity. Diameter $7\frac{3}{4}$ inches. c. 1805. *Godden of Worthing Ltd.*

4. A blue-printed impressed-marked 'M. Mason' plate of typical form and pattern, showing the influence of the Chinese 'Nankin' porcelain. Diameter $9\frac{1}{8}$ inches. c. 1805. *Victoria and Albert Museum (Crown Copyright).*

5. An unmarked Mason-type plate of similar shape to the marked examples shown in Plates 3 and 4 (see page 5). Diameter $8\frac{1}{2}$ inches. c. 1805. *Mr. & Mrs. B. Halls.*

6. A superb Mason-type 'British Nankin' soup plate in close imitation of the Chinese porcelain made for European customers (see page 5). Diameter $8\frac{3}{4}$ inches. c. 1805. *Messrs. Godden of Worthing.*

7. An early Mason porcelain sugar-box of pattern number 3, matching the impressed-mark plate shown below. 4½ inches high. c. 1805. *Messrs. Godden of Worthing.*

8. A Mason plate and teabowl and saucer of pattern number 3, the plate with impressed-name mark 'M. MASON'. c. 1805. *Victoria and Albert Museum (Crown Copyright).*

9. A very rare early Mason porcelain tea caddy (cover missing) bearing a popular printed design found on other marked ware. $5\frac{1}{4}$ inches high. c. 1805. *Miss M. Martin.*

10. A rare Mason porcelain sugar-box showing the full (uncut) version of a standard printed design—one coloured-over by hand in enamel colours (see also Plates 3 and 9).
c. 1810. *Messrs. Sotheby & Co.*

11. Representative parts of a Mason porcelain teaset of the 1810 period bearing a bat-printed design found on other Mason porcelain. The teapot is 6 inches high. *Messrs. Godden of Worthing.*

12. A fine Mason porcelain teapot, stand and creamer of the 1810–13 period decorated in orange and gold, with bat-printed classical-figure panels. *Messrs. Sotheby & Co.*

13. Representative parts of a rare Mason porcelain dessert service showing a variety of fine bat-printed subjects. Square dishes, 8 inches. c. 1805–10. *Messrs. Godden of Worthing.*

14. Three rare and colourful vases bearing the impressed mark 'M MASON', showing the fine quality of the early gilding and painting. The large vase is $11\frac{1}{2}$ inches high. c. 1810. *Messrs. Mason's Ironstone China Ltd., Works Collection.*

Colour Plate I.   A superb Miles Mason porcelain vase, richly gilt on a blue
ground, painted on each side with panels of birds in a landscape. Impressed mark 'M. MASON'. $6\frac{1}{4}$ inches high. c. 1810.

15.   A rare Miles Mason porcelain vase and cover, finely gilt and painted with flowers. Impressed-name mark. 7 inches high. c. 1810. *Beaverbrook Art Gallery, Canada.*

16.   Two of a set of three Miles Mason porcelain vases of the same shape as that shown in Colour Plate I but painted with animals and figures in landscape. Impressed-name marks. 8 inches and $6\frac{1}{4}$ inches high. *Messrs. Godden of Worthing.*

17. Representative parts of a Mason's Patent Ironstone dinner service of fine quality, of a design known as 'Table and flower pot pattern' (see page 25). The sauceboat is rarely found in such sets. c. 1813–20. *Messrs. Godden of Worthing.*

18.   This mark, showing the Prince of Wales' feather motif by the crown, is rare. In this case, on the tureen shown in Plate 19, it occurs with a standard 'Mason's' impressed mark.

19.   A rare oval-shaped tureen of the same pattern as the pieces in Plate 17. The finely engraved Royal Arms mark is reproduced above. The tureen is 13½ inches long. c. 1815. *Messrs. Godden of Worthing Ltd.*

20. A blue-printed Mason's Patent Ironstone tureen and cover of 'Blue Pheasants' pattern (see page 25). The impressed Royal Arms mark is as Plate 22A. c. 1815–20. *Messrs. Godden of Worthing.*

21. An early Mason's Patent Ironstone China tureen of pattern No. 1 'India Green Grasshopper' design (see page 25). Marks: 'Ironstone China Warranted' and 'N 1'. $12\frac{1}{2}$ inches long. c. 1815. *Messrs. Godden of Worthing.*

22. An early Mason's Patent Ironstone China tureen decorated with one of several Chinese-style so-called 'Japan' patterns. Tureen $13\frac{1}{2}$ inches long. c. 1815–20. *Messrs. Godden of Worthing.*

22A. The rare, moulded Royal Arms mark occurring on the tureen shown in Plate 22 above.

23. A rare and fine quality impressed-marked 'Mason's Patent Ironstone China' tureen, cover and stand. $6\frac{1}{2}$ inches high. c. 1820–5. *Messrs. Godden of Worthing.*

24. A rare sexagonal Mason's Patent Ironstone tureen and cover of the blue-printed 'Blue Pheasants' pattern. 7 inches high. c. 1820–5. *Victoria and Albert Museum (Crown Copyright).*

25. A rare Mason's Patent Ironstone two-division vegetable dish and cover with an impressed-name mark. 11 inches long. c. 1815–20. *Messrs. Godden of Worthing.*

26. An impressed-marked 'Mason's Patent Ironstone China' six-sided vegetable dish and cover with a typically broadly painted 'Japan' pattern. Diameter 11½ inches. c. 1820. *Messrs. Godden of Worthing.*

27. A Mason's Patent Ironstone China shaped oval tureen with post-1830 moulded feet. Printed crowned mark (page 47). 14½ inches long. c. 1835. *Messrs. Godden of Worthing.*

28. Representative pieces from a Mason's Ironstone dinner set with one of the gay but less expensive designs broadly painted, perhaps by child labour. c. 1825–30. *Messrs. Mason's Ironstone China Ltd., Works Collection.*

29. A rare and ornately moulded Mason's Patent Ironstone sauce tureen. Printed crowned mark (page 47). 7 inches long. c. 1835–40. *Messrs. Godden of Worthing.*

30. A Mason's Patent Ironstone China tureen, cover and stand (of the same basic shape as Plate 29, above), decorated with a fine quality printed design. Printed 'C. J. Mason & Co' mark. c. 1829–40. *Victoria and Albert Museum (Crown Copyright).*

31. A blue-printed soup plate of willow-type pattern, perhaps that called 'Blue Chinese landscape' in the 1818 sale. Printed mark. $9\frac{1}{2}$ inches. c. 1820. *Author's Collection.*

32. A blue-printed dinner plate bearing the rare impressed mark 'MASON'S CAMBRIAN ARGIL'. $9\frac{3}{4}$ inches. c. 1820. *Victoria and Albert Museum (Crown Copyright).*

33. A rare Mason's Ironstone plate of a shape registered on 16th April 1849 (see page 20). Printed mark as shown on the left. *Author's Collection.*

34. A very finely decorated impressed-marked 'Mason's Patent Ironstone China' soup plate with green border and central crest. This lobed-edged shape is also very rare. $9\frac{1}{2}$ inches. c. 1825. *Messrs. Godden of Worthing.*

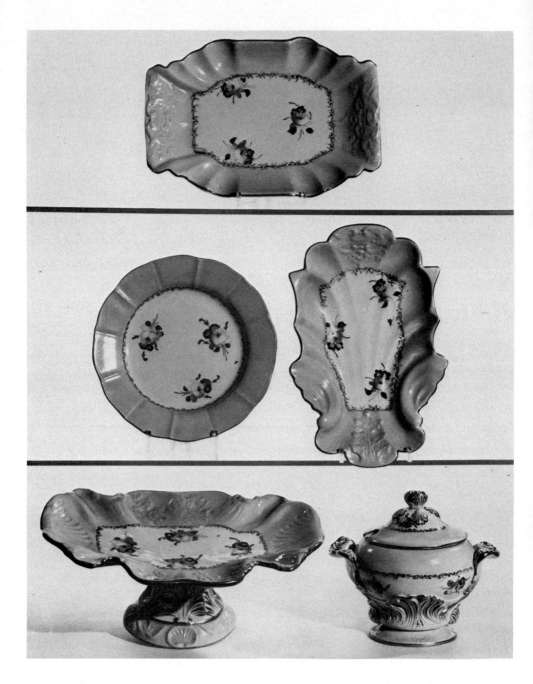

35. Representative pieces of an impressed-marked 'Mason's Patent Ironstone China' dessert set. Green and gold borders and hand-painted floral sprays. Centrepiece 12½ inches long. c. 1815–20. *Messrs. Godden of Worthing.*

Colour Plate II. Representative pieces of an impressed-marked 'Mason's Patent Ironstone China' dessert set. A typical 'Japan' pattern, perhaps that termed 'Old Japan pattern' in the 1818 sale (see page 25). Centrepiece 14¼ inches long. c. 1815–20. *Messrs. Godden of Worthing.*

36. An impressed-marked 'Mason's Patent Ironstone China' centrepiece and plate from a dessert service of the 1815–20 period. *Messrs. Godden of Worthing.*

37. Representative pieces of an impressed-marked 'Mason's Patent Ironstone China' dessert service of the 1820s, painted boldly with a 'Japan' pattern. Sauce tureen $7\frac{3}{4}$ inches high. *Messrs. Godden of Worthing.*

38.   Representative pieces of an impressed-marked 'Mason's Patent
Ironstone China' dessert service, showing unusual shapes of the 1820s.
Sauce tureen 7 inches high. *Messrs. Godden of Worthing.*

39. Representative pieces of an impressed-marked 'Mason's Patent Ironstone China' dessert service, showing unusual shapes of the 1820s. This pattern was termed 'Table and flower pot pattern' in the 1818 sale catalogue (see page 25). *Messrs. Godden of Worthing.*

40. Representative pieces of an impressed-marked 'Mason's Patent Ironstone China' dessert service of the 1820s. Richly decorated with a dark blue border over which the gilders have added a leaf design. Sauce tureen $6\frac{1}{2}$ inches high. *Messrs. Godden of Worthing.*

Colour Plate III.   Representative pieces from a Mason's Patent Ironstone China dessert service of the 1820s. This pattern, called 'Mogul', is made up from a printed outline which has been coloured-in by hand. A service of this pattern was sold for £5. 18. 0. in 1818 (see page 116). Printed crowned mark (page 46). Centrepiece 12½ inches long. *Messrs. Godden of Worthing.*

41. Representative pieces from an attractive and rare Mason's Ironstone dessert service of the 1820s, showing finely moulded shapes. Impressed Royal Arms mark as Plate 22A on some plates. Centrepiece 14 inches long. *Messrs. Godden of Worthing.*

42.   Rare representative pieces from a Mason's Ironstone dessert service
of the 1830 period. Printed crowned mark (page 46). Centrepiece $6\frac{1}{4}$
inches high. *Messrs. Godden of Worthing.*

43. A very rare impressed-marked 'Mason's Patent Ironstone China' small basket with pierced cover—perhaps the 'violet basket' of the 1822 sale (page 29). Similar baskets were made at other factories. $3\frac{3}{4}$ inches long. c. 1820. *Messrs. Godden of Worthing.*

44. A rare unmarked Mason's Ironstone bulb or bough pot. The coloured-over printed pattern is also seen in Plate 45. 9 inches long. c. 1815. *Messrs. Godden of Worthing.*

45. A Mason's Patent Ironstone China punch or 'sideboard' bowl, decorated with a coloured-over printed design. Printed crowned mark (page 46). Diameter 13 inches. c. 1815–20. *Messrs. Godden of Worthing.*

46. A Mason's Patent Ironstone China punch or 'sideboard' bowl, decorated in the style of Chinese porcelain. Printed crowned mark (page 46). Diameter 12½ inches. c. 1820–5.

47. Representative pieces of a finely moulded Mason's Ironstone breakfast service of the 1815–20 period. Note the egg cup, covered muffin or toast dish and large breakfast cup (see page 30). Impressed-name mark. Plate 7 inches in diameter. *Messrs. Godden of Worthing.*

48. A very rare pair of marked 'Mason's Patent Ironstone China' cornucopia of the 1830 period. '2 Flower horns' were included in the 1818 sale (page 31). Printed crowned mark (page 46). 8 inches high. *Peter Nelson, Stow-on-the-Wold.*

49. An impressed-marked blue ground Mason's Ironstone mantelpiece ornament, perhaps the 'card racks, mazarine' of the 1822 sale. $6\frac{3}{4}$ inches high. c. 1820–5. *Messrs. Godden of Worthing.*

50. A large impressed-marked 'Mason's Patent Ironstone China' dish, broadly painted with a typical 'Japan' pattern. 15½ inches long. c. 1820–5. *Messrs. Godden of Worthing.*

51. A large impressed-marked 'Mason's Patent Ironstone China' dish or platter from a dinner service. Such sets included dishes of this shape in graduating sizes from about 9 inches to 22 inches. c. 1820–5. *Marshall Field & Co., Chicago.*

52. An impressed-marked 'Mason's Patent Ironstone China' dish from a fine quality dessert service. The relief-moulded motifs are rare. $9\frac{3}{4}$ inches by $8\frac{1}{4}$ inches. c. 1815–20. *Victoria and Albert Museum (Crown Copyright)*.

53. An impressed-marked 'Mason's Patent Ironstone China' dish from a dessert service of the 1815–20 period (see Colour Plate II and Plate 37). $8\frac{1}{4}$ inches by $9\frac{1}{2}$ inches. *Messrs. Godden of Worthington*.

54. A small 'Mason's Patent Ironstone China' fireplace with relief-moulded decoration. This example was taken from Charles Mason's house in Fenton. c. 1830–40. *City Museum and Art Gallery, Stoke-on-Trent.*

55. A fine 'Mason's Patent Ironstone China' fireplace or chimneypiece relief-moulded and decorated in the Chinese style. A miniature example of this model, only 12 inches high, is in the Stoke Museum. Printed mark, as Plate 56. 62 inches wide, 48 inches high. c. 1830. *Messrs. Sotheby & Co.*

56. The special, printed mark found on the reverse side of the parts which formed the large Ironstone chimneypieces. 2¾ inches long.

56A. The large top section of a chimney piece, similar to that shown in Plate 55 but with relief-moulded floral motifs picked out in gold. 42 inches long. c. 1830. *Messrs. Godden of Worthing.*

57. A superb
'Mason's Patent
Ironstone China'
chimneypiece,
finely relief-moulded
and gilt, with hand-
painted panels of
flowers. 54 inches
high. c. 1835–40.
L. J. Allen, Esq.

58. A very rich
and ornate 'Mason's
Patent Ironstone
China' chimneypiece
moulded in high
relief. Blue ground
richly gilt with
flower-painted
panels. 72 inches
wide. c. 1835–40.
L. J. Allen, Esq.

59. A fine 'Mason's Patent Ironstone China' loving cup and cover, or perhaps the 'elegant mitre-shaped jars and covers' of the 1818 sale catalogue (page 34). Printed crowned mark (page 46). $13\frac{3}{4}$ inches high. c. 1825. *Northampton Museum.*

60. A very finely painted and gilt 'Mason's Patent Ironstone China' loving cup, of the same form as that shown above in Plate 59. Unmarked. $8\frac{3}{4}$ inches high. c. 1820. *Messrs. Delomosne & Son Ltd.*

61. A rare impressed-marked 'Mason's Patent Ironstone China' inkstand. One inkwell and one cover are withdrawn to show the loose component parts. $6\frac{3}{4}$ inches long. c. 1815–20. *Messrs. Godden of Worthing.*

62. A rare boat-shaped Mason's Ironstone inkstand, now lacking the loose inkwells. Printed crowned mark (page 46). $8\frac{1}{4}$ inches long. c. 1825–30. *Messrs. Godden of Worthing.*

63.   An impressed-marked 'Mason's Patent Ironstone China' jug of plain 'antique' shape but issued without a handle (page 17). $9\frac{3}{4}$ inches high. c. 1820. *Author's Collection.*

64.   A rare form of 'Mason's Patent Ironstone China' (impressed-marked) covered jug. $6\frac{3}{4}$ inches high. c. 1820. *Messrs. Godden of Worthing.*

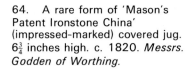

65.   An impressed-marked 'Mason's Patent Ironstone China' jug of rare form and better-than-average quality. $8\frac{3}{4}$ inches high. c. 1820. *Messrs. Godden of Worthing.*

66. A fine impressed-marked 'Mason's Patent Ironstone China' jug decorated with rich gold ground and gilt design. This 'antique shape' of the 1822 sale was copied by several other manufacturers, including Spode and Davenport (see Plate 107). $8\frac{3}{4}$ inches high. c. 1820. *Author's Collection.*

67. An impressed-marked 'Mason's Patent Ironstone China' jug of rare form. Gilt and enamelled over a rich blue ground. $5\frac{3}{4}$ inches high. c. 1825. *Messrs. Godden of Worthing.*

68. A Mason's Ironstone jug of rather unusual upright form. Printed crowned mark (page 47) with the name of a New York retailer— T. T. Kissam. 7 inches high. c. 1840. *Messrs. Godden of Worthing.*

69. Two Mason's Patent Ironstone jugs, the factory names for the shapes being 'Hydra' (*left*) and 'Fenton' (*right*). c. 1840. *Messrs. Mason's Ironstone China Ltd., Works Collection.*

70. A rare form of Mason's Patent Ironstone China covered jug. 12 inches high. c. 1840. *Miss F. R. Webster.*

71. A selection of Mason's Patent Ironstone China jugs showing typical shapes and patterns. Printed crowned marks. c. 1835–45. *The late Mrs. M. Symes.*

72. A relief-moulded 'C. J. Mason & Co. Granite China' jug in a pale blue earthenware. Printed mark as shown. $8\frac{1}{4}$ inches high. c. 1835. *Messrs. Godden of Worthing.*

73. A fine quality Mason's stoneware jug—perhaps similar to those described as 'stone figured jugs' in the 1822 sale catalogue. Printed crowned mark. $7\frac{3}{4}$ inches high. c. 1825. *Worthing Museum.*

Colour Plate IV. A selection of miniature or 'toy' objects in 'Mason's Patent Ironstone China' shown with an eight-inch vase for comparison of size. Many 'toy' pieces were included in the 1818 and 1822 sales (page 39). All pieces with impressed-name marks. c. 1815–25. *Messrs. Godden of Worthing.*

74. A superb quality 'Mason's Patent Ironstone China' miniature ewer and basin. Rich blue ground and finely gilt. Printed Royal Arms mark. Ewer $3\frac{1}{2}$ inches high. c. 1815–20. *Dr. M. Tanner.*

75. A fine pair of impressed-marked 'Mason's Patent Ironstone China' mugs richly gilt over a dark blue ground. $5\frac{1}{2}$ inches and $3\frac{3}{4}$ inches high. c. 1820. *The late Mrs. M. Symes.*

76. A very rare 'Mason's Patent Ironstone China' plate, the centre bearing a fine quality print of the 'Britannia' —the first steam Cundarder, launched in 1840. Printed crowned mark. c. 1840–5. *Author's Collection.*

77. A rare blue-printed 'Mason's Patent Ironstone China' soup plate. Diameter 9 inches. c. 1840. *Messrs. Godden of Worthing.*

78. An impressed-marked 'Mason's Patent Ironstone China' pot-pourri, with pierced outer cover and solid (removable) inner cover. Similar pieces —'1 pot pourri, rich Japan'—were included in the 1822 sale (page 37). 9½ inches high. c. 1820–5. *Messrs. Godden of Worthing.*

79. A large and rare impressed-marked 'Mason's Patent Ironstone China' pot-pourri painted with flowers on a pale yellow ground. 14 inches high. c. 1820–5. *Messrs. Godden of Worthing.*

80. A blue-printed Mason's Ironstone salad bowl from a willow-type pattern dinner service. This is a standard shape found in Chinese and other porcelain. Printed crowned mark. 8¼ inches square. c. 1830–5. *Messrs. Godden of Worthing.*

81. A rare form of Mason's Ironstone footed bowl with handles similar to that on the porcelain vases shown in Colour Plate I and Plate 16. Printed crowned mark. 6½ inches. high. c. 1820. *The late Mrs. M. Symes.*

82. A selection of early impressed-marked 'Mason's Patent Ironstone China' spill vases or 'match-pots' painted with typical 'Japan' patterns. Largest example 5¾ inches high. c. 1815–20. *Messrs. Godden of Worthing.*

83. A rare and attractive impressed-marked 'Mason's Patent Ironstone China' covered sugar box from a tea service of the 1815–20 period. 5 inches high. *Messrs. Godden of Worthing.*

84. A rare complete Mason's Iron-stone supper service decorated with the blue-printed 'Blue Pheasants' pattern (see Plate 24). Such supper sets were included in the 1822 sale—'A supper service, centre and 4 quadrants and covers . . . .' (page 38). Printed crowned mark (page 46). Diameter of complete set, 22 inches. c. 1820—5. *Messrs. Mason's Ironstone China Ltd., Works Collection.*

85. A fine quality impressed-marked 'Mason's Patent Ironstone China' teapot, hand-painted with flowers. This shape, with the moulded wicker-like border, would accompany a sugar bowl of the form shown in Plate 83. $5\frac{1}{4}$ inches high. c. 1815–20. *Messrs. Godden of Worthing.*

86. A rare and early impressed-marked toilet vessel, an example of many utilitarian objects made in this durable Ironstone body and richly decorated with 'Japan' patterns. 8¾ inches long. c. 1815–20. *Messrs. Godden of Worthing.*

87. An early impressed-marked 'Mason's Patent Ironstone China' chamber, decorated with a standard 'Japan' pattern. 6 inches high. c. 1815–20. *Messrs. Godden of Worthing.*

88. A large impressed-marked 'Mason's Patent Ironstone China' 'Japan' pattern vase shown with a miniature ewer. Vase 15 inches high. c. 1815–25. *Messrs. Godden of Worthing.*

89. Three Mason's Ironstone vases of unusual early forms, decorated with standard 'Japan' patterns. $5\frac{1}{4}$ inches to $7\frac{1}{4}$ inches high. c. 1815–20. *Messrs. Godden of Worthing.*

90. A large Mason's Ironstone vase, richly gilt over a dark blue ground —perhaps the 'sideboard vase, dragon handles, sumptuously gilt' of the 1818 sale (page 40). $18\frac{3}{4}$ inches high. c. 1815–20. *Messrs. Godden of Worthing.*

91. A pair of simple square-shaped vases decorated with the popular rich mazarine blue ground, overpainted and gilt in a typical manner. $13\frac{1}{2}$ inches. c. 1815–20. *Messrs. Godden of Worthing.*

92. An unusual impressed-marked 'Mason's Patent Ironstone China' yellow ground, covered vase with hand-painted panel. 9½ inches high. c. 1815–20. *Messrs. Chichester Antiques.*

93. An unusual impressed-marked 'Mason's Patent Ironstone China' open vase. Orange ground, gilt handles and borders and hand-painted panel. 6 inches high. c. 1815–1820. *Author's Collection.*

94. A magnificent impressed-marked 'Mason's Patent Ironstone China' vase decorated with a matt olive ground richly gilt and relieved by a border of white moulded flowers. The hand-painted panel is almost certainly by Samuel Bourne (page 43). The 1822 sale included several vases which are comparable with this example (see page 44). 27 inches high. c. 1820–5. *Messrs. Sotheby & Co.*

95. A fine quality Mason's Ironstone blue ground vase, the motifs being relief-moulded and gilt. 21 inches high. c. 1820–5. *Messrs. Godden of Worthing.*

Colour Plate V.   A very finely moulded 'Mason's Patent Ironstone China' vase after an 'antique' model. This shows to advantage the rich dark underglaze blue ground colour found on so many early examples, and the richness of the gilding. This shape, with that shown in Plate 94, is representative of the most imposing articles made in the Ironstone body (excepting the fireplaces, Plates 54 to 58) and these shapes may be found decorated in different styles. 28 inches high. c. 1820–5. *Messrs. Godden of Worthing.*

Colour Plate VI.   An attractive and good quality 'Mason's Patent Iron-stone China' vase decorated in the Chinese style—an example shown at the 1851 Exhibition, bearing the impressed crown mark, printed (angular) crowned name mark (page 47) and 1851 Exhibition inscription. Charles Mason exhibited a large range of goods in 1851, including 'Jars with raised enamel Mandarin figures and sea-dragon handles' (page 19). $17\frac{1}{2}$ inches high. *Messrs. Godden of Worthing.*

96. Two large 'Mason's Patent Iron-stone China' hall or alcove vases decorated in the Chinese style. 58 inches and 56½ inches high. c. 1840. *City Museum and Art Gallery, Stoke-on-Trent.*

97. An unusual and attractive Mason's Iron-stone vase decorated with a Chinese-style underglaze blue dragon design. Printed crown mark. 9¾ inches high. c. 1840. *Victoria and Albert Museum (Crown Copyright).*

98. A 'Mason's Patent Ironstone China' vase and cover (one of a pair) of a form popular in the 1830s and 1840s. Printed crowned mark. 15 inches high. c. 1840. *Messrs. Godden of Worthing.*

99. A set of three 'Mason's Patent Ironstone China' vases decorated with 'Japan' motifs on a green ground. Printed crowned mark. 8½ inches and 7 inches high. c. 1840. *Messrs. Godden of Worthing.*

100. A very fine quality impressed-marked 'Mason's Patent Ironstone China' wine or fruit cooler. Perhaps similar to the 'pair of wine coolers, gilt mask heads and ornaments' of the 1822 sale catalogue. c. 1820. *Messrs. Mason's Ironstone China Ltd.*

101. An Ashworth Ironstone bowl showing the re-use of a Mason's design (Plates 44 and 45). Printed Mason's crowned name mark, with post-1891 addition of the word 'England' (page 53). Diameter 10 inches. c. 1900. *Messrs. Godden of Worthing.*

102. Two blue-printed scenic plates, impressed-marked 'ASHWORTH'S REAL IRONSTONE', with potting date marks for April 1904 (page 53). The views are of 'Osborne House' and 'Balmoral Castle'.

Colour Plate VII. Representative parts of a colourful Ashworth Iron-stone dinner service, bearing both impressed and printed Ashworth 'Real Ironstone China' marks, with potting date marks '9.92' for September 1892. Pattern number 3623. Tureen 11½ inches high. *Messrs. Godden of Worthing.*

103. Two Ashworth plates from mid-Victorian dessert services. Colour-printed scenic plate has Royal Arms mark with initials 'G.L.A. & Bros'. The hand-painted floral plate has an impressed Ashworth name-mark. c. 1862–70. *Author's Collection.*

104. A selection of modern Ashworth Ironstone ware showing the earlier 'Japan' design adapted to modern shapes—ashtrays, cigarette holder, sandwich-tray, etc. Printed mark of the 1960s. *Messrs. Mason's Ironstone China Ltd.*

105. An impressed-marked 'Brameld' (Rockingham) stone china plate decorated with an underglaze blue print 'Parroquet'. Printed mark 'Parroquet. Fine Stone. B.' Diameter 8½ inches. c. 1830. *Author's Collection.*

107. A 'Davenport Stone China' jug, 'Japan' pattern—a very close copy of a standard Mason's shape (see Plates 66, 69 and 71). Printed mark—the first shown under 'Davenport' on page 65. 5¾ inches high. c. 1820. *Messrs. Godden of Worthing.*

106 (opposite). A superb quality underglaze blue print of York Cathedral, bearing the impressed 'CAREYS' name mark and a printed shield-shaped mark incorporating the name of the view and the wording: 'CAREY'S SAXON STONE CHINA'. 14½ inches by 12¾ inches. c. 1825–35. *Messrs. Godden of Worthing.*

108. A blue-printed 'Davenport Ironstone' plate. Impressed anchor and name mark with potting numerals for 1844; also oval printed mark with name of the pattern 'FRIBURG' (page 65). Diameter 10½ inches. *Author's Collection.*

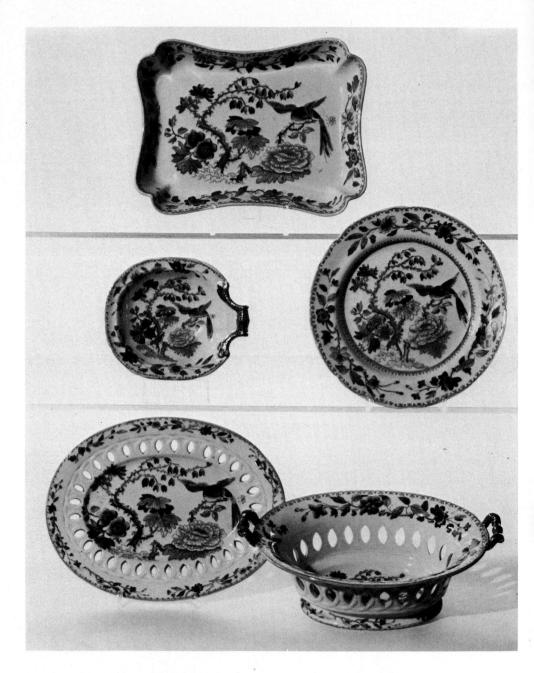

109.   Representative parts of a 'Davenport Stone China' dessert service
decorated with a standard design which was also made by other firms
(Plate 115). Printed 'Stone China' marks (page 65). Basket 10½ inches
long. c. 1810–20. *Messrs. Godden of Worthing.*

110. A finely moulded Hicks & Meigh 'Stone China' tureen from a dinner service. Printed Royal Arms mark (page 72). 13½ inches high. c. 1810–20. *Messrs. Godden of Worthing.*

111. A fine quality and colourful oval Hicks & Meigh Ironstone dinner service tureen. Printed Royal Arms mark (page 72). 12 inches high. c. 1815–22. *Messrs. Godden of Worthing.*

112. A finely moulded Hicks & Meigh 'Stone China' tureen, 'Japan' pattern, from a dinner service. Printed Royal Arms mark (page 72). 12 inches high. c. 1815–22. *Messrs. Godden of Worthing.*

113. A well-moulded Hicks & Meigh 'Stone China' tureen, cover and stand from a lengthy dinner service. Printed Royal Arms mark (page 72). 11 inches high. c. 1815–22. *Messrs. Godden of Worthing.*

114. A Hicks, Meigh & Johnson type Ironstone China tureen 'Japan' pattern. Printed mark 'Ironstone China Warranted'. $6\frac{1}{2}$ inches high. c. 1825. *Messrs. Godden of Worthing.*

115. Representative parts of a Hicks, Meigh & Johnson type 'Stone China' dinner service of a popular pattern made by several firms (Plate 109). Printed octagonal 'Stone China' mark (page 72). Tureen $10\frac{1}{2}$ inches high. c. 1825–35. *Messrs. Christie, Manson & Woods.*

116. Representative parts of a colourful Hicks, Meigh & Johnson 'Stone China' dessert service. Printed Royal Arms mark as shown in Plate 117, opposite. Oval comport 13 inches long. c. 1820–30. *Messrs. Godden of Worthing.*

117.   Representative parts of a fine quality and colourful Hicks, Meigh &
Johnson dessert set. The sugar tureen (*top left*) is a scaled-down version
of the dinner service soup tureen shown in Plate 112. Printed Royal Arms
'Stone China' mark is shown on the reversed plate. Diameter of plate 9
inches. c. 1825–35. *Messrs. Godden of Worthing.*

118. A Johnson 'Stone China' jug, of a typical type, shown with the printed mark. 4¾ inches high. c. 1825–35. *Messrs. Godden of Worthing.*

119. A Read & Clementson 'Stone ware' plate of good quality decorated with a coloured-over print. Printed mark as reproduced on page 84. Diameter 10½ inches. 1833–5. *Messrs. Godden of Worthing.*

120. A good quality 'stone china' dinner service soup plate by John & William Ridgway. Printed shield-shaped mark (page 88). Diameter 10 inches. c. 1814–20. *Messrs. Godden of Worthing.*

121. A John & William Ridgway 'Fancy Stone China' dish from a dessert service. Printed mark with initials 'J.W.R.' Pattern number 1226. 11¾ inches by 9 inches. c. 1815–25. *Messrs. Godden of Worthing.*

122.   A John Ridgway tureen and cover, the stand reversed to show
the Royal Arms mark with wording 'Imperial Stone China' above.
Tureen 13 inches high. c. 1830–40. *Messrs. Godden of Worthing.*

123.   A John & William Ridgway 'Fancy Stone China' tureen, cover and
stand, the small tureen turned to show the printed mark. Tureen 11 inches
high. c. 1820–30. *Messrs. Godden of Worthing.*

124. Underside of William Ridgway plate (Plate 125) showing the printed Royal Arms mark; and above, the impressed mark with the wording within the shield 'OPAQUE GRANITE CHINA. W.R. & Co'. c. 1834–54. *Messrs. Godden of Worthing.*

125. A 'Japan' pattern William Ridgway & Co. 'Opaque Granite China' plate. The impressed and printed marks are shown in Plate 124, above. Diameter $10\frac{1}{2}$ inches. c. 1834–54. *Messrs. Godden of Worthing.*

126.   A superb 'Spode Stone China' covered vase, 'Japan' pattern, having the appearance of fine, translucent porcelain. Printed 'Spode. Stone China' mark (page 93) with pattern number 2247. 24 inches high. c. 1820. *Messrs. Christie, Manson & Woods.*

127. A 'Spode Stone China' tureen, from a lengthy dinner service, decorated with a standard Spode design—number 2054. Printed mark (page 93). $7\frac{3}{4}$ inches high. c. 1820. *Messrs. Godden of Worthing.*

128. A rare form of Spode China dinner service tureen bearing the same pattern as that shown in Plate 127. Printed mark (page 93). $11\frac{1}{2}$ inches high. c. 1825. *Messrs. Christie, Manson & Woods.*

129.   Representative pieces from a 'Spode New Stone' dinner service of
an unusual pattern—number 3435. Large meat platter 19 inches by 13¾
inches. c. 1825. *Messrs. Godden of Worthing.*

Colour Plate VIII. Representative pieces from a 'Spode Stone China' dessert service, showing typical forms of the 1815–20 period—although the fruit coolers (*centre*) are only found in some of the finest sets, and the handled dish (*left, centre row*) is rare. This popular pattern, number 2118, copied from Chinese export market porcelain, is found in Spode porcelain and earthenware as well as in the Stone China body. Printed mark (page 93). Fruit cooler $12\frac{1}{4}$ inches high. *Messrs. Godden of Worthing.*

130. An impressed-marked 'Spode New Stone' three-piece vegetable dish, the bottom section of which held hot water to keep the contents above hot. 12 inches long. c. 1820. *Messrs. Godden of Worthing.*

131. An impressed-marked 'Spode New Stone' tureen, cover and stand from a large dinner service decorated with a 'Japan' pattern. Tureen $14\frac{1}{4}$ inches high. c. 1820. *Messrs. Godden of Worthing.*

132. A rare Stevenson & Williams 'Royal Stone China' tureen bearing a printed Royal Arms mark and the initials 'R.S. & W'. 12½ inches high. c. 1825. *Messrs. Godden of Worthing.*

133. An unusual Stevenson & Williams 'Royal Stone China' plate bearing a printed Royal Arms mark. Diameter 9½ inches. c. 1825. *Messrs. Godden of Worthing.*

134. An impressed-marked 'TURNER' stone-china-type plate decorated in the Chinese style. Diameter 9 inches. c. 1805. *Author's Collection.*

136. A matching mug to the presentation 'TURNER'S PATENT' jug shown in Plate 135. *City Museum & Art Gallery, Stoke-on-Trent.*

135. A superbly decorated 'TURNER'S PATENT' presentation jug decorated with rich, dark blue ground and finely gilt. Painted mark (page 97). $8\frac{1}{2}$ inches high. c. 1800–5. *City Museum and Art Gallery, Stoke-on-Trent.*

137. Representative pieces of a 'TURNER'S PATENT' dessert service, of the 1800–5 period, decorated with a standard Turner pattern and showing typical shapes employed by the Turners. Painted mark (page 97). Oval fruit comport 13¾ inches long. c. 1800–5. *Messrs. Godden of Worthing.*

138. A blue-printed 'Wedgwood & Co' plate bearing the very popular 'Asiatic Pheasants' pattern, one produced by many firms. Printed crest and name marks (page 98). Diameter 9 inches. c. 1860–70. *Author's Collection.*

139. Representative parts of a 'Wedgwood's Stone China' dessert service. Printed mark, with pattern number 1156. Oval fruit comport $11\frac{1}{2}$ inches long. c. 1827–35. *Messrs. Godden of Worthing.*

140. A 'Japan' pattern dish from a dessert service bearing the un-
identified printed 'TONQUIN CHINA' mark (page 103). $11\frac{1}{2}$ inches by 8
inches. c. 1820. *Messrs. Godden of Worthing.*

141. A blue-printed Ironstone platter from a dinner service made at the
Ynysmedw pottery in Wales. The printed mark shown includes the name
of the proprietor, 'Williams', the name of the pattern, 'Rio', and the body,
'Ironstone'. $11\frac{1}{4}$ inches long. 1854–60. *D. Harper, Esq.*

Catalogues of Mason's Stock Sold in
1818 and 1822

A
CATALOGUE
OF
A MOST VALUABLE AND EXTENSIVE STOCK
OF
ELEGANT AND USEFUL
CHINA
SUITED FOR DOMESTIC PURPOSES
OF ENGLISH MANUFACTURE

Recently consigned from the Manufactory for actual sale, and highly deserving the attention of Persons of Fashion and Private Families.

* It comprises

a large assortment of complete table and Dessert services, composed of strong and serviceable material, painted in imitation of the rich Japan and other Oriental Patterns; Breakfast, tea and coffee equipages, ornamental Dejeunes and Vases for flowers and essence, including about Twelve of noble size, suited to fill niches or Recesses in Drawing Rooms, superbly ornamented.

Which will be sold by Auction
BY MR. CHRISTIE
at his Great Room, Pall Mall,
on Tuesday, December 15th, 1818
and two following Days, at one o'clock

N.B. Few lots would appear to have been sold. Prices have been inserted against those few lots and these originate from the auctioneer's master, priced, catalogue. The original spelling has been retained where the meaning is clear.

FIRST DAY'S SALE
TUESDAY, DECEMBER 15th, 1818,
PUNCTUALLY AT ONE O'CLOCK

1   Two taper candlesticks, coloured and gilt, and 2 cabinet pitchers.
2   One toy ewer, bason, jug, and mug, and 2 tall taper candlesticks, roses and gilt
3   Two toy cups and saucers, japanned and gilt
4   Two Dresden pattern jars, 2 square essence burners; and 2 toy jars
5   One table service, India pheasant pattern, viz. 18 dishes in sizes, 2 soup tureens, covers and stands, 4 sauce ditto, 4 square vegetable dishes, 1 sallad ditto, 1 fish ditto, 72 table plates, 24 ditto soup and 24 pye ditto
6   Two square Chinese jars and covers. £1. 3. 0.
7   One coffee pot, antique pattern and shape
8   Two hexagonal antique beakers
9   Two handsome tulip cups and saucers, and 2 match pots
10 Two tall jars and covers, richly ornamented and gilt
11 Two elegant mitre shaped jars and covers, sumptuously gilt
12 One desert service, Mogul pattern, viz. 1 centre piece, 12 fruit dishes, 2 cream tureens and stands, and 24 plates. £5. 18. 0.
13 One breakfast tea and coffee service, corn flower sprig and gold lines, viz. 12 bowls and saucers, 12 tea cups and saucers, 15 coffee cans, 12 breakfast plates, 1 tea pot and stand, 1 salt box, 1 cream ewer, 1 pint bason, 2 bread and butter plates, and 2 butter tubs and stands
14 One toy ewer, bason, jug and mug for a cabinet
15 Two chimneypiece jars. 16/-
16 One table service, exact quantity as Lot 5, Chinese landscape pattern
17 Two cabinet cups and saucers, a toy ewer, bason, jug and mug
18 One Dejeune service, antique forms and ornamented. £3. 8. 0.
19 One desert service, old Japan pattern, blue, red, and gold, exact quantity as Lot 12
20 Two costly beakers, a la Chinoise
21 Two jars and covers, Chinese forms, richly enamelled and gilt
22 One table service, exact quantity as Lot 5, blue and gold border
23 One handsome sideboard jar, dragon handles and sumptuously gilt
24 Two rose and apple jars and covers, octagonal bronze and gold
25 Two square caddies
26 Two ornamental groups of flowers and gold
27 One antique coffee pot
28 Two tulips and stands, cabinet, and two square scent boxes. £1. 4. 0.
29 One table set, exact quantity as Lot 5, table and flower pot pattern
30 Two costly jars, a la Chinoise, beautifully pencilled, and gilt
31 One desert service, exact quantity as Lot 12, gold rose japanned and gilt, antique forms
32 One breakfast tea and coffee service, exactly as Lot 13 (only in lieu of butter tubs, 2 covered muffin plates) sprig and gilt
33 Two tea caddies, groups of flowers and gold lace border
34 One table service, exact quantity and pattern as Lot 5
35 One costly octagonal jar
36 Two taper candlesticks, toy ewer, bason, jug and mug, 2 lavender bottles, 2 flower beakers, and 1 cabinet teapot. £2. 12. 6.
37 Two dragon octagonal beakers
38 One desert service, plain Japan, exact quantity as Lot 12. £12. 12. 0.
39 One Italian formed jar, or vase, biscuit of elegant workmanship
40 One table service, exact quantity as Lot 5, old Japan pattern, in green, pink, mazarine, red, and richly gilt

41 One breakfast tea and coffee set, exact quantity as Lot 13, French ground, Dresden sprigs, and gold
42 One Trentham bowl
43 One splendid dragon jar, a la Chinoise
44 Two costly beakers
45 One watering can and 2 flat formed bottles. £1. 2. 0.
46 Two Chinese jars. £1. 3. 0.
47 One desert service, gold rose, exact quantity as Lot 12
48 One table service, blue and gold
49 One octagonal rose and apple jar
50 One breakfast tea and coffee set, white and gold, embossed and coloured sprigs, exact quantity as Lot 32
51 One table service, exact quantity and pattern as Lot 5
52 Two cabinet jugs and mugs and 2 flower beakers
53 One foot pail. £1. 1. 0.
54 Ditto and slop jar. £2. 2. 0.
55 One table service, exact quantity as Lot 5, basket Japan
56 Two bell jars, lion's heads
57 Two 3-handled fluted vases
58 Two hexagonal tea caddies. £2. 10. 0.
59 Ditto. £1. 10. 0.
60 Two low fluted jars
61 One fine octagon vase, a la Chinoise
62 One Table service, exact quantity as Lot 5, India gold jar pattern
63 One desert ditto, same as Lot 17
64 Two card candlesticks, 2 tall ditto, Dresden pattern, and 2 baskets
65 Two tall hexagonal embossed jars and covers
66 Two small griffin octagonal jars
67 Two cabinet jugs and mugs
68 One table service, richly japanned in red, blue, green, and gold, exact quantity as Lot 5
69 One desert service, ditto, exact quantity as Lot 12
70 Two low bat-head ornaments. 18/-.
71 Two hexagonal beakers
72 Two lavender bottles, 2 low bat-head ornaments, 2 beakers, and 2 cabinet coffee biggins. £2. 5. 0.
73 Two antique jars and covers.
74 One table service, exact quantity and pattern as Lot 5
75 Two sugar caddies
76 One desert service, gold thorn, exact quantity as Lot 17
77 One breakfast tea and coffee set, ditto, vine embossed, exact quantity as Lot 18
78 Two pot pourri jars. £1. 1. 0.
79 One ornamental landscape. £1. 1. 0.
80 Two small antique bottles
81 One table service, landscape, Japan, slightly gilt, exact quantity as Lot 5
82 Two lavender bottles, 2 ranunculus pots, and 2 card candlesticks
83 Two round jars, of rich pattern
84 Two caddies
85 Two toy churns, 2 Dresden pattern jars, and 2 toy cups and saucers
86 Two tripods, 2 coffee biggins
87 One table set, exact quantity and pattern as Lot 5
88 Two flower vessels, colour and gold. 10/-.
89 Two tall Roman shaped jars. £1. 0. 0.
90 Two toy churns, lavender bottles, 2 candlesticks

End of the First Day's Sale

SECOND DAY'S SALE
WEDNESDAY, DECEMBER 16th, 1818
at one o'clock precisely

91 One cabinet ewer, bason, jug and mug, 2 ditto, coffee biggins
92 Two Chinese beakers
93 Two three-handled dragon jars, fluted, richly coloured and gilt
94 One desert service, Indian figure pattern, exact quantity as Lot 12. £4. 14. 6.
95 One table service, India pheasant, japan, slightly gilt, exact quantity as Lot 5
96 Two dolphin-head bowls, rich in colours and gold
97 Two pot pourries
98 Two cabinet teapots
99 Two tea caddies
100 Two rose-handled bell-shaped jars, bronze and gold
101 One table service, exact quantity as Lot 5, richly coloured figure pattern
102 Two three-handled jars
103 Two watering cans, 2 low bottles and stoppers. £1. 7. 0.
104 Two octagon jars. 14/-.
105 Two curiously formed vases, of antique shape, elegantly enamelled and gilt. £3. 7. 0.
106 One desert service, landscape Japan as Lot 12
107 Two small antique bottles, 2 toy cups and saucers
108 One table service, blue pheasants with gold border, exact quantity as Lot 5
109 One elegant sideboard jar, damaged
110 Two ink stands, 2 tulip cups and stands
111 Two Dresden cans and stands, 2 ditto cups, etc.
112 One table service, blue Chinese landscapes, exact quantity as Lot 5
113 Two large beer jugs. 9/6.
114 Two small Dresden pattern cups
115 Two garden flower pots and stands
116 Two small octagon jars, 4 card candlesticks, 2 ink stands
117 Two elegant beakers and covers, a la Chinoise
118 Two antique coffee pots
119 Two Trentham bowls, highly finished
120 Two 3-handled Dragon vases. £3. 8. 0.
121 One table set, richly finished in colour and gold, exact quantity as Lot 12
122 One desert set, rock and rose japan and gilt, exact quantity as Lot 12
123 One costly jar
124 Two bell shaped jars
125 Two lavender bottles and 1 cabinet ewer, bason, jug and mug
126 Two watering cans
127 Two tall covered jars
128 Two low open jars
129 A table service, mandarin pattern in colours and gold, exact quantity as Lot 5. £15. 15. 0.
130 Two beer jugs
131 One desert service, pheasants, in colours and gold, exact quantity as Lot 12
132 One table service, red mazarine, and richly gilt, exact quantity as Lot 5
133 Two Dresden pattern tulips and stands, 2 ditto, cans and stands, and 2 flat formed bottles. £1. 4. 0.
134 Two large bottle-shaped perfume jars. £6. 6. 0.
135 One table service, pattern and quantity as Lot 5
136 Two small hexagonal bottles. 9/-.
137 Two beer jugs
138 Two tall octagonal embossed Chinese covered jars

139 Two low fluted open jars, a la Chinoise
140 Two low jars and covers. 9/–.
141 Two small octagonal jars and covers, red, blue and gold
142 Two Lizard-handled vases. 18/–.
143 One table service, of costly manufacture, in colours, mazarine and gold, exact quantity as Lot 5
144 Two fine large bottles, ornamented, a la Chinoise
145 One breakfast, tea, and coffee set, Parisian sprigs and gold lines, exact quantity as Lot 13
146 One desert service, gold rose pattern, quantity as Lot 12
147 Two essence burners, 2 lavender bottles, and 4 paint cups
148 Two open jars
149 Two singularly formed jars, a la Chinoise
150 Two low Dolphin vases
151 One table set, old India Japan pattern, exact quantity as Lot 5
152 One ditto, exact quantity and pattern as Lot 35
153 Ditto, blue, red, and gold, ditto
154 One antique formed coffee pot
155 Two beakers
156 Two tall hexagonal beakers
157 Two curiously formed beakers, a la Chinoise
158 Two small round jars and covers. 10/–.
159 Two ditto octagon jars and covers
160 One table set, quantity and pattern as Lot 5
161 Ditto, rich Japan pattern, in colours and gold, as Lot 9
162 One breakfast tea and coffee set, french sprigs, and gold lines, exact quantity as Lot 18
163 One Dejeune set, red and gold
164 Two small round jars and covers, and 2 cabinet cups and saucers
165 Two porter mugs
166 Two sugar caddies
167 One ewer and bason, and 2 cabinet cups and saucers
168 One table service, India grass-hopper pattern, in colours, and slightly gilt, exact quantity as Lot 5
169 One desert service, Japan, red purple and gold, exact quantity as Lot 12
170 One breakfast tea and coffee set, sun flower and gold, exact quantity as Lot 13
171 One drawing room lions head perfume jar, and 4 toy Dresden pattern cups and saucers. 12/–.
172 Two jars, and cups
173 One table service, pattern and quantity as Lot 35
174 One ditto
175 Two jars, colours and gold
176 Two jardiniers and stands. 13/–.
177 Two antique formed coffee pots
178 Two watering cans, rich pattern, 2 small round jars and covers
179 Two rich lizard-handled jars. 18/–.
180 Two Etruscan jars
181 Four chamber candlesticks
182 Two square scent boxes, 2 toy churns
183 Two perforated jars
184 Two lizard jars. 10/6.
185 One desert service, India gold vase pattern, as Lot 12
186 Four jugs for beer. 17/–.
187 One fine perfume jar, a la Chinoise
188 One ditto

End of Second Day's Sale

THIRD DAY'S SALE,
THURSDAY, DECEMBER 17th, 1818,
at one o'clock precisely

189 Two match pots, 2 Lizard handled vases, 2 ink stands
190 Two rich beakers, 2 toy pitcher jars, 2 handled embossed essence burners
191 One table set, quantity and pattern as Lot 5
192 Two handsome ornaments, a la Chinoise
193 Two rich tea caddies
194 Desert service, India flower basket Japan exact quantity as Lot 12
195 Breakfast tea and coffee set, coloured sprigs, gold lines, exact quantity as Lot 13
196 Two Ornaments and covers
197 Two Bottles
198 A table service, of rich Mogul pattern in colours and gold border, exact quantity as Lot 5
199 One desert service, gold rose Japan in colours and gold, exact quantity as Lot 12
200 One costly Hall jar, elegant Chinese designs
201 One ditto
202 One table service, pattern and quantity as Lot 5
203 Two caddies, flowers and gold
204 Two pot pourris, small
205 Two Lizard-handled jars
206 One table service, Pagoda pattern in mazarine red and gold, as Lot 5
207 Two fluted open jars
208 Two coffee biggins, toy size
209 Three handsome octagonal jars
210 Two small octagonal dragon-handled bottles
211 Two beakers, handsome patterns
212 One desert service, India grasshopper pattern
213 One breakfast tea and coffee service, quantity as lot 18, sprigs, gold lines
214 Two vase-shaped ink stands
215 Two elegant Trentham bowls
216 One table service, rose and rock pattern, a la Chinoise, richly gilt, quantity as Lot 5
217 Two caddies, mazarine colours and gold
218 Two flower horns
219 Four wafer cups
220 Two square essence boxes
221 Two toy churns
222 One elegant toilet ewer and bason, antique forms and pattern
223 One ditto
224 One table service, old Japan pattern, red purple and gold, quantity as Lot 5
225 One very large dolphin-headed bowl, richly embellished in colours and gold, damaged
226 Two watering cans, colours and gold
227 Two toy pitchers
228 One sideboard jar, dragon handles, sumptuously gilt
229 One desert set, Chinese thorn pattern, in colours and gold
230 Two rose and apple handled octagonal perfume jars
231 Two dolphin-headed bowls
232 One table service, India water-melon Japan, and richly gilt, quantity as Lot 5
233 Two beakers and covers, rich, in Mazarine, enamel and gold
234 Two handled open top fluted jars

235 Two lizard-handled vases
236 Two flat bottles
237 One breakfast tea and coffee set, French sprigs and gold border, quantity as Lot 13
238 One table service, Mogul pattern, enamelled and gilt, quantity as Lot 5
239 Two caddies
240 One table service, blue India pheasant (pattern and quantity as Lot 5)
241 Two antique pattern coffee pots
242 Two cabinet ink stands
243 One table set, gold jar pattern, gold border, quantity as Lot 5
244 Four card candlesticks
245 Two handsome vase inkstands
246 Two cabinet tea kettles
247 Two cabinet coffee biggins
248 Two flower horns
249 One table set, India figure pattern, as Lot 5
250 One breakfast tea and coffee set, grasshopper pattern, 85 pieces
251 Two open perfume bowls
252 Two Etruscan jars for pastiles
253 One desert set, flower basket pattern
254 One table service, richly finished in mazarine, green and gold; quantity as Lot 5
255 Two strawberry jars and covers
256 One fine hexagonal hall jar and cover, enamelled in compartments, and sumptuously gilt
257 Two Pan's head ornaments, landscapes in compartments of Mazarine, and splendidly gilt
258 Two cabinet tea pots
259 One desert service, Chinese subject, in compartments of Mazarine and gold
260 Two scollopt scent jars
261 Two three handled fluted jars
262 Two water bottles
263 Two toy churns
264 Two watering pots
265 Two elegant dragon head octagonal jars
266 Two octagonal embossed jars and covers
267 One table set, India pheasant pattern in colours
268 Two round jars and covers
269 Two ditto, ditto
270 Two Chinese beakers, richly ornamented
271 Two oak-leaf low vases and covers
272 One richly executed jar, Chinese subjects, on Mazarine ground
273 One ditto
274 Four toy cream stands
275 Two cabinet pitchers
276 Two ditto, ditto
277 Two griffin-handled vases
278 Two embossed jars and covers
279 Two ditto, ditto
280 Two ditto, ditto
281 Two octagonal rose and apple jars for perfume
282 Two curious antique formed jars, handsomely gilt, etc.
283 Two octagonal jars and Covers
284 One ditto embossed jar and cover
285 One ditto, ditto, ditto

286 Two beakers hexagonal
287 Two lizard-handle vases
288 Two flat bottles
289 Two Etruscan jars
290 Two small dragon jars
291 Two chinese-shaped jars
292 Four card candlesticks
293 Two toy jars and covers
294 Two ditto, ditto, ditto
295 Four ranunculus pots and covers
296 Two antique formed coffee pots
297 Two toy tea kettles
298 One table set, ditto, japan pattern, red purple, and gilt

FINIS

THE VALUABLE & EXTENSIVE
STOCK OF CHINA
OF THE LATE
MR. MASON,
PATENTEE AND MANUFACTURE OF THE
IRON STONE CHINA,
AT NO. 11, ALBEMARLE STREET.

A
CATALOGUE
OF THE
ENTIRE ASSEMBLAGE OF USEFUL & DECORATIVE
PORCELANE,
OF RICH AND ELEGNT PATTERNS;
comprising
SEVERAL HUNDRED
DINNER, DESSERT, BREAKFAST AND TEA SERVICES;
JUGS, EWERS, BASINS,
DISHES IN SETS, BOTH OPEN AND COVERED;
PLATES IN DOZENS, OF EVERY SIZE:
NOBLE ORNAMENTAL JARS & EWERS,
superbly gilt and beautifully enamelled;
AND
A GREAT VARIETY OF CABINET ORNAMENTS,
OF THE MOST TASTEFUL AND ELEGANT FORMS.
WHICH WILL BE SOLD BY AUCTION

BY MR. PHILLIPS,

ON THE PREMISES
AT NO. 11, ALBEMARLE STREET,
ON FRIDAY, the 14th day of JUNE, 1822,
And following Day, at Twelve for ONE precisely,
BY ORDER OF THE EXECUTORS,
WITHOUT RESERVE.

May be viewed Four Days preceding the Sale, and Catalogues had on the Premises; at the Auction Mart, and at Mr. Phillips, 73, New Bond Street.

NOTICE

This Sale will commence every Day PRECISELY at ONE, on account of the number of Lots in each Day.

FIRST DAY'S SALE,
TUESDAY, the 4th Day of JUNE, 1822,
commencing at One o'clock precisely

The Description of the various Pieces composing the Dinner, Dessert and Tea Services, will be found on the largest or principal Piece in each Service.

Lot		Reserve
1	Twenty-four jars and covers	12/–
2	Two blue and white pheasant toilet suites, 16 pieces	10/–
3	Six ditto jugs, and a toilet suite, dragon pattern	10/–
4	Eight jugs and 9 jars and covers	12/–
5	A tea and breakfast set, 56 pieces	16/–
6	Four antique shape jugs	14/–
7	A tea service, 43 pieces	20/–
8	Two match boxes and 3 paper cases, mazarine ground	30/–
9	A dejune, gold edge, japan	42/–
10	Two broth basins, covers and stands and 2 porus wine coolers	24/–
11	Five jugs from the antique and 5 kitchen jugs	16/–
12	A dessert service, 43 pieces	60/–
13	Two card racks and 2 violet baskets	30/–
14	A dinner service, dragon pattern, 142 pieces, as per label on tureen	9 gns.
15	A pair of wine coolers, gilt mask heads and ornaments	42/–
16	Glass	—
17	A pair of jars, Chinese landscape and figures	25/–
18	A pair of essence jars, gilt and painted in birds and flowers, faulty	30/–
19	Glass	—
20	A breakfast service, neat sprig, 100 pieces	90/–
21	Two large jugs, gold plaid and flowers	30/–
22	Eleven meat, 12 soup and 5 pie plates	42/–
23	A Stilton cheese stand and cover, and 3 trays	20/–
24	A pair of hexagon vases, gilt Chinese building, figures, flowers and moths	55/–
25	A pair of ice pails, covers and liners, gilt and painted in flowers	60/–
26	Six basins, covers and stands, painted in flowers	42/–
27	A DINNER SERVICE, in boquet, 142 pieces, as per description on tureen	12 gns.
28	A wine cooler, gilt and japanned flowers	30/–
29	A breakfast service, dragon pattern, 69 pieces	90/–
30	Two ink stands, green ground and flowers, gilt	24/–
31	Six jugs, formed from the antique	16/–
32	Four basins, covers and stands, gilt edge	20/–
33	A ewer and basin, Indian sprig, gilt edge	20/–
34	Glass	—
35	A pair of jars and covers, japanned flower and gilt ram's heads and edges	70/–
36	A supper service, centre and 4 quadrants and covers, japanned flower, gilt	80/–
37	Six jugs, pheasant and flowers from the antique	14/–
38	A ditto toilet suite, 8 pieces, and a tea set painted in flowers	30/–
39	A dessert service, gilt and painted in flowers, centre, 12 compotiers and 24 plates	150/–
40	A large chamber jar and cover, blue landscape and a foot pan	30/–

Lot		Reserve
41	A pair shaped jars and covers, japanned and gilt flower	100/-
42	Three jugs from the antique, fancy pattern	30/-
43	Glass	—
44	A pair of hand candlesticks with extinguishers and glass shades	42/-
45	A pair of biscuit vases, with bandeau of flowers and glass shades	35/-
46	A suite of three ditto with shades	45/-
47	A DINNER SERVICE, gilt and ornamented with flowers, 142 pieces, as described	30 gns.
48	A handsome tea set, 44 pieces	9 gns.
	'Very high indeed' [auctioneer's comment written in catalogue]	
49	A toilet suit in flowers, 8 pieces and a glass caraft and tumbler, fluted	55/-
50	A small ewer, basin and pair of candlesticks with glass shades	30/-
51	A DINNER SERVICE, rich japan pattern; sumptuously gilt, 142 pieces	£35.
52	A pair of Grecian form essence bowls, with handles, sumptuously gilt	£6.
53	A pair of blue essence bottles, 2 inkstands, wafer cup and cover and 4 glass shades	35/-
54	A pair of handsome urns on pedestals, richly gilt and glass shades	40/-
55	A NOBLE LOFTY JAR with cover, surmounted with griffins and blue ground, beautifully enamelled in birds and flowers	9 gns.
56	An essence cup and cover, pair of square bottles and a breakfast and tea set, blue border	65/-
57	A chamber slop pail and cover, painted in flowers, gilt edges and ornaments	40/-
58	A porous wine cooler and 9 jugs, formed from the antique	16/-
59	Glass	—
60	A lofty ESSENCE JAR and cover dragon handles, and top painted in flowers	63/-
61	Glass	
62	A dessert service, blue and gold flower border	190/-
63	A chamber suite of 9 pieces, caraft and tumbler	50/-
64	A DINNER SERVICE, peacock and flowers, 142 pieces	£14.
65	A suite of 4 jugs in flowers	30/-
66	A tea set, white and gold, 45 pieces	20/-
67	Glass	—
68	A dessert service, blue birds and flowers, 43 pieces	130/-
69	A DINNER SERVICE, hexagon shape, blue birds and flowers, 142 pieces	11 gns.
70	A pair of shaped jars and covers, gilt and painted flowers	40/-
71	A pair of flower urns, richly gilt and painted and 2 glass shades	35/-
72	A pair of handsome essence jars and covers, large hexagonal, gold plaid	30/-
73	A pair of blue sprinklers, gilt handles, embossed figures and glass shades	40/-
74	A DINNER SERVICE, rich old japan pattern, contining 142 pieces, as described	25 gns.
75	A ditto DESSERT SERVICE, 43 pieces	6 gns.
76	A pair of jars with dragon handles	35
77	Glass	—
78	Glass	—
79	Glass	—

Lot		Reserve
80	A pair of match cases, Dresden flower and glass shades	20/-
81	A center piece, fruit basket, radish tray, 2 sallad bowls, mustard, pepper, argyle and egg beater	26/-
82	Two chamber services, 16 pieces	32/-
83	A DINNER SERVICE, Dresden sprig, 142 pieces, as described	25 gns.
84	A ewer and basin, enamelled moths and flowers, and 8 jugs, blue bird and flower	30/-
85	A set of five Grecian shape urns, painted in birds and flowers, sumptuously gilt and 5 shades	130/-
86	Glass	—
87	Twenty-two meat, soup and dessert plates, Dresden flower and gold edge	40/-
88	A DINNER SERVICE, blue bird and flower, containing 142 pieces, as described	190/-
89	A dessert service, blue sprig, 43 pieces, ditto	5 gns.
90	Four jugs from the antique, enamelled border and flowers	10/-
91	Glass	—
92	A dejeune, festoon flowers and sprig	15/-
93	Two pink jars and covers	20/-
94	A DINNER SERVICE, blue birds and flowers, contents, 142 pieces, as described	190/-
95	Glass	—
96	A tea set, same pattern, 45 pieces	7 gns.
97	A pair of broth basins, covers and stands, japanned blue compartments	30/-
98	A pair of hexagon FLOWER POTS and stands, mazarine ground and gold edge	5 gns.
99	Two jugs from antique designs	16/-
100	A breakfast service, painted sprig, 30 pieces and 12 plates, melange	40/-
101	A ragout dish, cover and liner, a steak ditto, an ice butter tub, butter tub, and a pickle stand	50/-
102	A supper service, richly gilt, 10 pieces	70/-
103	Two ice pails, covers and liners, grasshopper and flowers, gilt edge	42/-
104	Glass	—
105	Twelve jugs and covers, blue birds, etc.	30/-
106	Glass	—
107	A chamber slop pail and cover, blue birds and flowers	16/-
108	Four antique form jugs, grasshopper pattern	11/-
109	Two fruit baskets, on feet	40/-
110	Three mugs, gold plaid, and shaving box, red rose, etc.	20/-
111	Five large jugs, embossed flower	15/-
112	Two japanned jars, dolphin handles	35/-
113	A DINNER SERVICE, dragon pattern, contents, 143 pieces, as described	9 gns.
114	A rich japan DESSERT SERVICE, 43 pieces	8 gns.
115	Glass	—
116	Glass	—
117	A DINNER SERVICE, hexagon shape, grasshopper pattern, 143 pieces, as described	15 ? gns.
118	Glass	—
119	Pair of rich jars and covers, sumptuously gilt	30/-
120	Twelve melange plates	18/-

Lot		Reserve
121	Twelve ditto, various rich patterns	18/-
122	A rich gilt and japan toilet service, 8 pieces	63/-
123	A DINNER SERVICE, Tourney sprig, 143 pieces, as described	11 gns.
124	Two ewers, gilt and japan flower, formed from the antique	20/-
125	A breakfast service, white and gold, 30 pieces	30/-
126	A broth basin, cover and stand and chamber slop pail and cover	24/-
127	A handsome essence jar, green ground and flowers and 2 match cases in landscapes	63/-
128	Two blue and white chamber sets, 16 pieces	35/-
129	Glass	—
130	A potatoe dish and cover, 5 potting pots and an eggstand with 6 cups	12/-

End of the First Day

SECOND DAY'S SALE,
WEDNESDAY, the 5th Day of JUNE, 1821,
commencing at One o'Clock precisely.

Lot		Reserve
131	Thirteen blue jugs, in sizes	30/-
132	Two blue chamber sets with carafts and tumblers	40/-
133	Twenty pieces sundry useful articles, white	30/-
134	Twelve white preserving jars and covers	32/-
135	A dejeune, Bourbon sprig	30/-
136	Glass	—
137	Glass	—
138	Two Stilton cheese stands and 2 fluted top wine coolers, willow	40/-
139	A dessert set, blue	63/-
140	Glass	—
141	Six coloured jugs and 12 mugs	27/-
142	Two ice pails, richly gilt (1 cover faulty)	37/-
143	A table set, willow	190/-
144	Glass	—
145	Glass	—
146	Three paper cases and 2 scent pots, mazarine	20/-
147	Three rich India pattern jugs	25/-
148	Two wine coolers, elegantly gilt	42/-
149	A breakfast service, 42 pieces	70/-
150	A breakfast and tea service, 93 pieces	50/-
151	Two chamber sets, japan, with caraft and tumbler	60/-
152	A table set, grasshopper, gold knobs	£16.
153	A ditto, flower pattern (not Ironstone)	£7.
154	Two porous wine coolers, 2 ditto butter tubs and 24 glass wines	36/-
155	Twenty one pieces of various articles, white	21/-
156	A dessert service, japan	105/-
157	Glass	—
158	Glass	—
159	Eight uncovered jugs and 5 covered ditto, blue	35/-
160	A supper set, rich japan, gold edge	38/-
161	Three jars, mazarine and gold chased figures, with shades	105/-
162	A breakfast set, Chinese sprigs, 77 pieces	60/-

Lot		Reserve
163	Two chamber sets, white, with carafts and tumblers	28/-
164	Two large flower pots and stands, mazarine	80/-
165	Glass	—
166	A set of lunch plates, tourney sprig, gold edge	30/-
167	A pair of ice pails, japan	60/-
168	A table service. Chinese Figures, gold edge, as described	£18.
169	A very richly gilt tea service	190/-
170	A white supper set	20/-
171	Glass	—
172	Six hunting jugs and 5 mugs	24/-
173	Three jugs, japan	20/-
174	Two antique coffee pots, with glass shades	35/-
175	One fine hexagonal hall jar	150/-
176	Six broth bowls, covers and stands	35/-
177	Twenty-four rich melange plates	50/-
178	Two antique jars	42/-
179	Glass	—
180	Two pastille burners, with glass shades	55/-
181	A breakfast set, coloured flowers, 61 pieces	75/-
182	A table service, japan, richly gilt	23 gns.
183	A blue supper set	25/-
184	Glass	—
185	Glass	—
186	Glass	—
187	Glass	—
188	Glass	—
189	A dessert service, white	36/-
190	One superb square very large hall jar, mazarine and Indian devices	17 gns.
191	A tea set, japan, 57 pieces	84/-
192	A chamber set, green border, enamelled, with caraft and tumbler	15/-
193	A Trentham plaid jar	35/-
194	Seven mugs, hunting, and 24 glass tumblers	25/-
195	Two toy ewers and basins, mazarine with shades	27/-
196	Two shell pen trays, 2 hand candlesticks and 2 glass shades	24/-
197	A dessert service, roses and gold edge, 41 pieces	6 gns.
198	Two porous wine coolers and 2 butter tubs	20/-
199	Glass	—
200	Glass	—
201	Glass	—
202	Forty-eight lunch plates	30/-
203	Two chamber sets, blue, with carafts and tumblers	40/-
204	A supper set, blue	30/-
205	A table service, blue	190/-
206	A dessert service, Dresden flowers, 37 pieces	7 gns.
207	Two ice pails, flowers in compartments, on blue border, richly gilt	4 gns.
208	Two elegant vases, with shades	40/-
209	Two flower pots and stands, japan, with shades	31/6
210	Three ragout dishes, pans and covers, white	60/-
211	A breakfast set, Indian dragon, gold edge, 94 pieces	110/-
212	A table service, white	6 gns.
213	Glass	—
214	Glass	—

Lot		Reserve
215	Glass	—
216	Eight jugs, blue, and 4 covered ditto	30/-
217	Six jugs, gold jar pattern	25/-
218	Twelve breakfast cups and saucers, white and gold	30/-
219	An elegant chamber service, with caraft and tumbler	60/-
220	Six very rich plates	52/-
221	Two elegant griffin jars, painted in fruit and flowers, sumptuously gilt	6 gns.
222	Glass	—
223	Glass	—
224	Forty-eight lunch plates, various	30/-
225	Two broth basins, covers and stands, japan, and 4 soup plates, rich melange	30/-
226	A table service, japan, gold edge	£25.
227	A dessert set, japan, ungilt	6 gns.
228	An oval set, japan, gilt, with mahogany tray	52/-
229	Glass	—
230	Glass	—
231	Glass	—
232	Glass	—
233	A tea set, coloured flowers, 45 pieces	30/-
234	A breakfast and tea service, India sprig, 111 pieces	84/-
235	A chamber service, Chinese figures, with caraft and tumbler	25/-
236	A table service, blue	190/-
237	Twelve plates, richly painted, with various arms and crests	60/-
238	Glass	—
239	Seven handsome dessert plates, melange	35/-
240	A splendid Neapolitan vase, painted by S. Bourne	£30.
241	Two hexagon vases, mazarine (1 faulty)	10/-
242	Glass	—
243	Glass	—
244	Twelve blue mugs and 12 horns	25/-
245	Twelve ditto and ditto	25/-
246	Five club top jugs and 6 stone mugs	25/-
247	Twelve lunch plates, blue bell japan, and dish and cover	25/-
248	Two vegetable dishes for hot water	60/-
249	Four chocolate cups and stands, and 4 odd dishes	20/-
250	Twenty-two lunch plates, gilt Japan	25/-
251	A lunch set, of basket pattern, gold edge, 68 pieces (plates not gilt)	96/-
252	Two chimney vases, Chinese pattern	20/-
253	Two ditto, japanned	25/-
254	Two porous wine coolers and 24 glass wines	30/-
255	Twenty-six pieces and sundry useful articles, white	40/-
256	Two foot pans, white	25/-
257	Eight jugs, blue, and 8 mugs	30/-
258		
259		
260		

End of the Second Day

THIRD DAY'S SALE,

THURSDAY, the 6th Day of JUNE, 1822,

Commencing at One o'Clock precisely.

Lot		Reserve
261	Two chamber sets, white, with carafts and tumblers	25/-
262	One foot tub and 1 slop jar, blue	20/-
263	Two ice pails, blue, and 2 wine coolers, white	25/-
264	Nineteen lunch plates and 3 jugs	45/-
265	Glass	—
266	Two blue large flower pots and stands	40/-
267	Glass	—
268	A breakfast set, tourney sprig, gold edge, 54 pieces	63/-
269	A ditto, japan, 22 pieces	35/-
270	Two bottles, mazarine, white figures with shades, and 1 centre jar	63/-
271	Nine hunting mugs	12/-
272	Two vegetable dishes, japan	30/-
273	A table service, white	6 gns.
274	A ditto, blue	9½ gns.
275	A ditto, blue japanned	12 gns.
276	A melange breakfast and tea service, 73 pieces	70/-
277	Three cheese stands and 1 vegetable dish for hot water, japan	42/-
278	Two new form blue chamber sets with carafts and tumblers	40/-
279	Glass	—
280	Glass	—
281	One large sideboard bowl, Indian pattern	105/-
282	Two richly gilt ice pails	80/-
283	Three jugs, japan	25/-
284	A supper set, richly gilt	60/-
285	Glass	—
286	Glass	—
287	Glass	—
288	A set of three vases, fruit and green ground, with shades	75/-
289	Two match pots, roses on black ground and 1 antique coffee pot, with shades	32/-
290	A japanned table service, grasshopper	£14.
291	A dessert service, japan	6 gns.
292	Thirty-five lunch plates, rich brown and gold border	90/-
293	Twelve rich melange plates	no price
294	A very rich ragout dish and cover	50/-
295	A table service, blue	£9. 10. od.
296	A breakfast service, blue, 87 pieces	40/-
297	Glass	—
298	A large hydra top jar, mazarine birds and flowers	9 gns.
299	Two Chinese jars and covers	no price
300	Four toy spouted mugs, rich japan, and 2 candlesticks, tourney and shade	35/-
301	Two candlesticks, flowers and orange ground, with shades	40/-
302	Glass	—
303	Glass	—
304	Glass	—
305	Two chamber sets, blue, with carafts and tumblers	40/-
306	Eight jugs, blue, and 24 liquere glasses	35/-

Lot		Reserve
307	Three ditto, rich japan	30/-
308	A rich japan table service	£25.
309	A very beautifully, painted landscape dessert service, by S. Bourne	£30.
310	A richly gilt and painted tea service	8 gns.
311	A breakfast service, green scroll and gold border, 77 pieces	5 gns.
312	A dejeunee, Indian garden	50/-
313	Two chamber sets, green leaf border, with carafts and tumblers	35/-
314	A ragout dish and cover, and 2 vegetable dishes for hot water, gold jar pattern	42/-
315	Twenty-four lunch plates	30/-
316	Six beautiful plates	35/-
317	Four hexagon jugs, mazarine and gold bands	50/-
318	Six broth basins and stands, grass hopper japan	24/-
319	A blue table service, willow	9½ gns.
320	Twelve species of useful articles, willow	18/-
321	Twenty-nine ditto, white	42/-
322	Glass	
323	Glass	—
324	A richly gilt table service, gold tops	£25.
325	A table set, tourney sprig	£20.
326	Two vases, mazarine, and 1 centre ditto, with shades	63/-
327	Two vases, Views in Rome	4 gns.
328	Glass	—
329	A very beautiful Italian formed vase, painted by S. Bourne, superbly gilt and burnished	35 gns.
330	Sixty-nine sundry pieces, peacock japan	90/-
331	Seventeen ditto	65/-
332	Two large myrtle pots and stands, mazarine	84/-
333	Two candlesticks, buff ground, with shades	40/-
334	Glass	—
335	Glass	—
336	Glass	—
337	Glass	—
338	Thirty-eight pieces of useful articles, white	40/-
339	Twelve jugs, blue	30/-
340	Two blue chamber sets, with carafts and tumblers	40/-
341	A Chinese jar, white, figures on mazarine	30/-
342	Two vases and shades	63/-
343	A dessert service, japan	6 gns.
344	A breakfast service, green ground, gold edge, 52 pieces	£5.
345	Five stone jugs and 6 mugs	25/-
346	Thirty-four lunch plates, blue and japan	35/-
347	Glass	—
348	A table service, gilt japan	£26.
349	A ditto, common japan	£14.
350	A ditto, blue	£9. 10. od.
351	A tea set, Bourbon sprig, 45 pieces	25/-
352	A breakfast and tea service, white and gold, 11 pieces	6 gns.
353	Two hexagon tall jars and covers, japan	42/-
354	Eight mugs and 8 ditto japan	£6. 16. od.
355	Three jugs, corbeau grounds	32/-
356	Two ice pails, peacock japan	40/-
357	Glass	—

K

Lot		Reserve
358	Glass	—
359	Eight jugs, blue, and 6 mugs	25/–
360	Two wine coolers and 2 ice pails, blue	25/–
361	Five punch bowls, blue	30/–
362	A table set, enamelled sprigs	14 gns.
363	A table service, Chinese characters on mazarine ground	£40.
364	A breakfast service, dragon pattern, 70 pieces	55/–
365	A tea service, richly japanned, 45 pieces	6 gns.
366	A beautiful melange dessert service	£21.
367	Three small vases with shades	35/–
368	A pagoda vase, japan	£5. 10. od.
369	Glass	—
370	Eight jugs and 4 covered ditto, blue	35/–
371	Glass	—
372	Glass	—
373	Glass	—
374	Fifteen bowls for various uses, white	27/–
375	Glass	—
376	Sixteen pieces of useful articles, white	27/–
377	Two card racks, mazarine	20/–
378	Four rich broth basins, covers and stands	32/–
379	Two very rich chocolate cups and stands	30/–
380	Three cheese stands and 6 bakers, rich japan	40/–
381	Eight hunting jugs	24/–
382	Two chamber sets, gold jar, with carafts and tumblers	£2. 10. od.
383	A table service, green flowers (only one tureen)	13 gns.
384	A table ditto, blue	9½ gns.
385	A dessert ditto, ditto	60/–
386	Two chamber sets, white, with carafts and tumblers	30/–
387	Two fruit baskets, japan	42/–
388	Six jugs, gold jar and 4 ditto grasshopper	26/–
389	Six mortars	30/–
390	Seventeen ice plates, japan	50/–

End of the Third Day

FOURTH DAY'S SALE,
FRIDAY, the 7th Day of JUNE, 1822,
Commencing at One o'Clock precisely.

Lot		Reserve
391	Two vegetable dishes for hot water, 2 cheese stands and 6 bakers, grasshopper japan	28/–
392	One ragout dish and cover and 2 vegetable dishes for hot water, japan	30/–
393	Two chamber sets, white, with carafts and tumblers	25/–
394	Nine jugs and 4 covered ditto, blue	30/–
395	Two small hexagon bottles, mazarine, with shades, and 2 small candlesticks, red ground, with ditto	27/–
396	A breakfast set, bourbon sprig, 54 pieces	30/–
397	A (dejeune), rich japan	50/–
398	Twenty-seven pieces of useful articles, white	20/–
399	Eight jugs, blue, and 24 liquere glasses	33/–

Lot		Reserve
400	Glass	—
401	Glass	—
402	Glass	—
403	Glass	—
404	One supper set and covers, blue, and 17 pieces various	30/–
405	Two lotus porous coolers and 12 [glass] fluted and diamond border tumblers	48/–
406	A tea set, white and gold, 45 pieces	50/–
407	Two chamber sets, green border, with carafts and tumblers	45/–
408	A table set, white	105/–
409	A breakfast service, blue, 101 pieces	35/–
410	Two soup tureens and stands, rich brown and gold border	70/–
411	Forty-eight lunch plates	30/–
412	A trentham jar, japan	25/–
413	A set of 5 vases, painted shells and landscapes, red ground	8 gns.
414	A table service, japan	11 gns.
415	A ditto, peacock japan	12 gns.
416	A dessert service, gold jar japan	80/–
417	A ditto, japan	150/–
418	A square supper set, rich japan	50/–
419	Twenty-four melange cups and saucers	15/–
420	One chamber set, Indian paintings, with caraft and tumbler	30/–
421	Nine stone jugs	25/–
422	Two vegetable dishes and 4 bakers, rich japan	63/–
423	A rich tea set, 45 pieces	8 gns.
424	Glass	—
425	Glass	—
426	One dragon jar	84/–
427	A splendid hall jar, mazarine and oriental device	12 gns.
428	Four cabinet pieces	12/–
429	Two rich toilet ewers and basins	63/–
430	Four broth bowls and stands	28/–
431	Glass	—
432	Two chamber services, white, with carafts and tumblers	25/–
433	Glass	—
434	A breakfast set, white and gold, 76 pieces	105/–
435	A table service, very richly japanned hexagon tureens, gold burnished tops	£26.
436	A breakfast set, white, 82 pieces	40/–
437	Seven jugs, jar pattern, 10 [Glass] fluted wines, and 12 tumblers	36/–
438	Glass	—
439	Glass	—
440	Glass	—
441	Glass	—
442	Three vases, with shades	95/–
443	Nine stone jugs and 12 goblets	24/–
444	Thirty-six goblets	18/–
445	A tea service, coloured sprigs, gold edge, 45 pieces	38/–
446	A dessert service, rich japan, gold edge	7 gns.
447	Six beautiful plates	30/–
448	Six ditto	34/–
449	Two fruit baskets and stands, japan	30/–
450	Three Indian sprig jugs	63/–
451	Twelve mugs, various	20/–

Lot		Reserve
452	A pair of ice pails, very richly japanned	63/–
453	Twenty-four lunch plates, enamelled	12/–
454	Six bakers, rich japan	15/–
455	Two hexagon vegetable dishes for hot water and 6 bakers, nosegay	30/–
456	Glass	—
457	Glass	—
458	Glass	—
459	Two tall Chinese jars	15/–
460	Two small Indian pattern tea pots, pair vases, and glass shades	30/–
461	An Italian formed vase, superior painting, richly burnished and finely modelled	18 gns.
462	A breakfast set, Indian coloured sprigs, 70 pieces, gold edge	35/–
463	A chamber service, very richly japanned, with carafts and tumblers	42/–
464	A table service, blue	£8. 10. od.
465	A dessert service, ditto	60/–
466	A tea service, red and gold border	30/–
467	A small breakfast service, japanned, 33 pieces	105/–
468	A ditto, ungilt, 68 pieces	63/–
469	Twelve jugs, blue	30/–
470	Two foot pans, blue	20/–
471	Two ditto	20/–
472	Thirty pieces of useful articles	30/–
473	Glass	—
474	A rose and apple jar	42/–
475	Five two-handle vases, enamel sprig, on mazarine ground	50/–
476	Six beautiful plates	40/–
477	Six ditto	42/–
478	Glass	—
479	Twelve melange plates	18/–
480	Two ice pails, japan	42/–
481	A hexagon temple jar	28/–
482	Six bakers and 3 cheese stands	25/–
483	Two vegetable dishes for hot water and a 22-inch dish, japan	63/–
484	A coloured table service	12 gns.
485	A handsome table service, rich Indian devices, hexagon tureens	£21.
486	A table service, bourbon sprig	12 gns.
487	Eleven hunting jugs	22/–
488	A pot pourie, ram's head, mazarine	42/–
489	Two Indian flower jars, mazarine	42/–
490	Glass	—
491	Glass	—
492	Three paper cases, beautifully painted and glass shades	42/–
493	A tea set, brown and gold border	80/–
494	A ditto, coloured wreath, gilt, and 12 breakfast cups and saucers	73/–
495	A dejeunee, rich japan	42/–
496	Twelve jugs, blue, and 24 liquere glasses	40/–
497	Two chamber sets, blue, with carafts and tumblers	40/–
498	Glass	—
499	Glass	—
500	Glass	—
501	Glass	—
502	Glass	—

Lot		Reserve
503	Two white ice pails and 2 blue coolers	20/-
504	Six jugs and 3 covered ditto, blue, and 24 liquere glasses	35/-
505	A shell ink stand, red ground, 1 toy watering can, and 2 tea pots	32/-
506	Four square canisters, japan, with shades	40/-
507	Two ditto and a shell ink stand	20/-
508	Two large jugs, richly japanned	42/-
509	A shaving box and 2 violet baskets, Dresden flower	20/-
510	A table service, blue	£8. 10. od.
511	A ditto, willow, japanned and richly gilt (only one tureen)	16 gns.
512	Glass	—
513	Eleven jugs, blue	25/-
514	Thirty-three preserving jars, white	50/-
515	Glass	—
516	Glass	—
517	Three jars, various	10/-
518	Two hexagon jars and covers, japan	21/-
519	A tea set, white, 45 pieces	15/-
520	A ditto, yellow and gold border, 45 pieces	25/-

End of the Fourth Day

FIFTH DAY'S SALE
SATURDAY, the 8th Day of JUNE, 1822,
Commencing at One o'Clock precisely.

Lot		Reserve
521	Glass	—
522	Five jugs, various coloured	no price
523	Two mantle jars, mazarine	40/-?
524	One soup tureen, 4 bakers and 2 vegetable dishes for hot water, Mogul japan	40/-?
525	Six stone mugs and 5 jugs	30/-
526	One tea set, gilt japan, 49 pieces	50/-
527	A Bourbon sprig breakfast set, 87 pieces	80/-
528	Glass	—
529	Glass	—
530	Glass	—
531	A table set, blue	9 gns.
532	Glass	—
533	Glass	—
534	Glass	—
535	A lot of useful articles, blue	no price
536	A breakfast service, red and gold, 74 pieces	no price
537	A table service, japan	no price
538	Two jars, sprigs, on mazarine	no price
539	A fine hall jar, Oriental design	no price
540	Four baskets, Dresden flowers, and 2 square bottles	25/-
541	Ten stone jugs	21/-
542	Eight jugs, blue	16/-
543	Glass	—
544	One chamber set, basket japan, with caraft and tumbler	20/-
545	Two sets, green leaf border	30/-
546	Six bakers, 4 boats and stands and 2 cheese stands, jar pattern	28/-

Lot		Reserve
547	A tea service, green ground	70/–
548	A dessert, richly gilt Indian pattern	147/6
549	Glass	—
550	A breakfast service, roses and gilt, 72 pieces	94/6
551	A breakfast service, blue, 100 pieces	30/–
552	A chamber service, japanned and gilt, with caraft and tumbler	25/–
553	Twelve stone jugs	27/–
554	A table service, birds, gilt	7 gns.
555	Two hexagon jars, with shades	73/6
556	Glass	—
557	Glass	—
558	A dragon vase and cover, Indian devices	73/6
559	Glass	—
560	A highly finished tea service, 45 pieces	9 gns.
561	A dessert service, coloured	70/–
562	A chamber service, blue	18/–
563	Glass	—
564	Glass	—
565	Glass	—
566	Eight jugs	16/–
567	Eleven ditto, Indian form	22/–
568	A large sideboard bowl	4 gns.
569	Two vases, with shades	£2.
570	Two paper cases, raised figures on mazarine	15/–
571	Two Indian formed jars and shades	4 gns.
572	A blue table service	9 gns.
573	A ditto, coloured	no price
574	Glass	—
575	Glass	—
566	Glass	—
567	A very rich dessert service, Oriental style	10 gns.
568	Two chamber services, white	35/–
569	A breakfast service, after the Chinese manner, 94 pieces	6 gns.
570	A tea service, blue and gold border	4 gns.
571	A small breakfast service, melange, 60 pieces	
572	A very rich pair of ice pails	
573	Six finely pencilled plates	
574	Six soup ditto	
575	Twelve melange plates and a fine round dish	
576	Two match cases, delicately finished, with shades	£3. 10. 0d.
577	Two beautiful antique coffee pots, with shades	£3. 13. 6d.
578	Glass	—
579	Glass	—
580	Eighteen preserving jars, white	20/–
581	Eight jugs, blue	no price
582	A dinner service, nosegay pattern	£12.
583	A ditto, very rich	£20.
584	A toilet ewer and basin, rich pattern	20/–
585	A flower bowl, mazarine and delicate sprigs	30/–
586	Two exquisitely painted satyr goblets	£5.
587	A blue table service	9 gns.
588	Twenty-six pieces of useful articles, blue	no price
589	A dessert service, blue sprigs and gilt	8 gns.
590	Twelve breakfast cups and saucers, gilt	15/–

Lot		Reserve
591	A breakfast service, enamelled roses, 77 pieces	3 gns.
592	Glass	—
593	Glass	—
594	Glass	—
595	Glass	—
596	Glass	—
597	Glass	—
598	Glass	—
599	Five rich mugs, various	20/–
600	Twenty lunch plates	20/–
601	Thirty-six ditto	35/–
602	Two potatoe dishes and covers, and 1 vegetable dish for hot water, japan	no price
603	A rich dessert service	£9. 19. 6d.
604	A tea service, white and gold border	£2. 10. 0d.
605	A rich tea service, 45 pieces	£7.
606	A table service, highly gilt, etc.	£22. 10. 0d.
607	Fourteen stone jugs	28/–
608	Twenty-two lunch plates	no price
609	Six richly pencilled plates	no price
610	Six ditto soup ditto	no price
611	Two wine coolers, richly japanned	£2.
612	A small lunch service, blue and gold edge, 27 pieces	no price
613	Two octagonal jars, Chinese	no price
614	A conservatory bowl	no price
615	Two Indian bottles with shades	no price
616	A mazarine toilet, ewer and basin, with shades	no price
617	Four small flower pots and stands, mazarine and delicate sprigs	no price
618	Glass	—
619	Glass	—
620	Glass	—
621	Glass	—
622	Glass	—
623	Glass	—
624	Two chamber sets, blue	no price
625	A hall jar, lion head handles	£2. 10. 0d.
626	A table service, enamelled and gilt in the Oriental manner	£22. 10. 0d.
627	A very highly japanned chamber service	45/–
628	A breakfast service, Chinese coloured sprigs, 116 pieces	90/–
629	A tea set, sprigs and gold	no price
630	A small tea set, melange, 30 pieces	no price
631	Twelve white jugs	no price
632	A two-handled Etruscan formed flower vase, highly finished in flowers and gold, with shade	no price
633	Glass	—
634	Glass	—
635	Glass	—
636	Glass	—
637	Twenty-six pieces of useful articles, blue	30/–
638	Sixteen preserving jars	no price
639	Glass	—
640	Glass	—
641	A pagoda vase, for vestibule	no price
642	Two very rich water jugs	no price

Lot		Reserve
643	Four mugs, richly gilt	no price
644	A trentham bowl	no price
645	Thirty-six small plates, japan	no price
646	Two vegetable dishes for hot water, 4 bakers, 1 cheese stand and 18 plates, coloured	no price
647	Two very rich chocolate cups and covers	no price
648	Three large and 2 small dishes, and 1 drainer, coloured	no price
649	Twelve stone jugs, of two shapes	no price
650	Two chamber sets, jar pattern	no price

End of the Fifth Day

SIXTH DAY'S SALE
MONDAY, the 10th Day of JUNE, 1822,
Commencing at One o'Clock precisely.

Lot		Reserve
651	A tea set, white and gold	35/–
652	A breakfast set, yellow and gold border, 64 pieces	70/–
653	A blue dessert service	50/–
654	Two chamber services, white	23/–
655	Four mortars and 2 porous wine coolers	30/–
656	Glass	—
657	Eight jugs, blue	18/–
658	Glass	—
659	Ten stone jugs	24/–
660	Two chamber services, gold jar pattern	35/–
661	Twelve melange breakfast cups and saucers	18/–
662	A table service, blue	9 gns.
663	A small tea and breakfast service, 51 pieces	40/–
664	A dessert service, coloured	84/–
665	A dejeunee, Indian sprig	35/–
666	Two chocolate cups and saucers and 7 useful pieces of table ware	27/–
667	Six highly finished plates	30/–
668	Six soup ditto	36/–
669	Two fruit baskets and stands, Oriental designs	35/–
670	Three paper cases, rich, with shades	35/–
671	Two octagon jars	63/–
672	Twelve beautifully finished plates, various	80/–
673	Two serpent handled jars	42/–
674	Two vases, green ground, fruit and shades	84/–
675	Glass	—
676	Glass	—
677	Eight jugs, blue	16/–
678	A table service, richly coloured and gilt, hexagon tureens	£26.
679	A ditto, blue, gold edge	£14.
680	A square supper service, finished japan	70/–
681	A small breakfast set, 30 pieces	30/–
682	A chamber service, richly gilt	35/–
683	Six stone jugs	12/–
684	A table service, green ground, Dresden border	15 gns.
685	Eighteen lunch plates	30/–

Lot		Reserve
686	Two handsome jars and covers	50/-
687	Glass	—
688	Ten jugs, blue	23/-
689	A table service, blue	9 gns.
690	Glass	—
691	A splendid hall jar, from an improved Indian model	16 gns.
692	Two delicate vases, with shades	24/-
693	Four japan candlesticks, mazarine	16/-
694	A very richly finished tea set, 45 pieces	8 gns.
695	An Indian pattern breakfast service, 77 pieces	30/-
696	Two chamber services	30/-
697	Twelve caddy basins [? Glass]	31/-
698	Ten jugs, blue	23/-
699	Glass	—
700	Glass	—
701	Four candlesticks and extinguishers, mazarine japan	15/-
702	Two large flat candlesticks, mazarine, with shades	42/-
703	Two handsome mantle jars, with shades	45/-
704	Four rich mugs	35/-
705	A table service, coloured hexagon tureens	17 gns.
706	A small breakfast service, 28 pieces	42/-
707	A rich chamber service	42/-
708	Glass	—
709	A dessert service, blue foliage	3 gns.
710	Two beautiful painted goblets	4 gns.
711	Four delicate cabinet pieces	24/-
712	Glass	—
713	Glass	—
714	Glass	—
715	Glass	—
716	Two porous coolers and 4 mortars	30/-
717	Glass	—
718	A tea set, dragon and gold border	36/-
719	A breakfast service, coloured sprig, 47 pieces	35/-
720	A table service, blue	9 gns.
721	A ditto, rich japan	25 gns.
722	Two toilet ewers and basins, and 2 chocolate cups, rich	30/-
723	Seven dishes, rich japan	30/-
724	Eleven stone jugs	25/-
725	Seven ditto	14/-
726	Four rich mugs	20/-
727	One large water jug, richly japanned	20/-
728	Six highly wrought plates	60/-
729	Six soup ditto	50/-
730	Two fruit baskets and stands, rich	35/-
731	Two sugar bowls, covers and stands, japanned	24/-
732	Three richly painted paper cases, with shades	50/-
733	Glass	—
734	Eight jugs and covers, blue	24/-
735	Twenty-six pieces of useful articles, blue	30/-
736	Glass	—
737	Two Indian beakers	35/-
738	An elegant flower vase, with shade	42/-
739	A small breakfast service, enamelled, 28 pieces	25/-

Lot		Reserve
740	A chamber service, green leaf border	20/–
741	A table service, nosegay pattern, hexagon tureens	12 gns.
742	Twelve breakfast plates	20/–
743	Six compotiers	20/–
744	Seven bakers, rich japan	30/–
745	Two vegetable dishes for hot water, a ragout dish and cover and 2 bakers, coloured	40/–
746	One 20-inch gravy dish, 1 cheese stand and 1 vegetable dish for hot water	25/–
747	Seventy-six pieces of table ware, coloured	90/–
748	Six bakers, coloured	21/–
749	Eighteen lunch plates	21/–
750	Two two-handled low vases, with shades	40/–
751	One toilet ewer and basin	21/–
752	Five scent jars and covers	42/–
753	Two large flat candlesticks, mazarine with shades	42/–
754	A hall bowl	42/–
755	Glass	—
756	A table set, plaid japan, richly gilt	£30.
757	A table set, blue	9 gns.
758	A breakfast service, japan, 54 pieces	105/–
759	A dessert service, japan	£8.
760	A square supper set, Indian pattern with border	40/–
761	Two chamber services and gold jar	40/–
762	A small melange breakfast set, 31 pieces	23/–
763	Two cream bowls and covers, gold thorn	18/–
764	Twelve handsome plates, various	30/–
765	Four vases, with shades	no price
766	Eight jugs, blue	16/–
767	Nine ditto	18/–
768	Glass	—
769	Glass	—
770	Glass	—
771	A table set, brown border	73/–
772	A dessert set ditto, 4 chamber sets ditto, with carafts and tumblers	70/–
773	Six ornaments	38/–
774	A tea set, dragon gold edge	35/–
775	A small tea set, 39 pieces	63/–
776	Eight jugs, blue	20/–
777	Eight ditto	20/–
778	Twenty-six useful pieces, blue	30/–
779	Glass	—
780	Glass	—

End of the Sixth Day

SEVENTH DAY'S SALE
TUESDAY, the 11th Day of JUNE, 1822,
Commencing at One o'Clock precisely.

Lot		Reserve
781	Twelve jars and covers	16/–
782	Sixteen jugs, blue	32/–

Lot   Reserve

783 Two porous wine coolers and 2 butter tubs   15/-
784 A DINNER SERVICE, blue   9 gns.
785 Ten jugs from the antique   23/-
786 Two blue chamber sets   30/-
787 Glass   —
788 Glass   —
789 Glass   —
790 Glass   —
791 Glass   —
792 Twenty-six pieces of useful articles   30/-
793 Two sprinkling bottles, 2 cups and covers, moths on mazarine
    ground with glass shades   30/-
794 A DINNER SERVICE, blue and white   9 gns.
795 A pair of toy chamber candlesticks and 2 buckets with glasses   23/-
796 A breakfast set, dragon, 43 pieces   50/-
797 Glass   —
798 A tea service, painted in flowers   no price
799 Glass   —
800 Glass   —
801 Two chamber suites, blue and white   30/-
802 A tea set, painted in roses, 45 pieces   no price
803 A dessert service, painted and gold flower, 43 pieces   8 gns.
804 A DINNER SERVICE, japanned flower   13 gns.
805 A shell ecritoire and pair of match cases, blue and gold   32/-
806 Ten mugs, embossed hunting figures   20/-
807 Twelve broth basins and stands   30/-
808 Six punch bowls   25/-
809 A pair of toy hand candlesticks, a pen tray, and sprinkling pot,
    gold edges and flowers   25/-
810 Glass   —
811 Twenty-four mugs   24/-
812 Two vegetable dishes and covers and a steak ditto   20/-
813 A chamber suite, blue and gold edge   20/-
814 A DINNER SERVICE, blue and white   9 gns.
815 Twelve fruit dishes   12/-
816 A pair of blue bottles, raised flower, an ink cup and canister
    and 4 glass shades   28/-
817 A pair of ice pails and 2 baskets and stands   25/-
818 A tea set, blue border, 45 pieces   30/-
819 A chamber set, japan gold edge   30/-
820 Glass   —
821 A pair of ditto ewers   no price
822 Twelve breakfast cups and 12 saucers, roses and gold edge   30/-
823 Eight baking dishes   no price
824 A DINNER SERVICE, blue and white   9 gns.
825 Glass   —
826 Two vegetable dishes and covers and a steak ditto   25/-
827 Two blue essence bottles, 2 wax hand candlesticks, gilt and
    painted flower, 2 inkstands and 4 glass shades   35/-
828 A chamber suite, japan flower   25/-
829 Eight broth basins and stands   20/-
830 Twenty-four blue mugs   24/-
831 A pair of handsome vases, richly gilt and painted in flowers,
    and 2 blue bottles in birds and glass shades   30/-

Lot		Reserve
832	A rich tea set, japan flower, 33 pieces	6 gns.
833	A breakfast service to match, 54 pieces	9 gns.
834	A DINNER SERVICE, blue and white	9 gns.
835	Glass	—
836	Nine melange dessert plates	25/-
837	A costly DESSERT SERVICE, exquisitely painted in SELECT VIEWS, by S. Bourne, enriched with burnished gold	35 gns.
838	Ten jugs, embossed flowers and figures	23/-
839	A handsome DINNER SERVICE, painted in roses	18 gns.
840	A DESSERT DITTO, japan and gilt flowers, 43 pieces	£8.
841	Eight baking dishes and 20 dessert plates	30/-
842	Two neat essence bottles, gold sprig, and 2 jugs with glass shades	35/-
843	Six rich dessert plates	30/-
844	A dinner service, blue	9 gns.
845	A breakfast service, white and gold, 84 pieces	5 gns.
846	Eight melange dessert plates	20/-
847	Glass	—
848	A ragout dish and cover and 5 bakers, japan	24/-
849	Six handsome soup plates	42/-
850	A handsome japan and gilt DINNER SERVICE	£21.
851	A dessert service, blue and gold border	9 gns.
852	Two blue essence bottles, small sprig, 2 hand candlesticks, a pot pourie and cup and cover	25/-
853	Twenty melange plates	30/-
854	A DINNER SERVICE, blue	9 gns.
855	A handsome DESSERT SERVICE, painted in boquets, relieved by sea green and gold devices	15 gns.
856	A pair of handsome jars, with glass shades	28/-
857	An ice pail, japan, and 1 ditto barbeaux	30/-
858	Two vegetable dishes and covers, 2 cheese stands and 4 bakers	25/-
859	A handsome ecritoire and 2 essence bottles	25/-
860	Glass	—
861	Twenty-six useful pieces, white	30/-
862	A pair of toy jars, gilt and painted in flowers, and a violet basket painted in landscapes	25/-
863	A pair of handsome ice pails	37/-
864	A DINNER SERVICE, blue	9 gns.
865	Twelve breakfast cups and saucers, India sprig	21/-
866	A NOBLE VASE, formed from the antique, beautifully painted in landscapes and figures, by Bourne, and sumptuously gilt	£21. 0. 0d.
867	A pair of ornaments in the style of the Portland vase, and shades	50/-
868	A pair of neat jars and covers	40/-
869	A handsome TABLE SERVICE, coloured japan	22 gns.
870	Twenty-six pieces of useful articles	30/-
871	Sixteen baking dishes, coloured japan	36/-
872	A violet basket, painted in a landscape, a toy jug, an ink stand and sprinkler	20/-
873	A pair of handsome candlesticks, painted in flowers and glass shades	30/-
874	A DINNER SERVICE, blue	9 gns.
875	A pair of jars, neat sprig, on blue ground	63/-
876	Glass	—

Lot	Reserve
877 Glass	—
878 A pair of jars, painted in landscapes and glass shades	40/-
879 A handsome TABLE SERVICE, japanned	13 gns.
880 A pair of beakers, painted in flowers, and a japan vase	20/-
881 A NOBLE ESSENCE JAR, painted in flowers, on celeste ground, relieved by burnished gold	20 gns.
882 A pair of reading candlesticks, Dresden flower, a pen tray and an ink stand with glass shade	30/-
883 A handsome jug, painted in landscapes and hunting subject	42/-
884 A DINNER SERVICE, blue	9 gns.
885 Twenty-six pieces of white articles	30/-
886 Two blue and white chamber suits	30/-
887 A handsome ESSENCE URN, blue ground, enriched by moths, flowers and gilt decorations	84/-
888 A ditto, its companion	84/-
889 Two ice pails, rich japan	84/-
890 Glass	—
891 Two broth basins, gold edge, and large jug	30/-
892 Twenty-four blue mugs	24/-
893 Twelve melange breakfast cups and saucers, gilt	25/-
894 A coffee ewer, richly gilt, from the antique, and glass shade	25/-
895 Ten japan jugs	30/-
896 A breakfast set, India sprig, 44 pieces	50/-
897 A pair of flower pots and stands, painted in moths, and an accurate sun dial with glass shades	25/-
898 Six handsome dessert plates, sumptuously gilt	36/-
899 A pair of neat reading candlesticks, with glass shades	25/-
900 Twelve blue jugs	28/-
901 Two violet baskets, 2 hand candlesticks, gilt and painted in flowers and 2 sprinkling pots	30/-
902 Twelve dessert plates, 2 patterns	18/-
903 A pair of blue jars, raised figures, on blue ground and glass shades	40/-
904 Two toy jugs and a sprinkler, japan flowers, 3 glasses and 4 toy candlesticks	40/-
905 A toy ewer and basin, painted in landscapes, 2 pair of candlesticks and glass shades	25/-
906 Glass	—
907 Six punch bowls	20/-
908 A breakfast set, 41 pieces, blue flower	35/-
909 Three japan jugs, gilt edge	24/-
910 Twelve breakfast cups and saucers, small sprig	20/-
911 Twenty-four mugs	24/-
912 5 Japanned jugs	25/-
913 Twelve dessert plates, melange	63/-
913 Glass	—
915 Twenty-six pieces of useful items	35/-
916 Seven breakfast cups & saucers and seven plates, India sprigs	15/-
917 Twenty-four plates, barbeaux	20/-
918 Twenty-six pieces of white articles	30/-
919 A soup tureen and cover, Japan	12/-
920 Four delicate cabinet pieces and shades	27/-
921 Glass	—
922 Glass	—

Lot		Reserve
923	Glass	—
924	Three dishes, 2 beakers, 3 boats, 1 stand. Japanned	25/–
925	Four Plaid Japan dishes and drainers	105/–
926	A tea service, 99 pieces, blue sprig	75/–
927	Glass	—
928	Glass	—
929	Three baking dishes and 8 melange coffee cups & saucers	15/–
930	Six cups and 7 saucers painted in roses, 6 breakfast ditto and muffin & cover	20/–

End of the Seventh Day

EIGHTH DAY'S SALE,

FRIDAY, the 14th Day of JUNE, 1822,

Commencing at One o'Clock precisely.

Lot		Reserve
931	Twenty-six pieces of useful ware, blue	26/–
932	Two vegetable dishes and steak ditto with covers and liners, for hot water	28/–
933	Two chamber suites, blue and white	30/–
934	Twenty-four blue mugs	23/–
935	Eleven breakfast cups and saucers, gold edge	23/–
936	A table service, coloured japan	14 gns.
937	Eight breakfast and tea cups and saucers, 2 plates, tea pot and sugar basin, rich mazarine pattern	4 gns.
938	Glass	—
939	Sixteen blue jugs	35/–
940	Glass	—
941	An ewer basin and slipper, japan	15/–
942	A DINNER SERVICE, blue	9 gns.
943	A dessert ditto	50/–
944	Glass	—
945	Glass	—
946	Glass	—
947	Twenty blue jugs	50/–
948	Sundry useful items	15/–
949	Glass	—
950	A TABLE SERVICE, blue	9 gns.
951	A tea and breakfast service, 103 pieces	80/–
952	Nine jugs, 4 covered ditto and 3 mugs	35/–
953	Glass	—
954	A breakfast set, yellow and gold, 89 pieces	£9.
955	Sixteen blue jugs	35/–
956	A DINNER SERVICE, blue	9 gns.
957	Twenty-one hexagon shape blue jugs	45/–
958	A pair of vases and covers, mazarine, 1 faulty	30/–
959	A dessert service, colour japan	4 gns.
960	Two chamber suites, blue and white	30/–
961	A TABLE SERVICE, blue	9 gns.
962	Two vegetable and one steak dish, with covers	28/–
963	Nine jugs	20/–

Lot		Reserve
964	A pair of hexagon essence jars, painted in flowers, and a glass shade	3 gns.
965	Glass	—
966	A tea set, India sprig and gold edge	60/-
967	A japan vase and shade	30/-
968	Two vegetable dishes and steak ditto, with covers and liners	28/-
969	Twenty-six pieces of useful articles	28/-
970	A DINNER SERVICE, coloured japan	14 gns.
971	Two sets of blue chambers	30/-
972	Two rich cabinet cups, covers and stands, painted in landscapes and shade	70/-
973	A japan ewer and basin, soap and brush trays	20/-
974	A TABLE SERVICE, blue	9 gns.
975	Two pastil burners with glass shades, and 2 match cases, mazarine	42/-
976	Twenty-four blue mugs	28/-
977	A breakfast set, dragon, 62 pieces	45/-
978	A sprinkling can, 2 shell candlesticks and 3 egg cups	20/-
979	Two chamber sets	30/-
980	A DINNER SERVICE, japanned and gilt	17 gns.
981	An essence jar, painted in flowers on green ground, and glass shades	31/6
982	Twenty-six pieces of useful ware	25/-
983	Glass	—
984	Five ornamental vases	46/-
985	A TABLE SERVICE, blue	9 gns.
986	Three handsome paper cases with glass shades	40/-
987	Two vegetable dishes, covers and liners, and a steak ditto	28/-
988	A tea set, blue sprig, gold edge	46/-
989	A pair of japan reading candlesticks and 2 paper cases, birds on green ground	42/-
990	A DINNER SERVICE, India sprig	14 gns.
991	A vase and 2 match cases, mazarine, and glass shades	46/-
992	A breakfast set, coloured and gold sprig and edge, 52 pieces	5 gns.
993	Glass	—
994	A TABLE SERVICE, blue	9 gns.
995	Two candlesticks, 2 vases, and 2 paper cases, mazarine glass shades	40/-
996	Glass	—
997	A lofty ESSENCE JAR, dragon handles, japan flower and gilt ornaments	70/-
998	Glass	—
999	Glass	—
1000	A TABLE SERVICE, blue sprig, gold edge	14 gns.
1001	An essence bottle, 2 vases, 2 scent pots, and 3 glass shades	46/-
1002	Glass	—
1003	A breakfast set, blue border, 73 pieces	46/-
1004	Two scent bottles, 2 candlesticks, 2 hexagon bottles, and 4 glass shades	35/-
1005	A DINNER SERVICE, blue	9 gns.
1006	A dessert ditto, dragon border	£5.
1007	A scent bottle, 2 ditto pots, and 2 paper cases and glass shade	25/-
1008	A noble square ESSENCE JAR and COVER, mazarine ground, enriched with flowers, etc.	20 gns.

Lot		Reserve
1009	Glass	—
1010	A TABLE SERVICE, green border	15 gns.
1011	Glass	—
1012	Two hexagon jugs, 2 ditto bottles and 2 taper candlesticks, and 4 glass shades	40/–
1013	A breakfast and tea set, Tourney sprig, 73 pieces	73/6
1014	Glass	—
1015	A DINNER SERVICE, blue	9 gns.
1016	A handsome NEAPOLITAN VASE, formed from the antique, beautifully painted in landscapes, enriched with burnished gold, by S. Bourne	15 gns.
1017	Six essence bottles and covers, 2 paper cases, in landscapes, and 6 shades	40/–
1018	A NOBLE CISTERN, japan flowers and gilt dolphin handles	10 gns.
1019	A tea set, blue border, 40 pieces	25/–
1020	A DINNER SERVICE, coloured japan	14 gns.
1021	A dessert ditto	£4.
1022	Five scent bottles, 3 match cases, painted in landscapes, with 2 shades	52/6
1023	Twenty-six pieces of useful items	28/–
1024	Two vegetable dishes and steak ditto, with covers and liners	28/–
1025	Twenty-four tea cups and 24 saucers, and basins	23/–
1026	Two chamber sets	30/–
1027	A breakfast set, 55 pieces	23/–
1028	Two essence bottles, toy tea pot, 2 ink stands, 2 paper cases in landscapes, and 7 glass shades	50/–
1029	A pair of handsome vases	46/–
1030	A DINNER SERVICE, coloured japan	£20.
1031	Twenty-six pieces of useful ware	30/–
1032	A breakfast service, barbeau sprig, 106 pieces	50/–
1033	Two match cases, birds on green ground, 2 jars and covers, a bottle and 2 vases, with glass shades	46/–
1034	A handsome tea set, rich japan, 41 pieces	69/–
1035	A table service, blue	10 gns.
1036	A dessert ditto	52/–
1037	Two chamber suites, blue and white	30/–
1038	Three paper cases, landscapes, a bottle, an inkstand, and 4 shades	50/–
1039	A LOFTY JAPAN ESSENCE JAR and COVER, with gold enrichments	8 gns.
1040	A DINNER SERVICE, coloured japan	14 gns.
1041	A DESSERT ditto	90/–
1042	A tea set, barbeau sprig	20/–
1043	Two wafer baskets in landscapes, 2 bottles and shades, 3 cups and saucers, and 2 glass shades	40/–
1044	Two vegetable and 1 steak dishes, with covers and liners	28/–
1045	Glass	—
1046	Two ewers and basins, japan	35/–
1047	A breakfast set, dragon pattern, 86 pieces	30/–
1048	Twelve breakfast cups and 12 saucers, barbeau gold edge	30/–
1049	Three ornamental vases and covers	60/–
1050	Two chamber suites	35/–
1051	Twenty-six pieces, various	30/–
1052	Twenty-four blue mugs	48/–

Lot	Reserve
1053 Twelve breakfast cups and saucers, tea, sugar and milk pot	25/-
1054 A tea set, japan, 21 pieces	10/-
1055 Twenty-four blue mugs	28/-
1056 Twenty-six pieces of blue and white ware	30/-
1057 Two toy jugs and shades, 3 paper cases and shades	35/-
1058 A toy ewer and basin, and 3 flat candlesticks and 3 shades	28/-
1059 A handsome ewer and basin, India sprig	20/-
1060 Six melange breakfast cups and saucers	20/-

End of the Eighth Day

NINTH DAY'S SALE,

SATURDAY, the 15th Day of JUNE, 1822,

Commending at One o'Clock.

Lot	Reserve
1061 Thirteen blue jugs	25/6
1062 Three breakfast cups and saucers, 2 plates and a butter tub	8/-
1063 Three vegetable dishes and a steak ditto, with covers and liners	30/-
1064 A TABLE SERVICE, blue and white	£9.
1065 Twenty-four white bowls	30/-
1066 A breakfast set, barbeau, gold edge, 50 pieces	60/-
1067 Ten jugs, corbeaux	40/-
1068 Twenty-two pieces of useful articles, blue	25/-
1069 Thirteen blue jugs	25/-
1070 A DINNER SERVICE, blue and white	£9.
1071 A steak dish and 2 vegetable dishes, with covers and liners for hot water	23/-
1072 A breakfast and tea set, barbeau sprig, 106 pieces	70/-
1073 Four large beakers, green dragon	25/-
1074 A pair of reading candlesticks and shades	40/-
1075 A blue and white TABLE SERVICE	£9.
1076 Three violet baskets, a wafer box, vase and 2 churns	15/-
1077 A roll tray, potatoe dish, 2 nappies, and bowl	14/-
1078 Two jars and covers, and 2 vases, green dragon (1 faulty)	40/-
1079 Six ewers and basins, and 6 slippers, blue	30/-
1080 A DINNER SERVICE, Tourney sprig	13 gns.
1081 A ditto, blue and white (1 soup tureen)	£6.
1082 Two jars and covers, a cup and saucer, and 3 vases	30/-
1083 A tea and breakfast set, 109 pieces	60/-
1084 A dessert set, blue	50/-
1085 A pair of candlesticks, and 2 small vases with shades	25/-
1086 A DINNER SERVICE, embossed, blue foliage (no soup tureens)	15 gns.
1087 Glass	—
1088 A breakfast set, blue sprig, 47 pieces	40/-
1089 Two japan vases, and a paper case	25/-
1090 A DINNER SERVICE, blue (1 soup tureen)	£9.
1091 Six ewers and basins, and 6 slippers, blue	30/-
1092 Six ditto, and 6 ditto	30/-
1093 A tea service, blue sprig, 43 pieces	30/-
1094 A DINNER SERVICE, blue	6 gns.
1095 Two mummy jars, and 2 octagon vases	40/-

L

Lot		Reserve
1096	An ink stand, 2 wafer baskets, and 2 candlesticks and shades	30/-
1097	Two card racks, and 2 incense burners, mazarine	46/-
1098	Two vases and covers, and 2 jars and covers	40/-
1099	Four large bottles, dragon	40/-
1100	A TABLE SERVICE, coloured japan	14 gns.
1101	A tea set, coloured sprigs, 45 pieces	26/-
1102	Four vegetable dishes and 3 small ewers and basins	40/-
1103	Four ditto and three ditto	40/-
1104	An ink stand, 2 canisters, 2 candlesticks and shades	35/-
1105	A DINNER SERVICE, blue and white	9 gns.
1106	A dessert set, ditto	50/-
1107	Six ewers and basons, and 6 slippers, white	6o/-
1108	Two vases and 4 bottles, dragon	40/-
1109	A tea set, barbeaux sprig, gold edge, 43 pieces	40/-
1110	A blue and white TABLE SERVICE	£9.
1111	Twenty-four white bowls	30/-
1112	Two jars and covers, and 2 vases	£2.
1113	Pair of ice pails, rich japan	3½ gns.
1114	Forty-eight cups and saucers and 24 basins, blue	28/-
1115	Six ewers and basins, and six slippers, blue	30/-
1116	Six ditto and ditto, and 12 jugs	30/-
1117	A TABLE SERVICE, coloured japan	£25.
1118	Two jars and covers, and 2 vases and covers	no price
1119	Six ewers and basins, and 12 mugs and jugs	23/-
1120	A blue and white DINNER SERVICE	£9.
1121	A breakfast set, 42 pieces	30/-
1122	Glass	—
1123	Forty-eight cups and saucers and 24 basins, blue	30/-
1124	A rich japan DINNER SERVICE	£21.
1125	Two jars and covers, and 1 vase	30/-
1126	Six ewers and basins, and 10 mugs and jugs	25/-
1127	A DINNER SERVICE, blue and white	£9.
1128	A very rich breakfast set, fawn and gold, 72 pieces	9½ gns.
1129	A breakfast set, blue, 150 pieces	30/-
1130	Six ewers and basins, and 6 slippers	30/-
1131	A blue and white TABLE SERVICE	£9.
1132	Six ewers and basins, blue	18/-
1133	A handsome TABLE SERVICE, blue, enamel and gold border	£20.
1134	A handsome lofty ESSENCE VASE and COVER, japan flower	8 gns.
1135	Three incense burners, mazarine	40/-
1136	A breakfast service, blue sprig, 70 pieces	50/-
1137	A blue and white DINNER SERVICE	£9.
1138	Two etruscan vases and covers, japan	42/-
1139	A pair of ice pails, richly coloured and gold border	90/-
1140	Two hexagon soup tureens, 4 sauce ditto, 4 dishes and covers, rich japan, and 2 sallad bowls, flower and gold decoration	25 gns.
1141	Glass	—
1142	A breakfast set, barbeau sprig, 42 pieces	35/-
1143	Two card racks and 2 incense burners, mazarine	30/-
1144	A DINNER SERVICE, blue and white	£9.
1145	Glass	—
1146	A pair of ice pails, rich japan	70/-
1147	Four vegetable dishes, and 3 small ewers and basins	35/-
1148	Two vases and covers, and 2 jars and covers	40/-

Lot		Reserve
1149	A breakfast set, 72 pieces	40/-
1150	A splendid japan DINNER SERVICE	£42.
1151	Glass	—
1152	Eight jugs, corbeau	40/-
1153	Six ewers and basins, and 4 slippers, white	42/-
1154	A TABLE SERVICE, blue and white	£9.
1155	Three dozen half pints and stands, printed	20/-
1156	36 breakfast cups and 36 saucers, ditto	18/-
1157	36 teas, 36 saucers, ditto	16/-
1158	36 bowls, ditto	15/-
1159	One dozen creams, ditto	15/-
1160	A TABLE SERVICE, blue and white	£9.
1161	Twenty-four white bowls	30/-
1162	Twenty-four pieces of useful articles, blue	30/-
1163	Six ewers and basins, 6 jugs and 6 mugs	30/-
1164	Six ditto, 6 ditto and 6 ditto	25/-
1165	A blue and white TABLE SERVICE	£9.
1166	Six ewers and basins, 6 jugs and 6 mugs	25/-
1167	Six ditto, 6 ditto and 6 ditto	25/-
1168	Twenty-eight white bowls	30/-
1169	A DINNER SERVICE, blue and white	£9.
1170	Thirteen ewers and basins, printed	30/-
1171	Three dozen tea cups and saucers	16/-
1172	Two dozen jugs	20/-
1173	A table service, blue birds	£9.
1174	Four vegetable dishes and 3 small ewers and basins	35/-
1175	Forty pieces of useful articles, blue	50/-
1176	Eight ewers and basins, white	50/-
1177	A DINNER SERVICE, blue and white	£9.
1178	Two dozen half pints and stands, printed	12/-
1179	Two dozen breakfast cups and saucers, ditto	11/-
1180	Two dozen tea, ditto	9/-
1181	Two dozen bowls, ditto	15/-
1182	Two dozen breakfast cups and saucers	11/-
1183	A table service, blue	£9.
1184	Twenty-four pieces of useful articles, blue	30/-
1185	Twenty-four ditto	30/-
1186	Two vegetable dishes and steak ditto, with covers and liners	25/-
1187	Six ewers and basins, and 6 slippers, white	30/-
1188	Five ewers and basins and 8 jugs, blue	23/-
1189	Six handsome chimney ornaments	60/-
1190	A DINNER SERVICE, blue and white	£9.
1191	Nineteen printed jugs	9/-
1192	Two dozen printed tea cups and saucers	10/-
1193	Four dishes, tea, sugar and milk pot	10/-
1194	Nine blue jugs	20/-

End of the Ninth Day

THE REMAINDER OF THE
STOCK OF CHINA
OF THE LATE
MR. MASON
PATENTEE AND MANUFACTURER OF THE IRON
STONE CHINA
AT NO. 11, ALBEMARLE STREET.

A
CATALOGUE
OF THE
ENTIRE ASSEMBLAGE OF USEFUL & DECORATIVE
PORCELANE,
OF RICH AND ELEGANT PATTERNS;
COMPRISING
SEVERAL HUNDRED
DINNER, DESSERT, BREAKFAST, & TEA SERVICES;
JUGS, EWERS, BASINS,
DISHES IN SETS, BOTH OPEN AND COVERED;
PLATES IN DOZENS, OF EVERY SIZE;
NOBLE ORNAMENTAL JARS & EWERS,
Superbly Gilt and Beautifully Enamelled;
AND
A GREAT VARIETY OF CABINET ORNAMENTS,
OF THE MOST TASTEFUL AND ELEGANT FORMS.

The Extent, Variety, and great Value of this Stock afford the most advantageous
opportunity to the public to provide themselves with Porcelane of every class,
and of peculiar strength, for which the Iron Stone China has long been distinguished.

WHICH WILL BE SOLD BY AUCTION
BY MR. PHILLIPS,
ON THE PREMISES,
AT NO. 11, ALBEMARLE STREET,
On THURSDAY, the 20th day of JUNE, 1822,
And Two following Days, at Twelve for ONE PRECISELY,
BY ORDER OF THE EXECUTORS
WITHOUT RESERVE

FIRST DAY'S SALE
THURSDAY, the 20th Day of JUNE, 1822,
Commencing at Twelve for One o'Clock precisely.

Lot		Reserve
1	Twelve breakfast cups and saucers and 12 tea ditto, earthenware	10/-
2	Twenty-four breakfast cups and saucers and 2 milks, earthenware	12/-
3	Twelve jugs, ditto	6/-
4	Five hunting jugs, stone	12/-
5	Twelve mugs, iron stone	14/-
6	Seven ditto, stone devices	12/-
7	A breakfast suite, 36 pieces, Tournay sprigs	30/-
8	Six antique jugs, iron stone	15/-
9	A pair of Chinese formed jars	52/-
10	A fine pot pourie	30/-
11	Glass	—
12	Two wine coolers and 2 butter tubs	20/-
13	A table service, blue, iron stone, 142 pieces (2 soup tureens, covers and stands, 4 sauce ditto, 18 dishes, 1 drainer, 4 ragout dishes, 1 salad, 60 plates, 18 soup, 18 dessert)	£9.
14	Two rich fruit baskets and stands	30/-
15	Eight stone jugs	20/-
16	Twelve mugs, iron stone (2 sizes)	18/-
17	Two match cases, an antique coffee pot and 2 shades	36/-
18	Five jugs from a beautiful Chinese original	30/-
19	Two chocolate cups and stands, very rich	18/-
20	Two pair of Chinese beakers	36/-
21	A breakfast set, 41 pieces	35/-
22	Twelve breakfast cups and saucers	30/-
23	Six coloured jugs	18/-
24	Six mugs, stone	10/-
25	Nine jugs, iron stone	22/-
26	A pair of well painted vases	42/-
27	Two chamber suites complete, 16 pieces	30/-
28	A table service, coloured, 87 pieces	9 gns.
29	Two highly finished candlesticks and shades	24/-
30	A table set, blue, iron stone, 142 pieces	9½ gns.
31	Two match cases and shades, mazarine	22/-
32	A breakfast service, japan colours and gold, 22 pieces	£8.
33	A pair of rich ice pails	£3. 10. 0d.
34	A pair of Chinese tea caddies	30/-
35	Four stone jugs	12/-
36	Two rich caddies and shades	42/-
37	A pair of beautiful hexagon flower pots and stands	£3. 10. 0d.
38	Four large and 1 small covered jug	16/-
39	Glass	—
40	A table set, japan, 142 pieces	17 gns.
41	Non-Mason china	—
42	A beautiful flower bowl, mazarine	18/-
43	Six jugs, iron stone	13/-
44	Glass	—
45	Glass	—
46	Two chamber suites, 16 pieces	30/-
47	Four broth basins and stands, blue	14/-

Lot		Reserve
48	A breakfast set, 52 pieces	40/-
49	A lofty hall jar	7 gns.
50	A dinner set, blue and white earthenware, 142 pieces	6 gns.
51	A set of 3 vases and shades	36/-
52	A breakfast set, 6 large and 6 small cups and saucers, 6 cans, 6 plates, 6 eggs, 1 slop, 1 cream, 1 roll tray, 2 dishes, and 2 cake plates	63/-
53	Seven stone jars	18/-
54	Two vases, landscapes, and crimson grounds	30/-
55	Two khan dragon beakers	30/-
56	A pair of rich chamber candlesticks and shades	30/-
57	Glass	—
58	Twenty-six useful articles, blue	32/-
59	A pair of card cases, mazarine and white embossed figures	24/-
60	Glass	—
61	Six rich plates, melange	30/-
62	Six ditto	30/-
63	A pair of mazarine water jugs	32/-
64	A fine dragon jar	4 gns.
65	A table service, basket pattern, 142 pieces	14 gns.
66	A set of 5 jars	50/-
67	A table set, coloured, and gilt japan, 142 pieces	£20.
68	Four jugs and 5 mugs, stone	18/-
69	Four antique jugs, corbeau	£1.
70	Gold edge, 6 breakfast cups and saucers, 6 cups and saucers, 6 coffee cups, 6 egg ditto, 6 plates, 2 large ditto, 1 tea pot and stand, and 1 sugar and cover	£2. 18. od.
71	Glass	—
72	Two very rich vases	£3. 10. od.
73	Six rich soup plates	30/-
74	Twelve rich melange plates	£3.
75	Two vegetable dishes, and 1 steak ditto	28/-
76	A dessert set, blue, 43 pieces	70/-
77	A pair of essence burners, mazarine	32/-
78	Five jugs and 4 mugs, stone	19/-
79	Three handsome vases, painted in landscape, and shades	4 gns.
80	Two vases, flies, on mazarine, and shades	28/-
81	A table service, white, 142 pieces	£7.
82	A rich melange dessert set, 43 pieces	18 gns.
83	Glass	—
84	One handsome japan vase and shade	£1.
85	Five vases and covers, japan	£2.
86	One ewer and bason, and 1 slipper, japan	30/-
87	Two blue ewers and basins, and 2 slippers	25/-
88	A table set, blue, 142 pieces	£9.
89	A dessert set, blue, 43 pieces	3 gns.
90	Glass	—
91	Twenty-six pieces of useful articles, blue	32/-
92	A handsome japan bowl	30/-
93	Two vegetable dishes and 1 steak dish	38/-
94	Glass	—
95	A tea set, blue sprig, gold edge, 42 pieces	48/-
96	Six breakfast cups and saucers, 6 plates, 6 egg cups, and 1 muffin plate and cover, ditto	36/-

Lot		Reserve
97	A dessert set, japan, gold edge, 43 pieces	8 gns.
98	Two rich cups, covers and stands, painted in landscapes and shades	58/-
99	Twelve jugs and 6 mugs, blue	38/-
100	A dinner set, blue, 142 pieces	£9.
101	A ditto dessert, 43 pieces	3 gns.
102	Two vegetable dishes, rich japan	50/-
103	Six beakers and 3 cheese stands, ditto	50/-
104	One cut sugar bason, 1 ditto milk, 1 ditto muffineer and 1 butter tub	24/-
105	Glass	—
106	Two vases and covers, green dragons	30/-
107	Four rich jugs, corbeau	20/-
108	Three paper cases, rich landscapes	30/-
109	Two ewers and basins, and 2 slippers, blue	25/-
110	Two bottles, mazarine, and shades, and 2 baskets, landscapes	27/-
111	A dinner set, blue, 142 pieces	£9.
112	A pair of ice pails, rich border	£4. 10. od.
113	One essence pot, mazarine, and 3 cabinet cups and saucers	28/-
114	A tea set, bourbon sprig, 33 pieces	30/-
115	Twelve cups and saucers, 1 bason and 1 plate	15/-
116	Five bottles, mazarine	30/-
117	Twenty-six pieces of useful articles, blue	32/-
118	Six jugs and 12 mugs, blue	33/-
119	Four mugs and 4 jugs, stone	16/-
120	Two vegetable dishes and 1 steak ditto, blue	28/-
121	Glass	—
122	Two paper cases, landscape, and 2 essence bottles and 4 shades	30/-
123	One toy tea pot, 2 inks and 3 shades	24/-
124	A dragon pattern earthenware breakfast set, 92 pieces	37/-
125	Glass	—
126	Six ewers and basons, blue, earthenware	21/-
127	Eighteen tea cups and saucers, ditto	18/-
128	A breakfast ditto, 89 pieces	35/-
129	Twenty white basons, in sizes (earthenware)	10/-
130	Twelve ditto jugs	18/-

End of the First Day

SECOND DAY'S SALE
FRIDAY, the 21st Day of JUNE, 1822,
Commencing at One o'Clock precisely

Lot		Reserve
131	Three ewers and basins, and 3 slippers, white	30/-
132	Six jugs, 3 ditto, covered, and 6 mugs, white	26/-
133	Two foot pans, white	25/-
134	Two dozen blue earthenware cups and saucers, 2 tea pots, 4 basins, and 2 milks	15/-
135	Seven basins in sizes, and 5 beakers, white	16/-
136	Six jugs, 3 ditto covered, and 6 mugs, white	26/-
137	A square supper set, 8 pieces, snipe pattern	40/-
138	Ten antique jugs, blue	23/-

Lot		Reserve
139	Two vegetable dishes, and 1 steak ditto, blue	25/-
140	A table service, blue earthenware, 142 pieces	110/-
141	A dessert service, India landscape, 43 pieces	£4.
142	Twenty-five pieces of useful articles, white	30/-
143	Two chamber sets, blue	28/-
144	Eleven antique jugs, blue	25/-
145	Eight baking dishes in sizes, peacock	16/-
146	Twelve jugs, blue	27/-
147	Two candlesticks, japan, and 2 paper cases, birds	25/-
148	Three paper cases, painted birds, and shades	40/-
149	Six breakfast cups and saucers, 6 plates and 1 milk pot, India coloured, and gold sprigs	50/-
150	A table service, blue, 87 pieces	110/-
151	A dessert set, ditto, 43 pieces	50/-
152	A pair of vases and covers, mazarine	35/-
153	Two hexagon bottles, 2 ditto jugs, and 2 taper candlesticks and 4 shades	36/-
154	Four breakfast cups and saucers, 4 plates, 4 egg cups, and 1 muffin plate, yellow and gold	50/-
155	Two hexagon vases and covers, dragon	30/-
156	Twenty-six pieces of useful items, blue	38/-
157	Twelve jugs, blue	27/-
158	A chamber set, japan	28/-
159	Two paper cases, and pair of candlesticks, mazarine	36/-
160	A table service, rich rock japan, 87 pieces	10 gns.
161	A square supper set, willow japan, 12 pieces	78/-
162	Two bottles, and 2 scent pots, enamelled	22/-
163	Two vegetable dishes and 1 steak ditto, blue	25/-
164	Glass	—
165	Glass	
166	Glass	—
167	Two handled vases, mazarine, and shades	24/-
168	Two vases, mazarine, and 2 essence bottles, japan and glass shades	30/-
169	Glass	—
170	A table service, blue, 142 pieces	£9.
171	A dessert set, ditto, 43 pieces	50/-
172	Twelve jugs, blue, no covers	27/-
173	Two match cases, and 2 essence bottles, japan, and 2 taper candlesticks, mazarine	36/-
174	Two Spanish vases and covers, japan	44/-
175	A tea set, sprigs and gold edge, 46 pieces	50/-
176	A breakfast set, coloured sprigs, 105 pieces	50/-
177	Glass	—
178	Glass	—
179	Glass	—
180	A table service, coloured, japan, 63 pieces	£10.
181	A dessert set, red and gold rose, 43 pieces	£8. 10. 0d.
182	Twelve mugs, blue	16/-
183	Four tea cups and saucers, 4 coffee cups, 2 plates, and 2 egg cups, yellow and gold	28/-
184	Two small bottles and 2 essence ditto, mazarine and shades	27/-
185	Glass	—
186	A vase, painted in flowers, and 2 paper cases	54/-

Lot	Reserve
187 Glass	—
188 A handsome antique jug	23/-
189 A very rich tea set, 45 pieces	8 gns.
190 A very rich coloured and gilt table service, 142 pieces	£35.
191 Glass	—
192 Twelve mugs, blue	14/-
193 Glass	—
194 A rich antique vase	35/-
195 Two Spanish vases, coloured and gilt	30/-
196 A paper case, and 2 small jugs, mazarine and shades	20/-
197 Glass	—
198 A pair of vases and covers, green dragon	15/-
199 A handsome antique jug	20/-
200 A table service, blue, 142 pieces	£9. 10. od.
201 A dessert set, ditto, 43 pieces	£2. 10. od.
202 Two baskets and stands, japan	50/-
203 Two tall hexagonal bottles, mazarine	35/-
204 Four flower pots and stands, mazarine	63/-
205 Glass	—
206 Two bottles, India figures and landscape	30/-
207 Two three-handled vases, mazarine	60/-
208 Two vases, views in Rome	80/-
209 Three vases, painted in landscape	70/-
210 A table service, white, 142 pieces	£6. o. od.
211 A vase, painted in shells	50/-
212 A tea set, rock pattern, 41 pieces	50/-
213 Two tall jars and covers, dragon	15/-
214 Twelve custard cups and covers, basket pattern	14/-
215 Glass	—
216 Four small vases, japan	23/-
217 An ewer and basin, and brush tray, handsome japan	46/-
218 Six jugs and 5 mugs, stone	20/-
219 A shell ink stand, and 2 paper cases, flower border	23/-
220 A table service, peacock, japan, 87 pieces	£8. 10. od.
221 A dessert set, japan, 43 pieces	8 gns.
222 Two bottles, and 1 vase, japan	17/-
223 A pair of card racks, and a pen tray, mazarine	28/-
224 A pair of violet baskets, a candlestick and 2 paper cases, mazarine	25/-
225 A handsome antique ewer, japanned and gilt	25/-
226 A pair of flat candlesticks and extinguishers, mazarine	25/-
227 A tea set, gold border, 44 pieces	50/-
228 Glass	—
229 Glass	—
230 A table service, blue, 87 pieces	£5. 10. od.
231 Two vases and 2 beakers, green dragon	30/-
232 A large essence jar, japanned and gilt	42/-
233 Glass	—
234 Two bottles, 2 vases, and a watering pot, mazarine	30/-
235 Glass	—
236 Two buckets, 2 ink stands, and 2 flat candlesticks	23/-
237 Two handsome vases and shades	28/-
238 Glass	—
239 A dejeune, coloured sprigs	35/-
240 A rich gilt japan table service, 142 pieces	£28.

Lot		Reserve
241	Twenty pieces of useful articles, blue	23/–
242	Twenty-six ditto	30/–
243	Two chamber sets, blue	28/–
244	Two ditto	28/–
245	Five punch bowls, blue	30/–
246	A breakfast set, blue, 54 pieces	23/–
247	Four broth basins, 3 pudding ditto, 5 mugs, and 2 boats, blue	23/–
248	Four candlesticks, 2 small ewers and basins, and 2 broth basins, blue	23/–
249	Two vegetable dishes and 1 steak ditto, blue	25/–
250	Three small vases, and an essence pot, flowers	18/–
251	A caddy, candlestick, jug, mazarine, and ink stand	15/–
252	Six ewers and 6 basins, blue earthenware	23/–
253	A breakfast set, blue sprig, 36 pieces	28/–
254	Ten jugs, blue earthenware	10/–
255	Twenty-seven pieces of useful articles, white	30/–
256	Twenty-four tea cups and saucers, 2 tea pots, 2 milks, and 4 basins, blue earthenware	14/–
257	Two vegetable dishes, 2 small ewers and basins, and 4 mugs, white	23/–
258	A dessert set, white, 43 pieces	40/–
259	Twenty-four tea cups and saucers, blue earthenware	11/–
260	Six jugs, ditto	6/–

End of the Second Day

THIRD DAY'S SALE,
SATURDAY, the 22nd Day of JUNE, 1822,
Commencing at One o'Clock precisely

Lot		Reserve
261	Two chamber sets, white	26/–
262	One potato dish, 3 hot water plates, 7 bakers, and 3 pudding basins, white	22/–
263	Six ewers and basins, blue earthenware	15/–
264	Sixteen pieces of useful articles, blue	16/–
265	Six mugs, and 4 jugs, blue earthenware	6/–
266	Two vegetable dishes, and 1 steak dish, blue	24/–
267	Twenty-six pieces of useful articles	20/–
268	Three jugs, japan flowers and gold edge	21/–
269	One chamber set, gold jar	31/–
270	A table service, blue, 87 pieces (1 soup tureen, cover and stand, 2 sauce ditto, 2 covered vegetables (or ragouts) sallad, 13 dishes, 36 meat plates, 12 soups, 12 sweets)	£5. o. od.
271	Twelve jugs, blue earthenware, and 12 cups and saucers	14/–
272	Ten ditto, formed from the antique, blue	20/–
273	Six breakfast cups and saucers, 1 muffin plate and cover, flowers, and 6 cups and saucers, roses	21/–
274	Six ewers and basins, blue earthenware	15/–
275	Twenty-four pieces of useful articles, blue	20/–
276	Twelve jugs, blue earthenware	—
277	Two vegetable dishes, and 1 steak dish, blue	23/–

Lot		Reserve
278	Eighteen tea cups and saucers, 2 milks, 4 basins, and 1 tea pot, blue earthenware	10/-
279	Two vases and 1 jar, green dragon	30/-
280	A table service, blue, 142 pieces	£8.
281	Twelve custard cups and covers, grasshopper	14/-
282	Twelve jugs, stone	25/-
283	A dejeune, japan	50/-
284	A tea set, rich japan pattern, 45 pieces	£6. 6. od.
285	Three beakers, mazarine sprigs	16/-
286	Two bottles, ditto and white figures	24/-
287	Two Grecian shape vases, flowers and green ground with shades	63/-
288	Nine antique jugs, blue	18/-
289	A handsome two-handle vase, mazarine and shade	42/-
290	A table service, blue, 142 pieces	£8. 0. 0.
291	A dessert service, ditto, 43 pieces	50/-
292	Two handsome satyr vases, painted in landscape and shades	90/-
293	Six rich plates	30/-
294	Six jugs, japan, antique form	12/-
295	Two candlesticks, green, and flowers with shades	28/-
296	A handsome one handled vase, fruit and green ground	30/-
297	Two hexagon vases, japan, with shades (1 faulty)	42/-
298	A handsome japan dessert set, 43 pieces	14 gns.
299	A pair of ice pails, ditto	90/-
300	A table service, blue, 87 pieces	£5. 0. od.
301	Eight jugs and 6 mugs, stone	24/-
302	Two rich vases, fruit and green grounds	50/-
303	Six rich soup plates	18/-
304	Two chamber sets, gold jar	50/-
305	A handsome Trentham bowl	24/-
306	Three handsome japan jugs	27/-
307	A small ewer and basin, 2 toy watering cans and 2 shell candlesticks	27/-
308	A very handsome tea set, 45 pieces	90/-
309	A rich antique formed ewer and basin	18/-
310	A table service, blue, 142 pieces	£8. 0. od.
311	A pair of four-handled vases, mazarine	42/-
312	Two Spanish vases, mazarine	42/-
313	A breakfast set, rock pattern, 94 pieces	8 gns.
314	A pair of urns, beautifully painted in landscapes, and glass shades	48/-
315	A pair of vases, mazarine, and shell ecretoire and 2 glass shades	48/-
316	A pair of flower pots and stands, painted in birds, with glass shades and two match cases	28/-
317	A pair of jars, japanned, flower and dragon handles	24/-
318	Six rich dessert plates	30/-
319	A pair of green dragon beakers	21/-
320	A table service, blue, 87 pieces	£5. 0. od.
321	A dessert service, japan, birds and flowers, 43 pieces	£5. 0. od.
322	Three ewers, blue dragon, from the antique	11/-
323	Four jars and beakers, green dragon	60/-
324	Pair of hand candlesticks and extinguishers, and 2 bottles, flowers on mazarine ground	28/-
325	Six handsome soup plates	30/-
326	A rich blue and gold ewer and basin with glass shade	38/-
327	A pair of ditto essence burners, and 2 cups and covers	30/-

Lot		Reserve
328	A pair of candlesticks, glass shades and 3 vases	32/–
329	A blue and gold coffee ewer and 2 tea cannisters	26/–
330	A table service, blue, 142 pieces	£8.
331	A dessert service, ditto, 43 pieces	50/–
332	Two flat candlesticks and extinguishers, 1 toy ewer and basin, 2 essence bottles and 5 shades	38/–
333	A chamber set, rich japan	70/–
334	Six handsome dessert plates	33/–
335	A dinner service, 142 pieces	15 gns.
336	Two broth basins, covers and stands, rich japan	28/–
337	Two hexagon vases and covers, mazarine	42/–
338	Two rich candlesticks and extinguishers, and 1 small vase, japan	28/–
339	A dejeune, rich japan	50/–
340	A table service, blue, 87 pieces	£5.
341	Six plates, birds and shells on gold border	30/–
342	Two match cases, mazarine, and shades	18/–
343	Five jugs, figured stone	11/–
344	Two Satyr vases, flowers and red ground	63/–
345	Two beakers and covers, Chinese pattern	20/–
346	Pair of ice pails, flowers and blue border	5 gns.
347	A table service, blue sprig and gold edge, 142 pieces	15 gns.
348	Six rich dessert plates	30/–
349	Two bottles and 1 beaker, green dragon	20/–
350	A table service, blue, 142 pieces	£8. 10. od.
351	A dessert ditto, 43 pieces	50/–
352	A breakfast set, yellow and gold, 47 pieces	90/–
353	Four breakfast cups and saucers, 4 coffee cups and saucers, and tea pot, blue and gold, and flowers	60/–
354	Two coolers, plaid Japan	50/–
355	A breakfast set, blue, 48 pieces	36/–
356	A ditto, blue sprig, 50 ditto	40/–
357	A supper set, 5 pieces, and tray, rose japan	63/–
358	Three handsome soup plates	15/–
359	Two bottles and covers, and paper case, japan	21/–
360	Two candlesticks, japan, and 1 antique vase	26/–
361	A table service, blue, 87 pieces	£5.
362	Two antique jugs, corbeau	10/–
363	Two chamber sets, blue	12/–
364	A rich flat candlestick and extinguisher, and a pair small bottles, mazarine	12/–
365	A table set, india sprigs	15 gns.
366	A breakfast set, blue sprig, 42 pieces	30/–
367	Six rich dessert plates	30/–
368	Four oval dishes and covers, blue	22/–
369	Four antique jugs, corbeau	20/–
370	A table service, blue, 87 pieces	£5.
371	A breakfast set, Bourbon sprig, 77 pieces	50/–
372	Six rich dessert plates	30/–
373	A breakfast set, blue sprig, gold edge, 28 pieces	40/–
374	A bottle, mazarine, and a jug, corbeau	16/–
375	A breakfast set, blue border, 32 pieces	20/–
376	Two foot tubs, white	24/–
377	A supper set, blue, 9 pieces	21/–
378	A breakfast set, coloured and gold sprigs, 25 pieces	50/–

Lot		Reserve
379	Twelve antique jugs, blue	24/–
380	A table service, blue, 87 pieces	£5.
381	A breakfast set, dragon, 62 pieces	48/–
382	Twelve white jars	24/–
383	Twelve ditto	24/–
384	Two vegetable dishes, peacock pattern	42/–
385	Twenty-six pieces of useful articles, blue	25/–
386	Eight beakers, blue	16/–
387	Twenty-four tea cups and saucers, dragon, earthenware	8/–
388	Twenty-four ditto, blue earthenware	8/–
389	Twelve jugs, blue earthenware	12/–
390	Twelve ditto, ditto	12/–

FINIS

THE LAST PART OF THE
STOCK OF CHINA
OF THE LATE
MR. MASON
PATENTEE AND MANUFACTURER OF THE IRON
STONE CHINA
AT NO. 11, ALBEMARLE STREET

A
CATALOGUE
OF
THE REMAINING STOCK
OF USEFUL & DECORATIVE
PORCELANE,
OF RICH AND ELEGANT PATTERNS;
COMPRISING
DINNER, DESSERT, BREAKFAST, & TEA SERVICES;
JUGS, EWERS, BASINS,
DISHES IN SETS, BOTH OPEN AND COVERED;
PLATES
AND A
VARIETY OF CABINET ORNAMENTS,
OF THE MOST TASTEFUL AND ELEGANT FORMS.

The Extent, Variety, and great Value of this Stock afford the most advantageous opportunity to the public to provide themselves with Porcelane of every class, and of peculiar strength, for which the Iron Stone China has long been distinguished.

WHICH WILL BE SOLD BY AUCTION
BY MR. PHILLIPS,
ON THE PREMISES,
AT NO. 11, ALBEMARLE STREET,
ON FRIDAY, the 28th day of JUNE, 1822
And following Day, at Twelve for ONE precisely,
BY ORDER OF THE EXECUTORS

May be Viewed One Day preceding the Sale, and Catalogues had on the Premises; at the Auction Marts; and at Mr. PHILLIP'S, 73, New Bond Street.

FIRST DAY'S SALE
FRIDAY, the 28th Day of JUNE, 1822,
Commencing at One o'Clock precisely.

Lot		Reserve
1	Twelve white jars	24/-
2	Twelve ditto	24/-
3	Twelve ditto jugs	18/-
4	Twelve ditto mugs	7/-
5	Two ditto ice pails	16/-
6	Fifteen ditto useful pieces	25/-
7	Twenty-four cups and saucers, 2 pint and 2 half pint basins, blue earthenware	10/-
8	Six jugs, blue iron stone	18/-
9	Twelve ditto, blue earthenware	13/-
10	A small table set, blue, 87 pieces	£5. 10. od.
11	Twenty pieces of useful articles, blue, iron stone	25/-
12	A breakfast set, 36 pieces	28/-
13	Eight stone figured jugs	20/-
14	Glass	—
15	Two porous wine coolers and 2 butter tubs	18/-
16	A Stilton cheese stand	44/-
17	A pair of fruit baskets, rich japan	18/-
18	A breakfast set, 37 pieces	28/-
19	Five beautiful jugs	24/-
20	A table set, blue, 142 pieces	£9. 10. od.
21	A pair of Indian beakers	28/-
22	A pair of blue iron stone coolers	14/-
23	Five figured stone jugs	15/-
24	Six ditto mugs	12/-
25	A pair of mantle ornaments	28/-
26	Sixteen pieces of useful articles, blue iron stone	18/-
27	A pair of jars	24/-
28	A dessert service, Indian landscape	4 gns.
29	Glass	—
30	A table set, blue, 87 pieces	6 gns.
31	A rich water jug [glass?]	36/-
32	A breakfast set, japan, 22 pieces	48/-
33	A pair of vases, painted in landscapes, and shades	42/-
34	Glass	—
35	A pair of candlesticks, high finished [glass?]	21/-
36	A pair of chinese vases	24/-
37	Glass	—
38	A very finely japanned jug	31/-
39	A pair of mazarine myrtle pots and stands	84/-
40	A table set, blue, 142 pieces, earthenware	£6. 10. od.
41	A rich pot pourie	36/-
42	Six melange plates, rich	30/-
43	A breakfast set, rich, 19 pieces	60/-
44	A pair of card racks, mazarine	24/-
45	Glass	—
46	Seven stone figured mugs	18/-
47	A pair of ice pails, blue iron stone	36/-
48	A pair of chinese flower vases	60/-

Lot		Reserve
49	Six handsome dessert plates	30/–
50	A table set, 142 pieces, tournay, gold edge	28 gns.
51	Four rich jugs	28/–
52	A breakfast set, 42 pieces	70/–
53	Two chamber sets, blue, iron stone	30/–
54	Two ditto	30/–
55	Two ditto	30/–
56	A pair of water jugs, mazarine and broad gold edge	32/–
57	Two green beakers	36/–
58	A rich pagoda formed hall jar	6 gns.
59	Glass	—
60	A table set, 142 pieces, tournay	12 gns.
61	A tea set, white and gold, 45 pieces	2 gns.
62	Six rich soup plates	30/–
63	A pair of elegant vases	120/–
64	A pair of ditto chinese	24/–
65	Two vegetable dishes and a steak dish, blue iron stone	25/–
66	Glass	—
67	A pair of fruit baskets and stands, japan	32/–
68	A pair of mantle jars	34/–
69	A tea set, 45 pieces	52/–
70	A table set, 142 pieces	16 gns.
71	Glass	—
72	Three vases and 2 shades	63/–
73	A breakfast set, 26 pieces	50/–
74	Glass	—
75	Two card racks and a pen tray	30/–
76	A breakfast set, 54 pieces	54/–
77	A set of 5 ornaments	44/–
78	One flower bowl and shade	30/–
79	A supper set, richly japanned and gold edge, 12 pieces	£3. 10. od.
80	A table set, 142 pieces, coloured	12 gns.
81	A pair of card candlesticks and shades	36/–
82	A rich toilet ewer and basin with shade	34/–
83	A pair of ice pails, japanned	£3. 10. od.
84	One water jug, neatly pencilled	36/–
85	A breakfast set, 20 pieces	48/–
86	A pair of wine coolers, rich japan	50/–
87	One pot pourie, rich japan	36/–
88	A dessert service, beautifully painted in flowers and green ground	18 gns.
89	Twenty-four plates, carnation, gold edge	36/–
90	A table set, 142 pieces, rose pattern	16 gns.
91	A tea set, 45 pieces, japan	6 gns.
92	Three vases, mazarine	42/–
93	Twelve custard cups	18/–
94	Fifteen pieces of useful articles, blue iron stone	15/–
95	A pair of flower jars and shades	£3. 10. od.
96	Six blue and white jugs	12/–
97	Two ewers and basins, green border	26/–
98	One slop pail, blue iron stone	16/–
99	Seven jugs, blue iron stone	15/–
100	A table set, 142 pieces, japan	21 gns.
101	A breakfast set, dragon earthenware, 34 pieces	14/–
102	A ditto iron stone, coloured, 42 pieces	50/–

Lot		Reserve
103	A chamber set, green border	27/-
104	Six jugs, blue iron stone	14/-
105	Twelve ditto, earthenware	14/-
106	Eighteen cups and saucers, earthenware	8/-
107	Two mantle jars	63/-
108	Twelve jugs, blue earthenware	14/-
109	Twenty-four breakfast cups and saucers, 2 pint basins, cream, 1 tea pot, dragon earthenware	21/-
110	A table set, 87 pieces, blue earthenware	62/-
111	Six stone figured jars	16/-
112	Two punch bowls, blue iron stone	15/-
113	A chamber set, ditto	15/-
114	Two broth basins and stands	10/-
115	Two punch and 2 pudding bowls, blue iron stone	11/-
116	Six ewers and basins, blue earthenware	24/-
117	Twelve jars, white iron stone	18/-
118	Twelve mugs, ditto	12/-
119	Three water jugs, blue iron stone	14/-
120	A table set, 142 pieces	6 gns.
121	Twenty dessert plates, japan, gold edge	42/-
122	Six jugs, dragon, iron stone	14/-
123	Fifteen pieces of useful articles, white iron stone	18/-
124	Five stone mugs, figured	10/-
125	A breakfast set, 42 pieces, earthenware	13/-
126	A pair of mantle jars	32/-
127	Four match cases	30/-
128	A breakfast set, blue earthenware, 18 cups & saucers	15/-
129	Ditto, 24 cups & saucers	18/-
130	Ditto, 24 cups & saucers	18/-

End of the First Day's Sale

SECOND DAY'S SALE,
SATURDAY, the 29th Day of JUNE, 1822,
Commencing at One o'Clock precisely.

Lot		Reserve
131	Five stone figured mugs	10/-
132	Eight jugs, ditto, 2 patterns	10/-
133	A breakfast set, 55 pieces, dragon, iron stone	30/-
134	Twelve jugs, blue, earthenware	18/-
135	Twenty pieces of useful articles, blue, iron stone	20/-
136	Glass	—
137	Glass	—
138	Glass	—
139	Glass	—
140	Four composition mortars and pestles	10/-
141	A table set, 87 pieces, blue, iron stone	£5. 10. od.
142	Twelve white jugs, iron stone	12/-
143	Twelve ditto, mugs	9/-
144	A dessert set, coloured	£5. 5. od.
145	A chamber set, green border	27/-
146	Six stone mugs, various	20/-

M

Lot		Reserve
147	A chamber service, green border	27/–
148	Four handsome jugs	21/–
149	Two vegetable dishes, and 1 steak ditto, blue, iron stone	25/–
150	A table set, 142 pieces, blue, iron stone	£9. 10. 0d.
151	Glass	—
152	Six ewers and basins, blue, earthenware	24/–
153	Glass	—
154	Glass	—
155	Glass	—
156	Glass	—
157	Glass	—
158	Glass	—
159	Glass	—
160	A table set, 87 pieces, blue iron stone	6 gns.
161	Four rich jugs [glass?]	20/–
162	Glass	—
163	Two vegetable dishes and 1 cheese stand, richly japanned	60/–
164	Two beautiful caudle cups and shades	84/–
165	A dessert service, Indian flowers, rich	£8. 10. 0d.
166	A set of 3 rich jars	58/–
167	Two bottles and 2 match cases, ditto	30/–
168	A tea set, enamelled, 45 pieces	34/–
169	Five stone mugs	8/–
170	A table set, 142 pieces	15 gns.
171	A white iron stone dessert set, 43 pieces	40/–
172	An ink stand and 2 wafer cups with 2 shades	28/–
173	Two vegetable dishes and 1 steak dish, blue iron stone	25/–
174	Twenty-four pieces of useful articles, blue iron stone	25/–
175	Glass	—
176	Three match cases and shades	30/–
177	Glass	—
178	Two richly painted flower baskets and 2 lavender bottles and shades	27/–
179	A dessert set, blue, 43 pieces	50/–
180	A table set, 87 pieces, white iron stone	70/–
181	Twelve melange breakfast cups and saucers	30/–
182	Two broth basins and stands	16/–
183	A set of 3 Indian formed jars	28/–
184	A set of 3 ditto	63/–
185	A rich water jug [glass?]	27/–
186	A fruit basket	14/–
187	Glass	—
188	Glass	—
189	A breakfast set, enamelled, 31 pieces	18/–
190	A table set, 142 pieces, rich Japan pattern	21 gns.
191	A pair of candlesticks, Japan	16/–
192	A chamber service, ditto	24/–
193	Six very rich dessert plates	30/–
194	Six ditto soup plates	30/–
195	A dessert service, Pekin sprigs	10 gns.
196	Three jugs and 2 mugs, figured stone	10/–
197	Three flower baskets, enamelled china	16/–
198	A pair of Chinese vases and covers	63/–
199	A very fine hall jar, mazarine hydra top	9 gns.

Lot		Reserve
200	A table set, 142 pieces	30 gns.
201	Glass	—
202	Glass	—
203	Glass	—
204	Glass	—
205	Glass	—
206	Glass	—
207	A pair of Chinese jars	50/-
208	Nine stone jugs	24/-
209	Three rich soup plates	15/-
210	A table set, 87 pieces, grasshopper, hexagonal tureens	£9. 10. od.
211	A breakfast set, 42 pieces, red and gold	78/-
212	Glass	—
213	Glass	
214	A breakfast set, richly japanned, 42 pieces	60/-
215	Three cabinet pieces	17/-
216	A rich chamber service	£3. 10. od.
217	Six beautiful dessert plates	30/-
218	Eighteen tea cups and saucers, blue earthenware	8/-
219	Five stone mugs, figured	9/-
220	A table set, 87 pieces, rich japan	12 gns.
221	Two wine coolers, blue iron stone	20/-
222	Twelve jugs, blue earthenware	18/-
223	Twelve cups and saucers, white and gold	28/-
224	Twenty-one useful pieces, blue iron stone	24/-
225	A handsome mantle jar, beautifully painted in shells	50/-
226	Twenty-four cups and saucers, blue earthenware	11/-
227	Glass	—
228	One rich ice pail	42/-
229	Six rich soup plates	30/-
230	A table set, 87 pieces, mandarine	£9. 10. od.
231	A pair of very richly painted goblets	£4. 10. od.
232	A pair of candlesticks and shades	48/-
233	A pair of cabinet jars and a vase	18/-
234	Eight rich plates, arms	40/-
235	A pair of vases and shades	50/-
236	A rich ice pail	42/-
237	Glass	—
238	Glass	—
239	Glass	—
240	A table set, 142 pieces, blue	£9.
241	Glass	—
242	Two beautifully painted candlesticks	28/-
243	A fine flower bowl and shade	£3. 10. od.
244	A breakfast set, blue sprig, 42 pieces	36/-
245	Twelve jugs, blue earthenware	18/-
246	Four broth basins and stands, blue iron stone	20/-
247	Twelve jugs, blue iron stone	26/-
248	Twelve mugs, ditto	18/-
249	Glass	—
250	A table set, 87 pieces, blue earthenware	70/-
251	Two chamber sets, coloured	£5. 5. od.
252	One ditto, blue, gold edge	28/-
253	A pair of rich broth basins and stands	12/-

Lot	Reserve
254 Twenty-six useful pieces, blue iron stone	26/–
255 Two toilet ewers and basins, and a candlestick, ditto	24/–
256 Two vegetable dishes, blue	20/–
257 A pair of porous wine coolers	16/–
258 Glass	—
259 Glass	—
260 Glass	—

FINIS

Bibliographical Note

Most ceramic reference books give some information on the Masons and their Ironstone, but in some cases the facts are incorrect or of a very general nature.

Apart from the present work the only published specialist books are Reginald G. Haggar's *The Masons of Lane Delph* (Lund Humphries & Co. Ltd., 1952) and J. V. Goddard's earlier *The Mason Family and Pottery*, published in 1910. Other source material has already been acknowledged in the appropriate places in the text; but in the main, the available information consists of isolated references in general works such as Simeon Shaw's *History of the Staffordshire Potteries* (1829) or J. T. S. Lidstone's *The Thirteenth Londoniad* of 1866 (see page 104). These books are long out of print and are available only through book dealers or specialist reference libraries.

One general work must be mentioned—L. Jewitt's *Ceramic Art of Great Britain* (J. S. Virtue & Co., 1878, revised edition 1883)—for this contains a wealth of information on the many firms which produced Mason-type 'Ironstone china' or 'Stone China'. The new revised fifteenth edition of Chaffers' *Marks and Monograms* (William Reeves, 1965) is also helpful in this respect.

Interesting information on the export trade in Ironstone-type bodies is contained in Mrs. E. Collard's *Nineteenth Century Pottery and Porcelain in Canada* (McGill University Press, Canada, 1967).

INDEX

Index